Mary Adelaide Walker

**EasternLife and Scenery**

Vol. II: With Excursions in Asia Minor, Mytilene, Crete, and Roumania

Mary Adelaide Walker

**EasternLife and Scenery**
*Vol. II: With Excursions in Asia Minor, Mytilene, Crete, and Roumania*

ISBN/EAN: 9783743384156

Manufactured in Europe, USA, Canada, Australia, Japa

Cover: Foto ©ninafisch / pixelio.de

Manufactured and distributed by brebook publishing software (www.brebook.com)

Mary Adelaide Walker

**EasternLife and Scenery**

# EASTERN LIFE AND SCENERY

WITH

EXCURSIONS IN ASIA MINOR, MYTILENE,
CRETE, AND ROUMANIA

By Mrs. WALKER

IN TWO VOLUMES
VOL. II.

LONDON: CHAPMAN AND HALL
LIMITED
1886

LONDON:
PRINTED BY J. S. VIRTUE AND CO., LIMITED,
CITY ROAD.

# CONTENTS TO VOL. II.

### I.—FESTIVITIES IN THE HAREM.

Preparations for the Festival.—The Talika.—The Mistress of Ceremonies.—Zeheïra.—The State Couch.—Scenic Effects.—Rich Presents.—Jew Mountebanks.—The Bastinado.—Dinner.—Bouyouroûn.—How to Vanquish a Stuffed Lamb.—Zerdè-pillaw.—Khoshab.—From behind the Cafesses.—"Tastes Differ."—The Kiosk in the Vineyards.—Rest . . . . . . . . . . 1

### II.—THE BETROTHAL OF DJENANIAH CALPHA.

A Valuable "Halaïk."—Difficult Courtship and "Kismet."—The Ceremony of the "Nikyah" (the betrothal).—The Imām's Questions.—The Marriage Contract.—The Shower of Coin.—Gifts of Jewellery.—Fear of the Evil Eye . 15

### III.—TAKING HOME THE BRIDE.

The New Name.—Bridal Gifts and Bridal Furniture.—Oppressive Finery; the Face Jewels and the Golden Veil.—Decorated "Talikas."—The Bride's Throne.—Free and Candid Criticisms.—The Prayer Carpet.—A Peaceful Home . . . . . . . . . . 21

### IV.—UNDERGROUND STAMBOUL.

Yéré-Batan-Seraï.—The Mysterious Lake.—A Palace of the "Djinns."—Lukium.—The Cistern of the Hippodrome.—Bin-Bir-Direk.—The Cistern of Theodosius.—The Cistern of Arcadius.—Tchukur Bostān.—The Cisterns of

Bonus, of the Emperor Anastasius, of the Church of Pantocrator, of Boudroum Djami, of St. John Studius.—Massive Subterranean Remains.—Fazli Pasha . . 29

### V.—TURKISH HOME LIFE.

The Harem.—Slavery . . . . . . . 37

### VI.—A WINTER IN THE SUNNY EAST.

Fancies and Facts.—A Dog's Luxury.—A Snowstorm.—The Hurricane.—Pleasure and Peril.—"Yangheun Var!" the Cry of the Night Guardian.—A Half-Buried City.—Stagnation.—The Fear of Famine.—The Black Sacks.—The Snow-clothed "Sunny East."—Great Disasters in Asia Minor.—Wild Boars and Wolves in the Suburbs.—The Fatal Snowdrifts.—Disasters at Sea.—An Impromptu "Montagne Russe."—Street Modelling.—A Thaw and a Breath of Summer . . . . . . . . 77

### VII.—THE ART OF LIVING, ACCORDING TO GREEK FOLK-LORE.

A Baleful Day.—How to Dismiss a Visitor Politely.—The use of Salt in a Slipper.—Further Value of Slippers.—"Na! Na!"—Giving and Taking.—Spilt Salt must be Peppered.—The Danger of a Half-open Door.—Sad Consequences of Sitting on a Box.—Unwinding a Spell.—The Risk of Tying up a Destiny.—How Vinegar becomes Musty.—An Easy Way of Ensuring Custom.—How to Mend a Broken Head.—Great Dangers connected with the "Wash" of a Household.—Three-legged Trivets have Grave Responsibilities.—Awful Result of Open Scissors.—The Three Cloves.—The Danger of Hasty Compliments.—The Evil Eye . . . . . 85

VIII.—BROUSSA . . . . . . . 93

### IX.—THE BATHS OF BROUSSA.

#### NO. I.

Contrast in Beauties of Broussa and the Bosphorus.—Getting on Board.—Travellers and their Bags.—The Harem of

the Boat.—Our Small Party.—The Princes' Islands.—
The Gulf of Nicomedia.—The Open Marmora.—Dislocated Perspective.—Collapse.—The "Talika."—Winding Roads and Leafy Lanes.—The "Durbend."—Luxuriant Vegetation.—Beautiful View from the Bridge.—"Tchekirghé."—The Baths.—"Hotel du Mont Olympe."—Giovanni.—A String of Camels.—Fine View from the Hotel.—Exploring Adventures.—The Jews' Quarter.—The Ruined "Fabrika."—In the Bazaars.—Kutaya Pottery.—Sketching under Difficulties.—Cream Ices.—The Heavenly Valley.—View from the Mills . . . . 110

## X.—THE BATHS OF BROUSSA.

### NO. II.—TCHEKIRGHÉ.

Mountain Trout.—The View and the Passers-by.—The Trysting Tree.—A Sober Traveller.—A Wild Zebek.—A Santon.—Hawks and Storks.—A Start.—The Mouradiyeh Suburb.—The Mosque and its Surroundings.—An Aggressive Umbrella.—Rustic Fountains.—The "Kief."—Bademli Bagtché. — Yeni-Kaplidja Hammam. — Cypresses. — Tchekirghé. — Eski-Kaplidja Hammam.—The Mosque of Mourad I.—A Fountain of Hot and Cold Water.—The Sultan's "Tonghra."—Interior of the Mosque.—The Ruined "Turbé."—A Flowery Lane.—A Rustic Resting-place.—The Mineral Waters of Eski-Kaplidja . 141

## XI.—BROUSSA SILK.

### NO. I.

Eastern Method of Rearing Silkworms.—Difficulties of Investigation.—Sensitiveness of the Worm.—Value of Mulberry-leaves, and of Silkworm Seed.—Great Care Needed.—The First Sleep.—A Healthy Appetite.—The Second Sleep.—The Third Sleep.—Voracity.—Repose and Work.—The Miniature Grove.—A Fairy Hamac.—The Cocoon.—Silk-rearing Establishment at Demirdesch.—Frames used in Removal.—The Moths.—The "Graineurs."—The Riches of a Peasant that "Make themselves Wings."—The Public Ovens.—The Quality of the Water used in Washing the Silk . . . . . . . . 170

## XII.—BROUSSA SILK.
#### NO. II.—THE SPINNING FACTORIES.

A Spinning "Fabrika."—Unpleasant Odour from the Boiling Cocoons.— Native Workgirls.—Their Pay.—Clever Workers.—The Finished Hank.—Broussa Gauze.—Handkerchiefs.—Towelling.—The Bath Bornous.—"Burundjik" . . . . . . . . . . 180

## XIII.—THE MINERAL BATH.

The Yeni-Kaplidja Hammam.—A Shifting Crowd.—The Djamékian, or Robing-room.—The Hammamdji.—The Sookluk.—Screened Compartments and Dwelling-rooms. —Great Heat of the Springs.—Picturesque Scene in the Djamékian. — Swing Cradles. — Youth and Age. — A Betrothal Party.—Two Brides Elect. — Ceremonious "Sela'ams."—A Handsome Swimming-bath.—Mosaics and Coloured Tiles.—A Beautiful Bather.—Touching Solicitude for an Aged Negress . . . . . 186

## XIV.—THE PEARL OF THE EASTERN ARCHIPELAGO.

Mythology and Legend.—The Home of Erinna.—Genoese Castles.—An Open Roadstead.—Fine View from the Promontory.—A Prosperous Island —Careful Cultivation of the Olive.—Lesbian Wine.—The Harbours.—Fine Harbour of Hïera.—Valuable Hot Springs.—The Tomb of Kiatib Oglon.—His Fate.—A Ruined Téké and Cemetery.—Curious Epitaphs.—Bâhhl Ghenghizz Khan, the last Prince of the Crimea.—Beauty of the Mytileniotes.— The Daughters and their Fortunate Destiny.—Unequal Laws.—Custom stronger than Law . . . . 19

## XV.—ROUMANIAN MONASTERIES. NO. I. . . 209

## XVI.—ROUMANIAN MONASTERIES.
#### NO. II.—ADAM, JASSY.

From Bucharest to Berlad.—Jewish Coachmen.—A "Foolwoman."—Monastery of Adam.—The "Fundarik."—The Maïca.—The Maïca Staritza.—The Call to Service by the "Bar and Mallet."—Interior of the Church and Costume of the Nuns.—Church Ornaments.—Comfortable Homes of the Maïcas, their Confectionery, their Industry, and their Dress.—The New Monastic Regulations.—In the Staritza's Garden.—The Procession and the Prayers for Rain.—A worthy Lady Superior.—An Early Drive.—An inevitable "Difficulty."—Soothing Scenery.—At Jassy —Great Jewish Population.—Beautiful old Church, Treï Sfetitili.—St. Nicholas . . . 216

## XVII.—ROUMANIAN MONASTERIES.
### NO. III.—SÉCU AND SIKLA.

Charming Drive.—The Monastery of Sécu.—The Parenté Arfundrah.—Hospitality.—Foundation of Sécu.—Nestor and Metrofana.—Fortifications.—The former importance of the Monastery.—The Refectory.—"Mamaliga."— Start for Sikla.—The Bullock Cart.—Our Escort.— Parenté Samuel.—Armed Monks.—Sylvan Glades.—The Forest.—A Wild Mountain Track.—Magnificent Scenery. An uncomfortable Slope towards the Precipice.—The Monastery of Sikla.—A Venerable Staritz.—Origin of the Chapel of St. Theodora.—A Peaceful Scene —Parenté Samuel's Curls.—A Mountain Storm.—Sobastria . . 233

## XVIII.—ROUMANIAN MONASTERIES.
### NO. IV.—DURÂU, TCHAKLÂU, THE BISTRITZA.

From Piatra.—Picturesque Environs.—The Monastery of Bistritza.—Tomb of Alexander the Good.—A Beautiful Church.—Bisericanu.—Pingariciora.—Village of Hangû. —Moldavian Peasantry.—Costume.—Difficult Mountain Track.—The Monastery of Durâu.—A Tradition of Tourists.—From the Little Balcony.—Parenté Hilarion and the Neophyte.—Transylvanian Peasants.—Eidelweis. —A Little Miser.—Floats along the Troughs.—Repchiuni.—Leisurely Construction of the Raft.—Obstructions.—Lowering Clouds.—The Master Raftsman.— Rain and Rapids.—Skilful Guidance.—The Eddies.— A Sad Landing.—A Compassionate Traveller.—At Piatra.—Maritza.—Zeckler Harvesters.—Homewards . 249

## XIX.—IN CRETE.

### NO. I.—CANEA AND ITS ENVIRONS.

In the Harbour of Canea.—Rethymo.—Brother Geronimo.—Arrival at Canea.—The Convent Parlour.—An Improvised Home.—A Street Scene.—Our Opposite Neighbour.—The Grocer's Shop.—Cretan Costume.—Funerals.—Twelve o'clock.—The former Lords of the Island.—Ancient Costumes.—Raouf Pasha.—Unusual Visitors.—The Rhiza and the White Mountains.—Aloes . . 270

## XX.—IN CRETE.

### NO. II.—CANEA AND ITS ENVIRONS.

Church Mosques.—The Ancient Arsenal of the Galleys.—Venetian Fortifications.—The Negro Village.—Arab Huts.—Street Carriages.—The Leper Settlement.—Red Earth and Olive-trees.—Murniés.—Georghi, the Coffee-seller.—Honey and Travelling Bees.—"Lâvdanum."—The Spring of Perivoglia.—View from the Terrace.—The Garden of Munir Agha.—Fine Orange-trees.—Khalépa . . . . . . . . . . 284

# SKETCHES OF EASTERN LIFE AND SCENERY.

## I.

### FESTIVITIES IN THE HAREM.

Preparations for the Festival.—The Talika.—The Mistress of Ceremonies.—Zeheïra.—The State Couch.—Scenic Effects.—Rich Presents.—Jew Mountebanks.—The Bastinado.—Dinner.—Bouyouroûn.—How to Vanquish a Stuffed Lamb.—Zerdè pillaw.—Khoshab.—From behind the Cafesses.—"Tastes Differ."—The Kiosk in the Vineyards.—Rest.

At the country house of T—— Pasha there are great preparations for the festival of his three elder sons. This is a very important event in the life of a Mussulman family; long and costly preparations are made for it; all relations, friends, and even acquaintances, are invited to share in the feasting and rejoicing, and it is usual for persons of position and means to collect from the poorer families of the neighbourhood all who can take part in and benefit by the occasion.

We started from Pera (in acceptance of a pressing invitation), driven by poor old Eli, a Bulgarian, and one of the best talika-drivers in Constantinople. His was a rickety vehicle, and the old grey horse looked almost past work, yet Eli being fortunately sober, we felt that nothing short of an inevitable collision could upset us, and we jumped and thumped and swayed, and plunged—resigned and suffering—until at length we came to a halt on the summit of a steep hill.

Being accustomed to this uneasy method of locomotion, we had seized opportunities between the convulsions to admire, in passing, the fresh country in its bright May garments; the grassy, flowery slopes around Bebek; the black tents of a gipsy encampment; the rural lanes, the evergreen hedges, where ilex, myrtle, and scented bay form a glistening screen, parting now and then to frame delicious little vignettes of the sapphire Bosphorus and the violet hills of Asia.

Eli, leaving his talika to take care of itself for a while, descends the steep slope with us, and proceeds to knock lustily with a large stone on a yellow wooden gate which we suppose to be the entrance to the property of T—— Pasha. There is no response: more pounding with the stone; still no result. At length a man hails us from a neighbouring cottage window. The "dughiun" (festival) is at the great yali near the water. We must descend to the foot of the hill. He furthermore vouchsafes to lounge out in course of time, and, after some parley, consents to guide us and to carry our bags for a consideration. So we go down a sort of cataract of boulders and brambles, until at length, faint with heat and exertion, we find ourselves landed at the harem door.

A strange unknown woman shouts a boisterous welcome from the top of the flight of steps. She wears a white dress, very short, as ready for active service; her eyebrows are painted to meet in severe precision in the centre, her eyelids are touched with "surmeh" and her finger-tips dyed with henna; a mighty bunch of flowers on the forehead denotes the festive character of the occasion. She proves to be the hired mistress of the ceremonies, deputed to welcome the guests on their first arrival, to see that every one receives a due share of attention, and to keep up the spirits of the company generally.

The hall is quite full of women and girls in their gayest dresses; amongst them Zéheïra Hanum, who comes forward to us, both hands extended in eager and affectionate welcome. How charming and graceful she looks, in a light dress of white and gold-coloured muslin; on her head a coronet adorned with flowers, an ostrich plume, and some very handsome diamonds!

In a cool saloon overhanging the Bosphorus the

ladies of the family are assembled : the Têzé Hanum (the aunt), her witty daughter, the daughter-in-law, and some others, all richly dressed, principally in white, and blazing with diamonds. After the sweetmeats and coffee, the ladies wander away into another room, where a heavy curtain has been stretched across to screen off the entrance to the selamlik. From behind the curtain a hum of many voices and sounds of music reach us; the little boys are there with all the masculine portion of the family and guests. After spending some time listening to the monotonous rasping of the native instruments, the ladies—weary of peeping by turns round the edge of the goats'-hair " perdeh "—propose a visit to the room where the state bed has been prepared for the young brothers.

It is a magnificent construction : the coverlet is of rose-coloured satin stiff with gold embroidery, and there are richly ornamented silk and satin pillows and quilts laid about in profusion; above, a canopy formed of wreaths of artificial flowers, with feathers of many colours mingled with pearl ornaments, amulets, and charms. A feather fan is leaning in one corner, and, at the back of the bed, very prettily grouped, are clusters of imitation fruit, with grass and little toy lambs and cows and birds. A table beside the bed is heaped with oranges, toys, and presents.

Whilst we are yet admiring the delicate gold embroideries, there is a movement amongst the company; the distant sound of music has ceased, and we are all invited to leave the room, which is divided from the landing at the head of the staircase by a glazed partition shaded by curtains. Here all the women are crowded together to look on through the transparent muslin. It has all the effect of a theatrical representation: the empty room with the decorated bed is the stage. First of all enters on the scene the Pasha: he passes a slow and careful inspection of the preparations and withdraws; next, a *troupe* of Jew mountebanks take up their station in front of the bed, with tambourines and instruments of music. After a long pause of expectation, they receive a signal from the selamlik and suddenly burst into animation—the cymbals clash horribly, the tambourines jangle, the Turkish drums are banged into a deafening discord; then silence, a pause, another wild burst, and a man rushes in, bearing Mustafa Bey in his arms. He places him on the gorgeous couch. There is another pause of expectation; the mothers of the little beys, gazing anxiously through the muslin, are beginning to weep hysterically, the nurses and elder slaves weeping for sympathy. Again a fierce clang of the instruments, and Ethem Bey is carried rapidly in and laid beside his brother. Every one shouts, the women cry " Mashallah ! " several times, and before the shouts have ceased the third blast of triumph heralds the arrival of Osman Bey, who is also placed upon the bed. Then the instruments and shouts burst forth with renewed vigour; the Pasha comes in, and with the feather fan begins himself to fan the children, and a negress, shrouded like a ghost, makes her appearance to attend upon them. Friends crowd round to present their offerings; they bring toys of all sorts, gold and silver cups and spoons, jars of sweetmeats, a cannon, a large toy goat—anything, in short, that may amuse the three beys, who are nestled all in a row amongst the silks and satins and gold embroideries, their caps heavily adorned with pearls and diamonds. The children are from eight to ten or eleven years of age.

All this time the Jews are dancing and playing antics before them; a small mountebank boy, on the shoulders of a man, strives to catch their attention by his contortions; the crash and din of the music overpowers every other sound.

There is a pause in the performance, and the men withdraw from the room; the folding-doors are thrown back, and the tearful mothers are at length admitted into it. On a nearer view, many of the presents prove to be of considerable value. A diamond ring, a watch, or objects equally costly, are very customary gifts from the father, whose fortune has on this occasion to meet heavy charges, as, in addition to the outlay of all kinds incurred for the family, he is expected to lodge and feast for several days all the children who participate in the ceremonies and festivities of the "sunnet," as well as all their families; besides which each child receives a present in money and clothing. It may be well imagined that these occasions of almost boundless hospitality and expenditure are a terrible strain upon incomes already overburdened by a needlessly numerous household.

The mountebanks being about to resume work, the women are warned to vacate the premises once more; and we accordingly take up our stations behind some movable lattices stretched across the opening of folding-doors. Here we have an excellent view of the puppets. They are managed cleverly enough by the Jewish mountebanks, who are undeniably the most degraded type of humanity that can be met with here. A tall, villainous-looking man sits cross-legged on one side of the dark curtain that conceals his confederate. He wears a fantastic peaked cotton cap and holds a tambourine. The chief wit of the puppets seems to consist in running full tilt at the Jew and dashing off his cap, for which outrage they have to be bastinadoed on the spot—made to lie down, the soles of their feet turned up, and the punishment administered with great science and evident experience. One black puppet amongst them — exceedingly ill-behaved and coarse in his manners — did not certainly receive his due share of this same stick; but every one seemed satisfied and delighted with the performance.

A little before sunset, escaping from the heat of the crowded rooms, we made an attempt to visit the gardens, through a door leading out on to the hillside. The door was fast locked, however, the key was nowhere, and we were obliged to return into the house, finding, at length, a cool retreat in a room overlooking the water, where the pretty ladylike niece of Besmè Hanum came to entertain us with her conversation.

Dinner was served at sunset, on two tables in the great marble hall, or rather on round trays, beneath which, on the ground, was spread a white cloth embroidered in colours, the guests sitting around on cushions. The numerous company could not, of course, be accommodated at one time. The custom of eating from a dish placed in the centre makes a round table indispensable, and it must not be so large as to prevent a person from reaching the middle of it with ease; consequently, it is difficult to seat more than six or eight people together at the festive board. Several tables are therefore spread in the great hall, and the guests must be served in relays, the most honoured passing first in order.

They paid us that compliment. Water was poured over our hands from a slender "ibrik" into a "sayan," or perforated basin, both vessels being of silver, exquisitely chased and ornamented; a soft gold-embroidered Broussa towel was thrown lightly over the hands by another attendant. This serves also as the dinner napkin, one end being passed over the left shoulder; and we were established as comfortably as could be contrived round a steaming tureen of delicate white soup. Dipping our tortoiseshell spoons into this was easy—you must "do as they do at Rome" on these occasions—but the next dish was embarrassing. A lamb stuffed with rice, raisins, and pistachio nuts, and roasted whole, was borne along by two stout slaves and placed in the centre of the dining-tray. It is a high festival dish, and most excellent, but difficult of access with no other implements than a slender spoon and fingers. When dining with the family in this hospitable harem, knives and forks are always provided for our benefit, but on this public occasion we had begged that no invidious distinction might be made, and that we should be allowed to share the fortunes of war with our neighbours. But how to open the attack. We hesitate, reconnoitring. It is our part to follow the lead of the lady deputed to head the table and inaugurate the proceedings. She has pronounced the courteous "bouyouroûn," without which no well-mannered person begins action. "Bouyouroûn! bouyouroûn!" shouts the official mistress of the revels, hovering around and nodding her roses at us, excited and hospitable. "Bouyouroûn!" murmurs a gentle and famished neighbour, anxious to commence operations and too polite to rush on before. But how? From what limb of the formidable "rôti" can we grasp and secure with delicacy and decorum a dripping portion with only Adam's forks for weapons? People are hungry. The difficulty is solved by two ebony arms, adorned by blue glass bangles, that pass suddenly over my shoulder; the monkey-like fingers seize a leg, a guest on the opposite side grasps a shoulder. The lamb is torn asunder briskly, energetically, dismembered in an instant. Every one rushes at once into the vanquished mound of meat and stuffing, and the friendly negress selecting a tempting piece, deposits it benevolently on my slab of unleavened bread. Could one show hesitation where so much hospitality and good-will were intended? The readiest escape is certainly the prompt use of one's own fingers in such emergencies, if you have a natural objection to be fed by those of other people.

The repast was excellent—the usual amount of stuffed cucumbers, cheese puffs, vegetables of many kinds, the gala dishes of "baklawa," "tawouk mohalibé" (the white of chicken pounded into a "blancmange" of rice-flour, milk, and sugar), and the inevitable "zerdè pillaw," made of boiled rice, ornamented with cinnamon, saffron, and pomegranate-seeds. This zerdè pillaw is also an indispensable delicacy at every marriage feast. Pillaw is invariably the last dish served; it is followed by bowls of "khoshab" (a thin syrup flavoured with dried fruits), which is frequently the only liquid taken, although water is brought when asked for.

On rising from table the silver ewers are once more presented; the water is slightly warmed and scented, and there is a delicate ball of soap supported on the raised centre of the basin. The coffee, tchibouks, and cigarettes are handed round in the "sofa," the large central saloon on the first floor.

The drums and tambourines could be heard from a distance hard at work in the children's room, and the company soon move off to secure the best possible places behind the trellised screens. It is very trying to the unaccustomed eye, this peering through the small apertures of the cafesses, but we did our utmost to gaze with the best appearance of interest that we could command, in order not to disappoint our kind and gentle hostesses. They, poor women! were enchanted with the spectacle. There is so little to vary the monotony of their lives that the childish jugglery and buffoonery of these miserable jesters was to them an amount of entertainment that could hardly be sufficiently enjoyed. They put us in the best places, but we soon contrived to yield the position to more appreciative eyes, and I was very near falling to sleep in a quiet armchair in the dim background. This would not do. A strong effort, and I rouse myself once more. The Jews are still banging and clashing in the lighted chamber beyond the grating, and six stout elderly pashas are sitting very solemnly on a row of crimson seats, smoking six long tchibouks, and gazing and nodding grave approval of the show, which is a modified representation of Karaghenz (the Turkish Punch). The old gentlemen sat through the whole of the long performance with great steadiness and determination.

At midnight we at length ventured to withdraw to a room where mattresses for fourteen had been arranged upon the floor. It was only necessary to fancy it the cabin of a crowded steamer, and it did very well. Certainly no care or attention had been omitted by the hanums that might make our visit agreeable under the difficult circumstances. We slept from utter fatigue, but the native ladies remained above stairs until the pale dawn marked the swelling outlines of the Asiatic shore, the music and noise continuing also all through the night.

A few weeks later I paid, with a friend, another

visit to the harem of T—— Pasha, and found the family installed for the hot months in a charming kiosk nearly on the summit of the hill, amongst the vineyards and gardens of the property. The approach is rustic enough: a piece of string and a latch give admittance to a pleasant garden, fragrant with roses and clematis. A sound of voices drew us through the shady paths to the neighbourhood of the dwelling, where I came upon a black cook washing vegetables at a fountain—a large fine-looking woman, with splendid teeth gleaming as she uttered a joyous welcome; her sable head was adorned with scarlet blossoms. She seemed to know me well, and with much volubility and beaming smiles explained where the ladies were to be found.

They were seated in such a delightful room—so cool and breezy and flower-scented. The kiosk has been much improved lately: a broad verandah, running round three sides of it, is thickly draped with westeria, jessamine, and roses—a perfumed bower, from which you look out upon one of the most glorious panoramas of this part of the straits. The massive towers of Mahomet II. rise out of a world of heaving foliage; a few brown and red wooden houses are dotted here and there amongst the trees. Lower down a wilderness of sharp grey rocks and tangled shrubs, backed by the blue water and the swelling lilac-tinted hills of the opposite shore; on the left-hand, in strong relief, the gnarled and twisted form of a majestic pine-tree.

All is so calm and restful, so quiet, soft, and homelike, as we sit there a little later in the day, over the after-dinner coffee; the children are playing in the verandah beyond the open windows; the musical chant of a muezzim rises faintly from far beneath, where the white minaret gleams amongst the cypresses; a goat's bell tinkles from a neighbouring brow; the insects hum drowsily. My friend, unable to speak to the ladies, is nestled amongst soft pillows in the corner of a divan, where the breeze comes through the clustering jessamine; she dozes gently, the elder hanum smokes a pensive cigarette; Zéheïra is slowly re-stringing the pearls of her necklace, which had served to deck the fez of her little son on the occasion of the late festivity; and Leila Hanum, the Pasha's second daughter, seated in a quiet corner with her frame, is at work upon a towel of Broussa stuff which she embroiders in gold at either end as a present for her papa.

## II.

### THE BETROTHAL OF DJENANIAH CALPHA.

A Valuable "Halaïk."—Difficult Courtship and "Kismet."—The Ceremony of the "Nikyah" (the betrothal).—The Imām's Questions.—The Marriage Contract.—The Shower of Coin.—Gifts of Jewellery.—Fear of the Evil Eye.

DJENANIAH is to be married. She is only a Circassian slave. What can it signify how she is disposed of, how put out of the way, now that her services are no longer required? It signifies a very great deal, for Djenaniah is a humble dependent of one of those old-fashioned Mussulman families where the halaïk or slave is, in her degree, esteemed and cared for as one of themselves, for whose welfare they are responsible, and towards whom the tie of good-will and protection continues through life. Ibrahim Bey, the worthy master of that household, had bought her, a tiny girl of three years old, and putting her under the care of his young wife, the little halaïk grew up with the children of the house, to which no second wife was brought to disturb its peace and harmony. She was trained in habits of exquisite cleanliness and order; and the making of most of the garments of the household, the embroidery of the linen, the washing and ironing, the pickles and preserves, the zerdè pillaw and the kadaif for times of festival, the sherbet and the delicate creamy coffee, the cauldrons of ashourah, and the Ramazan distribution to the poor, all bore witness to Djenaniah Calpha's careful supervision and labour. She has indeed given a longer time of service than is generally expected from a halaïk, for she was too valuable to be easily dispensed with: during many years she nursed and waited on the bedridden mother of the bey, but the old lady is now dead, and it is time to give the faithful, patient woman her paper of liberty and a home of her own.

Ibrahim Bey and his wife made many and anxious inquiries to find a good steady man, with some small means and settled employment, as husband for their calpha, and finally made choice of Osman Effendi, the imām of a small mosque in one of the Asiatic villages of the Upper Bosphorus.

Djenaniah is no longer young, and has never had a claim to good looks; but she has a gentle, calm face, a quiet manner and soft voice, and the imām consents to take her as his wife on the report of her good qualities and house-keeping talents, as well as for the benefit of the connection with the bey's family. Whether she be pretty or otherwise is a matter to be left entirely to "kismet," for it is not to be supposed that he could obtain even a glimpse of her features. Djenaniah, however, has the advantage of him in this respect: there are many chances of observation through the cafesses or by the chink of the perdeh of the harem door, so she knows that her intended is about thirty-five, with a pleasant countenance, soft dark eyes, and an expression of placid good temper.

It is the day of the betrothal; a small group of men has assembled in the hall which separates the harem and the selamlik. The party consists of the vakeel, or representative of the bridegroom, his two witnesses, and one or two near relatives, with the imām of the quarter acting as civil magistrate, for the nikyah, or betrothal, which is the only marriage ceremony, is a civil rather than a religious rite. On the part of the bride, there are present her vakeel, two witnesses, Ibrahim Bey, and his eldest son. The door leading from the harem into the hall is slightly ajar, and Djenaniah, brought by two of her companions, is stationed behind it. The imām has recited a prayer, and the bride's vakeel comes to the other side of the gap and asks, "Do you, Djenaniah, accept me as your vakeel, to arrange the marriage with Osman Effendi, the son of Mahmoud Agha, of Koyoundjik? There is no answer, but a trembling rustle and agitated whisper from the friends. The question is repeated a second and yet a third time before a faint "Yes" concludes this part of the ceremony, for it is the correct thing for the fiancée to show the utmost reluctance and not to yield consent until three times solicited. Then the marriage contract is signed by the vakeels and the witnesses, the amount of dowry stated, and a new name agreed upon for the bride. Djenaniah is no longer a halaïk, and she will be called Hafiza Hanum. A messenger has ridden off in hot haste to convey the news of the signature of the contract to the bridegroom, who remains at home. The bearer of good tidings receives a handsome present. It is to be remarked that the amount of dowry acknowledged in the marriage contract must be paid to the wife if her husband should wish eventually to divorce her, and this law often acts as a check to maintain her in her position, from which she could otherwise be but too easily displaced.

Djenaniah is led back to her room, and the mother and nearest female relatives of the bridegroom begin to arrive at the konak. They are received at the entrance of the harem by an old calpha acting as mistress of the ceremonies, attended by a group of women. She holds a silver tray on which are a small dish with a piece of lighted charcoal and a silver filigree vase of incense. She waves this about the hands of the visitors as they cross the threshold; yashmaks and ferádjés are then taken off and the incense-bearer precedes them up the staircase. She pauses on the top step, and the guests bow their heads towards the perfumed vapour as they pass on into the sala. This use of incense is supposed to overcome all evil influences.

The visitors are now seated on the principal divan, the bridegroom's mother in the place of honour, and with a clashing sound of instruments a small procession makes its appearance from the opposite direction. Some girls with violins, cymbals, tambourines, and castanets are escorting the bride, who approaches slowly, upheld on either side by the kiayah and the hanum's old nurse; they grasp her arm above the elbow as if she must sink to the ground without this support. As she enters the hall, a shower of small silver coin is thrown into the air above her head.

Djenaniah is dressed in all the finery that could be got together; a rich velvet antary and schalwars embroidered in gold has been hired for the occasion in the bazaars; the heavy mass of diamonds on her head are lent by the hanum and by other ladies of the family; the fine brilliant on her finger is a present from the bey, and the handsome jewelled earrings a collective offering from the children of the family. She comes forward to salute the ladies, kissing the hem of their robe or the hand according to age and rank, and is then for the first time seated, by right, in the presence of her mistress. As soon as she is placed, facing the row of ladies, her future mother-in-law steps forward to offer her gifts of jewellery.

The tambourine and castanet players dance round and round the bride as she sits with folded hands and downcast eyes, and coins are again thrown, which occasions a vigorous and noisy scramble amongst the spectators. Refreshments are handed and the day of betrothal comes to an end. It is exceedingly difficult to witness the ceremony of betrothal just described, as the fear of the evil eye, always weighing on the Oriental mind, has an overpowering influence on these occasions.

The interval between the ceremony of the nikyah and the taking home of the bride is usually ten or fifteen days, but sometimes the delay is much greater. Children are even occasionally betrothed in infancy, and must wait many years for their marriage festivities.

Widows are re-married on a Sunday, after sunset; young girls are taken to their new homes on Thursday afternoon. No marriage takes place during the Ramazan or in the second month of the Mussulman year, Sefer; it is considered unlucky.

## III.

### TAKING HOME THE BRIDE.

The New Name.—Bridal Gifts and Bridal Furniture.—Oppressive Finery; the Face Jewels and the Golden Veil.—Decorated "Talikas."—The Bride's Throne.—Free and Candid Criticisms.—The Prayer Carpet.—A Peaceful Home.

DJENANIAH—now called Hafiza Hanum—no longer a halaïk, but a nikyahli (a betrothed one), was not taken to her new home until more than a fortnight had passed since the ceremony of the betrothal and the marriage contract. During this interval the customary interchange of presents has been conscientiously made. The imām, Osman Effendi (the bridegroom), acquits himself of his obligations with great propriety and a strict observance of the etiquette that regulates these offerings, bringing to the door of the harem fruits, flowers, and sweetmeats; he was even found there, one morning, patiently waiting with a boiled chicken in his hand as a testimony of regard for his—as yet unseen—betrothed.

On the fourth day, however, a more important bridal gift made its appearance, and was borne at once into the presence of the buyuk hanum, for her inspection and approval. On loosening the green ribbons that tied up the shrouding muslin, it proved to be a handsome tray, bearing in the centre a vase filled with inferior bonbons, surrounded by bottles of perfume and ornamental pots of mastic, cloves, cardamums, and other spices; but the crowning glory of the offering—the finishing touch of elegance—appeared in the form of a solid pair of high-heeled black leather boots! On a previous day a small bag of gold coins had been sent to the bride, as also the naléyn, or bathing-clogs, inlaid with mother-of-pearl, never omitted in the list of bridal gifts.

The wedding furniture has been taken, with some ceremony, to the house in Stamboul where the newly married couple are to pass the winter. The greater part of this plenishing is most liberally provided by Ibrahim Bey (who bears all the expenses of the marriage), and some things are gifts of friends of the family: there are stuffs for the divans and hangings, and camels' hair door curtains; a handsome store of bedding and household linen, with every requisite for the bath, and all the furnishing of the kitchen, everything as much as possible tied up in coloured gauze, bedecked with tinsel and streamers of ribbon, and carried in triumphal state on men's heads, or in talikas decorated with gay stuffs. The simple halaïk's worldly goods are taken home in an hour : the bridal furniture of a sultana (some years since) was carried from the Seraglio to her new palace in an uninterrupted procession lasting an entire week!

On the Tuesday before the marriage, Hafiza has been taken in state to the bath, accompanied by all the ladies and serving women of the harem; her fingers and toes are dyed with henna and her hair perfumed, after which, completely draped in her new takim, or set of bathing wraps, she clatters about on her bright new clogs, to kiss the hands of all the hanums in their order of precedence.

It is Thursday, the day of marriage. The customary present of fruit has been sent in by the bridegroom, and Hafiza, nearly crushed by the weight of her ponderous bridal finery, sits anxiously awaiting the signal of departure. Her dress is a crimson velvet antary, embroidered in gold (hired for the occasion), and, in addition to the mass of jewels composing her headdress (lent for the day), she has four diamonds fastened on her face : on the forehead, cheeks, and chin. A veil, like a cloud of long gold threads, falls on either side, from the top of her head. When she prepares to quit the harem, she wears no feràdjé, and, instead of the yashmak, a dark gauze handkerchief sprigged with gold entirely conceals her features.

The young daughter of a family, as she leaves her home, bends to kiss the father's hand and to ask his blessing, upon which he clasps a girdle round her waist and leads her to the foot of the stairs; the liberated halaïk respectfully kisses the hands of master and mistress, and departs in charge of an ancient dame, the kiayah or housekeeper of the harem.

The wedding procession is not very long; but the talikas are duly ornamented with their strips of bright stuffs wound round the lamps; the vakeels and witnesses, riding in front, display gaily coloured scarves, everything indicating a well-ordered bridal party, and the bride's carriage reaches the door of her new home; but here a difficulty arises. At the sound of the approaching carriages the bridegroom has hastened to the entrance; he stands at the wide-open door ready to hand in his bride, but she draws back and at first refuses to leave the carriage. It is thought right and becoming that she should hesitate and require great and respectful solicitation before entering her husband's home. Some young ladies will boast that they have kept their bridegrooms standing on the pavement for an hour, in vain. Hafiza, a gentle, unassuming woman, steps down after a short delay, and is supported very slowly up the staircase, held under the elbow by Osman Effendi, her veil still closely drawn down. The women in the great hall through which they pass hastily veil their faces, and money is thrown over the bride's head as she is led into the principal room and seated on a sort of throne, under a canopy of artificial garlands. Having thus disposed of his veiled charge, the husband comes back, again scattering money, and vanishes into the selamlik to rejoin his friends; the rest of the day is passed in festivity and in going to mosque, accompanied by the whole party.

In the harem, all the gossips of the neighbourhood are making the most of their golden opportunity. The entrance is free to every woman who may choose to wander in to criticise the bride, who sits immovable and speechless, her eyes cast down, her hands crossed, and her feet tucked under her. The veil is now thrown back, the gold threads carefully arranged, and she must endure unflinchingly the remarks which are uttered with as much freedom as though she were a lay figure. "Mashallah! yes, it is true, neighbour; seen quite near she is not so bad-looking as they say, but is there not a cast in that left eye? And the eyebrows! not fine and bushy, and meeting on the bridge of the nose, but a thin soft line, quite mean and shabby! Vuï! vaï! they have done her face painting very badly! The diamonds fine, do you say? Who denies that? I think I know a diamond when I see it, respected neighbour, though every one may not have *my* opportunities, but who knows how many hanums have lent their jewels for the wedding? And it is few enough she'll have when all is returned honestly, as, inshallah! we must *hope* they will be. Now, her head looks as if it would tumble off if that black girl wasn't helping to hold it up. Have you seen the husband, Muniré Hanum? A poor weak reed of a man, and not half so well off as they pretend. Old Ayesha wanted me to give him my Fatma, but I look higher than *that* for a son-in-law!" And so the shifting crowd passes and stares. They discuss the trousseau, the new house, the prospects of the household; and the poor victim of stringent ways and customs must remain thus until the muezzim calls the fifth prayer, when the bridegroom, spreading his prayer-carpet just within the entrance, goes slowly through his devotions, the wife standing up with folded hands, after which he raises her veil and, for the first time, looks upon her face, while he offers his marriage gift of jewellery. Now, if the bride is quick and self-possessed, while the veil is being raised, and before he has clearly seen her features, she must (says superstition) advance her foot and tread on her bridegroom's toe, as a certain means of securing for ever after her ascendancy in the household. Refreshments are immediately brought in, and the bride performs her first act of wifely duty in handing to her lord his pipe and coffee. When the lady is of superior rank this ceremony is omitted.

Marriage festivities frequently continue for three days, during which almost open house is kept. Zerdè pillaw, sweetened rice coloured with saffron and sprinkled with grains of pomegranate, is a dish never forgotten on these occasions.

On the day after the marriage, a present of clotted cream is sent by the bridegroom to the family of the bride, and he comes soon afterwards to pay his respects to the gentlemen and to send in elaborate messages of compliment to the harem.

A bride remains at home a month or six weeks, but she may receive her friends. Her first visit must be to her husband's mother.

The wedding festivities of our gentle Hafiza have been as simple as could be consistent with scrupulous attention to every necessary detail. The most important feature in the transaction—the choice of a husband—has proved singularly fortunate. The imām, Osman Effendi, and his wife, though with straitened means, are very happy in their marriage. We saw them in their modest home but a few days since; it is a poor place, but exquisitely clean and orderly. They have been married a year, and "during that time," said the worthy man, "we have not had one difference of opinion—not one unkind word!"

Hafiza has but one regret, but that is very keenly

felt—her longing to see once more the family of Ibrahim Bey, now removed to a distance. "I have been with them all my life," she said, with tears in her eyes; "the effendi and the hanum have been my father and mother; and, oh! little Zéheïra, the grandchild, she never left me until I came away. My heart is withering, my eyes ache to see them once again."

We withdrew, musing. This aspect of the condition and treatment of a "slave," a simple and everyday experience in the great mass of Mussulman households in this country, has it not as good a claim to honest judgment and fair appreciation as the popular theory of neglect and ill-treatment so tenaciously clinging to the name of "slave," and justified only in the small minority of those harems that are painfully striving to throw off their old rules of life without attaining to any higher and better principles of guidance?

# IV.

## UNDERGROUND STAMBOUL.

Yéré-Batan-Seraï.—The Mysterious Lake.—A Palace of the "Djinns."—Lukium.—The Cistern of the Hippodrome.—Bin-Bir-Direk.—The Cistern of Theodosius.—The Cistern of Arcadius.—Tchukur Bostan.—The Cisterns of Bonus, of the Emperor Anastasius, of the Church of Pantocrator, of Boudroum Djami, of St. John Studius.—Massive Subterranean Remains.—Fazli Pasha.

WERE it necessary to strengthen the impression of the culpable neglect with which the great question of the water supply of Constantinople has been—until lately—left to the chances of rain or drought, it would suffice to visit some of the ruined cisterns constructed for the benefit of the ancient city, and to note, even in the abandonment and decay of those mighty works, the startling contrast between the actual absence of all adequate provision, and the costly labour and anxious care bestowed on this important subject by the Roman and Byzantine rulers of this great metropolis.

Amongst these little-known remains of the stately and beautiful capital of the East, the cistern named by the Turks Yéré-Batan-Seraï (the subterranean palace) is the most remarkable for its solid construction, the mystery of its unknown extent, and the legends that haunt its sombre wilderness of granite columns. The proper entrance even is unknown, probably filled up or destroyed by fire or earthquake. It is now reached through a narrow opening in the paved courtyard of a Turkish konak, behind the "souterasi," or water-tower that overlooks the great square of St. Sophia, at a stone's throw from the line of the tramway.

The master of this konak is obliging, and his servants alive to the advantages of backshish, so that there is little difficulty in gaining admittance, and with some bits of candle and a guide, you struggle down the irregular hole and reach a small slimy platform. A few steps descend to the level of the water. Out of the dark, motionless lake rise —weird and solemn—the granite columns with their finely wrought Corinthian capitals; here, looming greyly in the livid darkness; there, faintly touched by some wandering ray streaming through an opening in the roof. Far as the eye can reach, the dark water, the massive pillars, and the trembling threads of light, pass away into distance, as if the extent were indeed illimitable. The legends of the place relate that one adventurous explorer started in a boat, and was seen no more; that another, warned by his mysterious fate, unwound, as he advanced, a cord fixed near the entrance, and so, after a long interval, returning in safety to the little platform, told how for hours he had steadily rowed on and seen no limit to the dark silent lake.

Turkish superstition holds that djinns, and ghouls, and malignant water-spirits hold gruesome revel in the fearful shadows of this unearthly "palace." These sinister ideas cling fittingly to the place, and it is distressing to find one authority who, defying all thought of mystery, boldly ventures to affirm that " the roof rests on three hundred and thirty-six pillars, divided as to length into sixteen rows, in breadth into twenty-eight;" but the statement can neither be challenged, nor accepted, as all verification would seem to be impossible. The picturesque effect of this wonderful work has much decreased since the rebuilding of that quarter of Constantinople. Those who visited it some years ago, after a great fire had cleared some openings in the upper earth, can never forget the solemn majesty of the picture.

Yéré-Batan-Seraï is generally called the "Royal Cistern of Constantine the Great," and thought to receive its principal supply of water from a small river at the head of the Golden Horn. Some authorities give it a much more ancient date, and hold a theory that it is filled from a source at a considerable distance from the city.

Texier, in his description of Nicomedia, speaking of a great ruined cistern in the neighbourhood of that city, says: "The interior had three coatings: the first, applied directly on the brick, was a mixture of lime and cement; the second, a compound of powdered charcoal and lime; and the third, a very hard stucco made of pounded stone, lime, and oil." In White's "Constantinople," this mixture is called "lukium," and he remarks: "The impervious quality of this mixture is so efficacious that, although some tanks are entirely beneath the earth, and thus perpetually exposed to outward infiltration as well as inward pressure—and undoubtedly coeval with the earliest Byzantine monarchs—yet there is no record of their requiring repair, or of their having ever leaked."

Several important reservoirs are grouped about this, the highest and central point of old Constantinople. Leaving the "subterranean palace," you cross the ancient racecourse—the Atmeïdan—to its western limit; pass by the industrial schools and workshops, and entering the building in which the Janissaries' costumes are exhibited, pause at the foot of the staircase, where a small wooden door looks like the entrance to a cellar or dustbin. Behind that door, a few feet along the wall on the left hand, is an opening through which the vaults and pillars of a large reservoir, occupying the circular end of the hippodrome, can be distinctly seen. The little door is now jealously closed, and the people on the spot deny, perhaps ignore, the existence of this monument. But it is there nevertheless, and some further evidence is found by following the rounded line of the old wall on the sea side. One of our best local authorities calls this a cistern of Constantine.

Turn back now, and climb the short ascent towards the unbuilt ground behind the ruined palace of the German ambassadors. Amidst the mounds of stones and rubbish are openings fringed with rank grass and tangled briers, through which a strange, sad sound, a sort of mournful droning wail, rises, as if from the bowels of the earth. It is the hum of reeling wheels, and the smothered stir of human voices. We are standing above the "Bin bir direk" (the thousand and one columns). The entrance is through a mean doorway and down a steep flight of rough stone steps. The name of the thousand and one columns is misleading, there being only two hundred and twenty-four. They are in marble, of great height and divided into sections: the lower part is now embedded in the accumulations of earth and rubbish. Seen from the flight of steps, the effects of light and shadow are very striking. This is often called the cistern of Philoxenus, a Roman senator who came to Constantinople in the time of Constantine.

Quite near to this spot, in a northerly direction, is situated the ancient cistern of Theodosius, also dry. It is smaller than either of those already mentioned, and is chiefly remarkable for some handsome columns with fine Corinthian capitals. This ruin was brought into notice by the great fire of 1865. When we last looked down into the gulf-like cavity, an ancient Turk was dreamily engaged there in making twine for fishing nets.

The cistern of Arcadius, which, although not the most extensive, is, in point of workmanship and careful finish, the handsomest of these wonderful remains of former splendour, is situated at a considerable distance from the hill of the Hippodrome, near the mosque of Sultan Selim, that overlooks the Golden Horn. Passing the Gul Djami, the way lies up the valley, then, by a very steep and narrow street, winds past a fine old dark red and green konak, beyond which and still higher up, a ruinous brick building appears on the left hand, entered through a heavy iron door. You push this open, if possible, and a beautiful cluster of noble columns and sculptured capitals rises in the softened twilight of the great vaulted enclosure. The workmanship of these columns is remarkably fine and of varied designs; each pillar bears one or more crosses, some on the capital, some on the shaft. The whole height of the pillars, from the base, being visible, the effect is extremely majestic and imposing.

The largest of the open reservoirs, called " Tchukour Bostan" (the sunken garden) is found rather higher up the same hillside, beyond the cistern of Arcadius. It is a square of about two hundred yards, and serves as a vegetable garden and orchard. The white mulberries grown there are singularly abundant and fine. The water of some fountains in this quarter of Sultan Selim is the purest and best in Constantinople.

Another Tchukour Bostan, also a market-garden, lies near the side of the Divan Yol, not far from the Adrianople gate. It is by some called the cistern of Bonus, a patrician of the time of Heraclius. There is yet, again, a dried-up reservoir of the same kind near the mosque of Hekim Ali Pasha, in the quarter of Silivria Kapoussi. It is thought to have been built by the Emperor Anastasius.

Of the large cistern built by the tyrant Phocas, close to the Church of Pantocrator (Zeïrek Djamissi), only the massive outer wall can now be seen. The entrance is at present unknown; four rows of Corinthian columns formerly supported the roof.

Below the Boudroum Djami, on the side overlooking the Sea of Marmora, is found a cistern built during the reign of the Emperor Valens.

In connection with the once beautiful church and monastery of St. John Studius—now the mosque of Emir Ahkor—there exists a fine cistern; the roof rests on twenty-four columns with handsomely wrought capitals. It serves at the present time as a cowhouse and stable.

Besides the cisterns, other underground remains are from time to time brought to view by fire or demolition, and important parts of the city rest, unsuspectingly, over vast subterranean vaulted passages, blocks of masonry, buried columns, and other evidences of long forgotten monumental structures. This is the case in the neighbourhood of the Porte, at the Seraskierate, and in the quarter known as Fazli Pasha. In this last-named spot, the ground near the mortuary chapel and tomb of the eminent statesman, Fuad Pasha, is completely honeycombed with passages and walls of enormous thickness and strength. These were visible for a short while amidst the ruins of that fearful conflagration that swept across from the Horn to the Marmora; they have probably disappeared beneath the new buildings that now cover all that slope.

The site of the Seraskierate, and particularly the space between the building and the western wall of the enclosure, cover remains similar to those at Fazli Pasha, but of still grander proportions. When the foundations of the present War Office were laid, columns of marble, granite, and porphyry of enormous size were disinterred, and lay for some months upon the ground amongst fragments of richly carved capitals, and heathen funereal tablets.

# V.

## TURKISH HOME LIFE.

### The Harem.—Slavery.

Notwithstanding all that has been written about Turkey and the Turks, very little information has been offered on the subject of Turkish home life, as to which the most erroneous ideas still prevail in Western Europe.

An intimate acquaintance with the daily life of Turkish families shows us households where we find much that is far below and grievously opposed to our own estimate of the beauty and sanctity of family ties; yet the impartial observer cannot fail to recognise as still in force amongst them many old-fashioned homely virtues which the hard fret and strain of our eager, hurried Western life would seem to have weakened and outgrown amongst ourselves.

None but residents in a Mussulman country can thoroughly realise how difficult—it may be said how impossible—it is that even the most painstaking and conscientious of travellers or correspondents should be able to form an unbiased and correct opinion on the difficult subject of Turkish home life. The reason of the difficulty is, however, obvious; in non-Mussulman countries intelligent travellers can procure at least admittance into the native society, and are enabled to arrive at some approximate idea of the manners and ways of life peculiar to the country. The opinions thus formed are, doubtless, superficial, for to gain any accurate knowledge of the home life of a people you must live amongst them and with them; and, more, you must meet them half way on the road of human sympathy and kindly feeling; you must endeavour honestly to judge them according to their opportunities, and not according to our own standard of right and wrong; but yet some idea may be formed of the status of the different members composing a household. In Turkey this information even is unobtainable by the inquirer of the sterner sex, such visitors being rigorously excluded from the society of the feminine portion of a Mussulman household. No husband or master of a family would, under any circumstances, receive a friend within the limits of the harem, and the information on domestic matters can very rarely be gained but at second-hand, most often from sources inaccurate and untrustworthy. This rule of rigid exclusion has been relaxed, only within the last few years, in the case of medical men in the exercise of their profession.

Few even among the Christian ladies resident in Constantinople have time, opportunity, or inclination to make themselves acquainted with the Mussulman homes around them. The difference of religion, manners, and language form an insurmountable barrier to frequent intercourse; while there can be little community of thought and feeling and few subjects of common interest between the English lady and the Turkish " hanum ; " and so it frequently happens that intelligent and educated women will pass a great part of their lives in the Turkish capital without acquiring one new idea to correct those originally imported from their Western homes, to which they eventually return with the supposed experience gained by their long residence amongst the Mussulmans, and thus help unconsciously to confirm many errors on the subject.

But there are travelling ladies eager, energetic, truly desirous of gaining an insight into this secluded harem life. They are taken to pay a few visits in some of the less " civilised " homes ; they accept sweetmeats and coffee, endeavour to smoke a tchibouk or a cigarette, get through a somewhat tedious amount of mild conversation with the help of a native lady acting as interpretress, and the enthusiastic travellers are supposed to have mastered in this easy and rapid manner the intricacies of female life in Turkey.

Neither can a more truthful idea be formed of Turkish life from the gay groups of veiled women lingering in their carriages in the square of the "Sultan Bayezid," or animating like moving flower-beds, the meadows of the Sweet Waters of Europe and Asia. These women do not represent the mass of the feminine population. The ladies of a very strict and orthodox Turkish household are seldom seen in the promenades frequented by the "ghiaour" inhabitants of the capital; some of them deem it almost a sin to pass, even in a carriage, through the Christian suburb of Pera; so the world knows little about them, and forms its opinion on the subject of Turkish households from such as are gradually adopting in some degree the manners and usages of the "Franks." The strictly educated Turkish lady shrinks from innovations so strongly opposed to her sense of propriety, preferring as a safer rule of life the law of seclusion in which she has been brought up.

Far from envying the liberty of the Frank woman, many Turkish hanums look upon the care with which they are surrounded as a proof of the high estimation in which they are held by their male relations; and they bestow a half-contemptuous pity on the Christian lady, whose life and occupations are so untrammelled and so energetic. The Mussulman woman is generally content to lounge through her existence, with its household duties, the visits made and returned, the inspection of the wares of female pedlars, and an occasional family picnic in some shady spot on the shores of the Bosphorus, while those whose activity of mind takes a housewifely direction are busy with the homely cares which a numerous household must entail. They make or superintend the preparation of great stores of pickles and preserves; they cut out and assist in the making of all the clothes of the harem, slaves' included; they embroider the towels, the coverings for the pillows, and many other articles of daily use; and at certain times and seasons they superintend the distribution of vast cauldrons of pillaw given to the poor, and of ashoora, a sweet soup, which is dispensed freely to all who present themselves to claim it on the tenth day of the month of Moharrem—the first month of the Mohammedan year—at which time they commemorate the deaths of Hoseïn and his followers at Kerbela.

A great deal of time is spent by Turkish women in the examination of the goods of the female pedlars above-mentioned. These women infest the harem. They are for the most part Jewesses, and are the principal source of the great evil of lavish expenditure and debt which causes so much distress and ruin amongst them. They encourage the Mussulman women to take their greatly overcharged merchandise on credit, and all the savings of the poor slave girls generally pass in this manner into their dishonest hands; and, worse than this, they are the medium of unauthorised communications with the outer world, and of intrigues, to which, indeed, some Christians of Pera do not scruple to lend themselves.

As may naturally be imagined, the ceremony of visiting forms an important element in Turkish home life. The most punctilious etiquette regulates this method of killing time in the harems. Upon all occasions of festivity, public or private, visits are interchanged, those of respect and duty taking the first place, children visiting parents, younger brothers and sisters their elders in the family, all dependents hastening to compliment and to salute their benefactors. During the festivals of Bairam the first day is devoted to the reception of the family, household, and nearest relations; on the other days those less nearly connected with the family offer their congratulations. The slightest change in the daily routine supplies occasion for complimentary visits; even the removal to summer quarters, or the return to town for the winter, is a sufficient reason for the children and friends to felicitate the heads of the house on the auspicious change of residence.

When a lady arrives on a visit she brings with her, according to her position and means, one or two attendants. She is received at the foot of the staircase by the superior women of the harem or by a lalla, if the condition of the family admits of these dependents. The visitor is then carefully and slowly assisted upwards, supported on either side by the elbow, and on reaching the head of the stairs her yashmak and feràdjé are removed. The visit may be only a morning call; in that case the visitor frequently retains a band of muslin across the forehead (a part of the yashmak) as a sign that she does not intend to remain to dine, and, perhaps, to sleep; but, nevertheless the veil which has been removed is carefully ironed out, the ferâdjé neatly folded, and the whole out-door costume enclosed in a wrapper until the lady moves to take leave. These wrappers are frequently made of silk or satin, richly embroidered. As the visitor advances into the room she makes the salute called " téméné," touching the mouth and forehead. She is then seated on a line with her hostess, who retains the seat of honour in the corner of the divan, unless her visitor be of decidedly superior rank; the téméné are then recommenced, and minute inquiries are made after each member of the respective families. In these inquiries even the babies are included, with the ceremonious title of bey or hanum.

When the coffee is handed round a well-bred person will make a slight téméné addressed to the hostess; the same little politeness is repeated as the cup is returned to the hand of the attendant. When it is desired to show the utmost amount of respect and regard toward a visitor, the tiny coffee-cup in its filagree or jewelled "yarf" is offered by the daughter of the house; the creamy froth, called "caïmak," which usually forms on the surface of the cup first poured out, is considered as especially complimentary,

Unmarried girls, or even young married women, accompanying their mother or aunt on a visit, seldom speak unless personally addressed, and then only in a subdued and respectful manner. A younger sister never seeks to perform the duties of politeness which properly devolve on the elder, but is found quite prepared to do her part when, in her turn, she arrives at the dignity of eldest unmarried daughter. Young girls do not in general take coffee or smoke, those indulgences being considered as the privilege of married or elder ladies. No member of a harem enters or leaves the house—though only for an hour or two—without saluting the mistress of it. Children kiss the hand of the hanum, then touch it with the forehead. Dependents kiss, or rather endeavour to kiss, the hem of her robe, for good breeding requires that the lady should withdraw her dress from this salutation, as anxious to avoid the act of homage.

While praising much that is admirable in the manners and deportment of the young daughters of well-conducted families, we must not omit the fact that the mode of bringing up little children, especially of those belonging to the higher ranks, is sadly deficient in the careful moral training which, with religious teaching, we in England consider as the indispensable basis of sound education. They are reared, it is true, in habits of respect and submission towards their parents and elders, but no healthy control is exercised over their minds and dispositions. They are weakly indulged—in infancy by their mother and nurses, in childhood by the lallas and the domestics of the selamlik, where little girls, until they adopt the yashmak, may wander in freedom. They are thus constantly in the society and under the care of uneducated people, whose excessive indulgence, as well as the conversations carried on without restraint before the children, are most injurious to them in every way.

It is usual to accuse Turkish women of great freedom and want of delicacy in this matter of conversation. The blame may have been formerly fully justified, but of late years a very great improvement has been observed in this respect, although in many harems there is yet much to be amended.

The above remarks apply more especially to families that still retain the punctilious and stately manners of the good old times. With the march of progress some familiar usages and customs have been relaxed, others altogether abandoned, and it is impossible to deny that in proportion as European civilisation has made its way into a household, so also many habits and observances—descriptively known by Englishwomen as "nice ways of doing things"—have been set aside, as old-fashioned and out of keeping with modernised ideas.

The Turks as a people are exceedingly charitable. This bright trait of the national character is too well known to need proof, yet I cannot refrain from repeating the opinion of a French writer, who calls the East "the land of benevolence . . . where pious asylums are opened for science, for indigence, and for sickness; where private charity has bordered the public roads with fountains for the refreshment of the wayfarer, and where the poorest village maintains a 'moosafirlik' or guests' room, where the traveller may find lodging and simple nourishment at the expense of the community." Beside the cloisters where the imāms and students are lodged, are found the khans for the poor and the traveller, and the hospitals for the sick; while colleges and public libraries are also a dependence of the mosque that provides for their maintenance. "Let the torrent of your liberality," says a Turkish proverb, "flow from the hand, so that the sound of it may not reach the ear."

In Turkish households, on every occasion of family joy or grief the poor are remembered, and the inmates of the harem are no less benevolent than the men of the family. The hanum, who seldom leaves her home, takes with her when she does so a well-filled alms-bag; and though the charity is indiscriminate and often bestowed on unworthy objects, she endeavours at least to fulfil one of the first precepts of her religion.

A devout and scrupulous Moslem should perform some act of charity or benevolence on every day of his life. It is common here to see even the poorly clad and rarely paid soldier drop, as he passes, his mite into the bowl of the street-beggar. There are no workhouses in Stamboul; none of the establishments for the relief of poverty so liberally provided, and, alas! so insufficient, in our own country. But neither are they required in the same degree; not that the poverty is less in proportion to the population, but the charity exercised in the simplest and most patriarchal form is unbounded. For instance, a poor woman arrives at the door of a harem with her little bundle containing all her worldly possessions. Perhaps she shows a few written words proving that she is known to some friend of the family; she is a stranger, but it is enough. She enters unquestioned. Her place is set at the family table or amongst the domestics according to her class in life; mattresses and padded quilts are spread for her at night, and she remains for several days a guest in the house. On her departure she receives a letter or recommendation for another friendly harem, with some new articles of clothing. It would be considered "ayib" (a disgrace) to let her leave without, at least, one new garment, and the poor woman is frequently entirely reclothed. There are many women, most of them widows in very poor circumstances, who pass their lives roaming from house to house. "A deplorable waste of life and time," we should say in busy, hardworking England. But the utter absence (until lately) of any attempt to educate Turkish women to habits of self-dependence and labour, throws a vast class of the population upon the kindness of their richer neighbours, and they might perish but for the charity so ungrudgingly bestowed upon them in these little-known Mussulman homes, where many persons, especially women and children who have lost their natural protectors, are received and supported permanently as members of the family.

At this terrible time of bitter suffering and distress, the homes of Stamboul—impoverished and ruined though they be by the war—yet find means to shelter, feed, and clothe thousands of the starving refugees from the Russian invasion, whom all the munificent charities of pitying Europe cannot suffice to reach.

I can recall, as an instance, the admirable charity of an excellent Mussulman lady, the wife of one of the highest ministers of the State, who received, fed, and sheltered forty of these unhappy exiles. She did more. One woman amongst them, suffering from some terrible illness, was an object of repulsion even to her own people, and lay neglected and dying. Did the delicate lady order her slaves to minister to the poor outcast? Calling one or two attendants, she went herself, with her own hands washed and dressed the wounds, and soothed the last hours of the unhappy " refugee " with the tenderest care and pity.

The animals also have their part in the benevolent nature of the Turkish character. It is a common custom, especially at the season of Ramazan, to buy a cage full of birds in order to liberate them; and even the dogs, though accounted by Moslems as impure, are never ill-treated by the Turkish inhabitants of the city. They feed them frequently at their doors, provide a sort of litter and a rude covering in winter for the mothers and their puppies, and even in many cases leave money in their wills to continue the distribution of food.

## The Harem.

A few words are necessary in explanation of the term " harem," as no word in connection with

Turkish homes has been more thoroughly misunderstood by Western nations. "Harem,"—signifying literally "inviolable, sacred"—has two meanings. It is used to express in a collective sense the whole feminine portion of a family, whatever the rank, condition, and employment. By the word "harem" we also understand that part of a dwelling or locality reserved for the residence or use of Mussulman women, in contradistinction to the "selamlik" (the place of salutation), inhabited solely by the men of the family. There are harems in the steamers and tramway carriages, keeping the Mussulman women apart from the general passengers, as there are harems in mosques and dervishes' tékés, where from behind latticed screen-work they can participate unseen in the devotions of the hour.

A Turkish dwelling of the better sort is called a konak when in the city, a yali when it is a country residence on the shores of the Bosphorus. A genuine, old-fashioned konak is built in two equal parts, and may almost be described as two houses under one roof, the selamlik and the harem; the gardens also are separated.

The position of the harem may be ascertained by the cafesses, or trellised wooden blinds, which are fitted into the windows on the outside. These blinds reach rather more than half-way up the window; ground-floor windows are usually entirely screened.

No harem windows are without cafesses, excepting such as are on the side of gardens from which they cannot be overlooked.

Large wooden doors in the centre of the building —similar to the *portes cochères* in France—give access to a vast unpaved court, serving as *remise* for the carriages of the family; four or five carriages of different kinds, covered with sailcloth, may generally be seen standing there: as in France, the family can thus enter their equipages under shelter. The great staircase leading to the selamlik faces the entrance gates; the door leading into the harem is on one side, protected by a tall wooden screen-work, which shuts it out from the view of the courtyard. In many konaks the door-porter attached to the harem lives in a small room outside of it, and near his quarters, fixed into the wall, is the pivot box in which all small articles called for from within are deposited.

In the crowded quarters of the city, the lower part of the konak towards the street, not required for the courtyard, is usually filled by shops, the inhabited portion of the house being on the first floor; few of the old-fashioned dwellings possess a second story. Between the selamlik and the harem a large intermediary apartment is called the "mabèyn." It may be used by either division of the family, according to circumstances. From the term mabèyn is derived the title mabèyndji, given to the chamberlains of the Sultan. The kitchens of a Turkish konak are mostly, but not always, attached to the selamlik, from which the meals are sent into the harem twice a day.

In old-fashioned houses there are no rooms especially furnished as bedrooms; the mattresses and bedding, brought out at night, are kept during the day in large closets, with which almost every room is furnished. You may frequently find also in these dwellings of the olden time two large knobs projecting from the walls at right angles, intended for suspending the baby's hammock.

Every suite of rooms in a house is provided with a " khaziné " (pronounced khaznah), literally the treasury; in this all stores of clothing and great supplies of bedding are kept. Sometimes articles of particular value are deposited in a fireproof stone room called the " magaza."

The scrupulous cleanliness that in a well-ordered house regulates the smallest details of domestic arrangement is very rarely to be met with elsewhere out of England. Nothing is prettier or more dainty than the white marble basin of ablutions, with its row of snowy towels suspended above it and lightly covered with a gold-embroidered muslin, a ball of Adrianople soap standing on one side, and " nâlin " (high clogs), lined with scarlet cloth, ready to protect the unslippered feet from the marble flooring.

In the apartments the invariable custom of leaving the outer shoes at the foot of the staircase keeps the carpeting or matting free from soil. This is necessary, not only to secure the cleanliness of the floor, on which all cutting out, spreading, and folding of garments is generally performed, 'but because any stain brought from the street would render it unfit for the use of the prayer-carpet. A detail of household organisation may be mentioned here, without which the fires so sadly frequent in Stamboul would be infinitely more numerous than they are at present. It is the duty that devolves on the halaïks of large harems to pass the night, in turn, as watchers. The female "beckdji" on duty walks constantly about the galleries and corridors, and but for this precaution few families would sleep in safety.

When we speak of a harem as applied to members of a family it simply means the womankind. Thus we use the word to indicate the feminine part of the household of a sultana, in which all the women belong to, or are dependent upon, herself; as we speak of the harem of a householder, although several of its members may be almost unknown to him— such as a brother's wife, some female relations and poor dependents residing under his roof—yet they form a part of the feminine division of his family, and consequently of his harem.

Enthusiastic travellers meeting a procession of carriages filled with veiled women are told that they contain the harem of a bey or pasha. They forthwith take careful note, and eventually discourse on the supreme felicity of the omnipotent owner of so much beauty. Those who can see behind the yashmak know that several of these houris are terribly old and wrinkled; that the veiled group so fascinating in its mystery comprises the "kïaya," or housekeeper, an old nurse or two, and a plentiful proportion of negresses. There are younger and prettier women in the party, but it is possible that they may, for the most part, belong to the rich mistress of the household, in which case the master himself is not entitled even to look upon their unveiled faces without the consent of his wife, who often holds steadily and jealously to her rights in this particular.

No Mussulman may see the uncovered face of any woman of his own faith except his wife, his own slave, or any very near relative within the prohibited degrees of marriage, such as mother, sister, daughter, niece, or daughter-in-law. The law of Mohammed allows to his followers four legally wedded wives and as many slaves as his means can purchase; but the doubtful privilege of polygamy is now very rarely exercised, and it is in the present day extremely unusual to meet with more than one wife in the household of a Turkish gentleman of moderate fortune. In many of these harems the halaïks, or slaves, are simply the attendants, performing all the duties of domestic servants. These duties are light, as the labour is much subdivided, while for the heavier work of the house rayah women, Greek or Armenian, are employed.

Polygamy is still to be met with, though as the exception, not the rule, at the two extremes of the social scale, amongst the very great and wealthy and amongst the poorer classes. With these latter a second wife may be taken in order to obtain the benefit of her money or of her labour, and there is an ungallant proverb which declares that " the acquisition of a woman is more useful than the acquisition of an ass!" Surédjis, men in charge of baggage horses, for instance, and others whose duty takes them to two or three places in succession, will be provided with a wife at either end of their line, to make a home and look after their interests.

In the harems of men of wealth and high position the possession of two or three wives and of a very numerous retinue is regarded as a mark of rank and importance, although there are well-known exceptions to this among the first statesmen of the present day. In these lavish establishments each lady must have her separate dwelling, her carriages, and servants. The cost of this style of living is very great, and the man of limited fortune cannot venture on such extravagance. He is fond also of "kïef" (repose), and dreading (as who would not?) the quarrels, heartburnings, and jealousies of a multiplied *ménage*, he settles placidly down into a respectable domestic character, even according to our own standard of respectability. Many a quiet patriarchal harem could be named where the one wife and mother of the family is truly the house-mother, looking after the welfare of children and slaves with unremitting care; she is the undisputed mistress of her household, but she is the first to set the example of tender and dutiful respect towards the aged grandparents, of almost boundless charity to the poor, and of hospitality to the " stranger within the gate." Gentleness towards little children and respect for age are amongst the most pleasing features in Turkish family life. The little ones, even though they may be only halaïks, are never, under any provocation, treated with roughness; while the filial love and care with which many a world-worn man soothes the declining years of his parents, particularly his mother—the validé—is well known to all who are acquainted with the daily life of the harem.

With regard to feminine titles and designations,

a short explanation may help to correct the mistakes which are so often made by strangers. The title of sultana is given *exclusively* to daughters and sisters of sultans and to the mother of the reigning Padishah. It is *never* borne by those ladies who occupy the recognised position of his wives, as the sultan does not (except under very rare and exceptional circumstances) go through the ceremony of marriage, and his partners, of whom seven are permitted, as officially acknowledged, are simply called kadinn. The mother of the eldest prince, taking the highest rank, is styled bash (head) kadinn; then follow the second, third, etc. After the kadinns four ikbals, or favourites, hold a sort of titled precedence over the rest of the women forming the imperial household. The mother of the reigning monarch is called the validé sultana; she acquires this rank on her son's accession, becoming at once a personage of great importance and influence in the State, in which she holds the second place, and enjoys immense revenues drawn from the Civil List. In the harems of pashas and private gentlemen the mother of the master of the house, if she reside with her son, is the "buyuk hanum," or great lady, and the head of the harem; if there be no mother it is the wife who is styled buyuk hanum. In the case of a second wife the title "kutchuk hanum"— the little lady—is used; and the same is applied to the daughters of the house, or they may be addressed by their name, followed always by the title hanum. This style is maintained in family intercourse; parents will frequently, but not always, use to an unmarried child the simple name, but children, even when grown up, never mention their parents without affixing the designation of respect, best expressed by the French " Monsieur mon père," " Madame ma mère," and it is invariably used between brothers and sisters, an elder sister being always addressed or spoken of by a younger as " abla," an elder brother as " agha bey."

In all matters of domestic etiquette and precedence the strictest rules are observed, and the respect due to age never set aside; sons and daughters, though they be themselves heads of families, invariably rise when the father or mother enters or quits the room. This respect for the parental tie, admirable in many cases, is yet carried among the Turks to a length which we should think incompatible with the due freedom of reasonable men and women; for instance, a married daughter continues always subject to the control of her father, and custom, if not law, forbids her to enter on any undertaking, even with the willing consent of her husband, when the father refuses his sanction. Divorce is easily obtained; a husband needs only to pronounce the words of separation, without the necessity of assigning any reason for the act. In this case, however, he is called upon to pay over to the divorced wife the sum of money which he has acknowledged in the marriage contract as her dowry, and in needy families this obligation frequently secures to the hanum the continuance of her position. A wife also can claim the right of divorce, but some reason must be assigned for the demand; amongst the reasons defined by law, the impossibility in which a man may find himself of maintaining his wife in a style suitable to her rank, is regarded as sufficient to justify it.

A liberated halaïk must, from the time of her liberation, veil herself in the presence of her former master. He may be the father of her children, but as a free woman, and not his wife, he is no longer entitled to see her features, more than he would those of a stranger. As an instance, Hourié had been for many years the devoted companion of a man of some position, and the careful and loving mother of several children. Their eldest daughter married, and upon this occasion it was fully expected that Hourié would receive the nikyah, or pledge of espousal, and gain the name, as she had for many years faithfully fulfilled the duties, of his wife. It was not so. The pasha, with a harshness loudly condemned by his friends and by the "neighbourhood," gave the poor woman her liberty. She lives in a small dwelling apart from the handsome house that was once her home, and if she sometimes sees her former husband it can be only when enveloped in the shrouding yashmak and feràdjé.

## Slavery.

The word "slave," so frequently in use when speaking of a Turkish household, is a term conveying to the English mind an impression very different to its true meaning in this country. A Circassian slave should be, according to Western ideas, a beautiful girl torn from the arms of her distracted parents and carried off from their happy mountain home, to pine and die in the gilded prison of a Stamboul harem. The picture may be filled in by the figure of a black harem agha in untiring exercise of his cruel "courbash" of rhinoceros hide. This estimate of the condition of slaves in the East is not entirely false, and yet it bears a strong affinity to Tennyson's celebrated "half a truth." The courbash does in reality sometimes seek its victims. Circassian women are sometimes decoyed or stolen from their homes, but it does not all come to pass in the dramatic manner so dear to novelists. I turn to notes and information collected with great care and with no small difficulty, as it rarely happens that a halaïk, or slave, will consent to explain to a foreigner the circumstances connected with her first arrival in this country. If the girl has been bought in infancy, all remembrance of her Circassian home has passed from her mind, but if she was brought here at a later age she invariably asserts that she was stolen; a feeling of pride and shame forbid her to own that she was sold by her own people, although careful inquiry will establish the fact in most cases. Circassian husbands not unfrequently decoy their wives from home and sell them to the slave-dealers, who dispose of them in Stamboul as wet-nurses.

The traffic in slaves, or rather, the importation of Circassians for sale, was forbidden by law a few years since. The importation has, in fact, nearly ceased, as the mass of the Circassian people emigrated into Turkey after the occupation of their country by the Russians, but the internal traffic in slaves goes on as vigorously as ever. The Circassians, indeed, as a rule, rear their offspring with no other object than to get out of this live-stock the best possible profit, sending them from miserable homes to make their fortunes in the capital. They have an eye also to their personal advantage in this venture, for if the daughter should chance to become the wife of a good, benevolent man, he may probably (there are many such instances) seek out her relatives to assist and benefit them. The parents are then cared for, the brothers and sisters educated and maintained: the whole family gets a lift in the world.

Halaïks are usually bought very young, at three or four years of age, and, as the Turks are proverbially tenderhearted towards children, these little ones are treated with great care and kindness. They are the pets of the household, and are not unfrequently adopted by the hanum, in which case they become free, sharing in all the advantages of the children of the family, and in due time are suitably married. A pretty, intelligent slave girl or adopted daughter is very often chosen and carefully educated to become the wife of a son of the house. Little slaves who continue to be halaïks are brought up as servants. All receive a slight smattering of education, *à la Turque*, being taught to recite some portions of the Koran and sometimes, in great households, to write a little, when, if they show remarkable aptitude, their education is continued in order that they may become in time, kiatibs—readers and writers of a more advanced order—or kiayas—housekeepers. They learn also to embroider and to make their own clothes, while some are taught music, dancing, and a little French. These accomplishments increase their value considerably, and it becomes with some people a matter of revolting speculation to educate batches of little Circassians, as you may fatten rabbits for market, buying them cheap in their infancy and native dirt, and selling them a few years later, with all their acquired graces, at a high price. The value of a halaïk begins at about £80 or £100; an accomplished musician or dancer may bring her owner nearly ten times as much.

When a little slave is newly brought into a harem —arriving, it may be, from Circassia or from some miserable hovel in the interior—the first thing done is to put her into a bath and to cut off her hair. She receives, at the same time, a new name of a fanciful and descriptive kind, and, thus cleansed, dressed, and transformed, she is handed over to the care of an elder slave. If newly separated from the "distracted parents," she must be for a few days very miserable, poor little waif, for she can only speak "Tcherkess," and as the dialects in that tongue are as numerous as the tribes, it is probable that no one in the house can understand her; but she learns the Turkish rapidly, and quickly becomes a member of the family, sufficiently contented with her lot, which in many respects is by no means a hard one. In great houses, an elder slave, a calfa (one who has the direction of others), will have the charge of two or three of the children. She teaches them to work, trains them in household duties, looks after their clothing, and takes care of them generally, receiving in return all the services that they can perform. They clean and arrange her room (if old enough), wash and iron her clothes, and wait upon her. The child in process of time becomes a calfa in her turn.

In imperial harems (those of married members of the Sultan's family) there are frequently as many as a hundred women and girls; the labours of the household are consequently almost nominal duties for many of them, but a large retinue of slaves being considered indispensable to the maintenance of high rank, eight or ten women are required to get through the work that one stout, active, maidservant in our own country could accomplish with ease. In quiet families of moderate fortune the number of halaïks is, of course, very much smaller, but even then, where only two or three persons require attendance, it would appear necessary to have five or six handmaidens; and the mistress herself frequently takes an active part in domestic matters. It follows that on the question of labour the life of a slave here is infinitely less laborious than that of any one of our maids-of-all-work, and (setting aside that which should never be lost sight of—the very great moral wrong of the whole system) their advantages may be said, in one sense, to be considerably greater. Every slave in a household is well-fed, lodged, and clothed. In very rich harems they are surrounded with much comfort and even luxury, and in these households it is very usual to make presents of money, sometimes to a considerable amount, for dress, ornaments, etc. These sums being distributed monthly have come in many houses to be regarded in the light of aïlik, or monthly wages, although slaves are not, of course, entitled to wages from their owners. The gifts are voluntary; they are made partly from natural generosity and kindly feeling, in order to gain the attachment of the household, partly in order that it may make a handsome appearance, and contribute, with other property —carriages and horses—to maintain the state of the family. It is usual to double the customary present at the festival of Bairam, when two or three new dresses are also given.

Handsome gifts are made upon all occasions of great family rejoicing. In a harem which might be named, the eldest daughter, still unmarried, has about ten halaïks belonging to her, and a younger sister has three as her personal attendants. In this mansion the chief lalla, or black guardian, receives 500$p$. per month (about £54 per annum), the kiaya nearly the same sum, and the rest of the women and girls various amounts, down to 50$p$. a month given to the little ones. In another establishment of high rank, the kiaya receives as much as 10 liras (more than £9) a month; the rest of the harem, on the same liberal scale. In this family, as is frequently the case with others of the same class, the slaves who have been married and settled out of the house continue to receive a sum for maintenance, paid monthly. These engagements are regarded as binding in honour if not in law, and should circumstances occur to stop for a time the regular payments, they are considered as a debt to be discharged as soon as practicable. There is a deep sense of faithfulness in the Turkish character, a strong clinging to old ties and associations, and in well-conducted families those friends or dependents who have once known or served them are very rarely—unless for serious reasons—set aside or forgotten.

A little ceremony in connection with the distribution of the new dresses may be mentioned here. When the stuffs are brought into the harem, the mistress of the family will direct the selection and allotment of them, according to the age, complexion and known taste of the wearer. In this matter the humble negress and the little newly-arrived halaïk are not overlooked. Then the stuffs are spread upon the ground to be cut out, and the lady or her kiaya, or perhaps the head calfa, with an immense pair of scissors, inaugurates the work for each garment, saying as she gives the first cut, "Bismillah!" (in the name of God).

As already mentioned, the white slaves in a harem are seldom called upon to perform any of the rough work of the house. They wash their own and their mistress's linen, work for her and for themselves, serve the table, and sweep the rooms. When scouring and house-cleaning are required, it is either done by the negresses or by women hired by the day. The meals are most usually cooked in the selamlik and sent into the harem in covered dishes. Whenever food is dressed within the dominions of the women, it is almost invariably a negress who is the cook, and she is sure to appear on the scene before the end of the repast to receive the compliments of the guests on her achievements, which are by no means inconsiderable.

There is no legal limit to the term of service due by halaïks to their owners; the customary time varies very much in different families. A slave bought in infancy, being of no great use in a house before the age of ten or twelve, it is very usual to exact from them after that time several years of active service. Slaves begin to expect their liberty after seven years of work, but they do not often obtain it so speedily, it may be not at all, especially if they are bright and clever, and their attendance has become valuable to their mistress. Some ladies will, however, forego their own comfort in justice to a girl who has behaved well. She is considered as having gained her paper of freedom, and is married from the house if opportunity offers. Handsome presents are made at the time of the marriage, in money and furniture, and they remain humble friends of the family, coming frequently to visit their former home and companions, from whom they always receive a hearty welcome. If a calfa who has been many years in a house does not marry, she remains with the family very much at liberty to do whatever she likes, and it often happens that a halaïk will refuse to leave a home where she enjoys comfort and abundance, for the liberty of a house of her own with its humbler means of existence. In many harems the rooms of the slaves are exceedingly comfortable, and even luxurious, carpeted and warmed in winter, and sufficiently furnished. The principal women, such as the kiaya, the nurse, and the bash or head calfa, have apartments given to them which many ladies might be glad to occupy.

The kiaya is a personage of great importance in the household, and holds a post of much responsibility. She is the female house-steward; looks after the change of houses between town and country, makes all the important purchases for the family, negotiates matters of business in the department of the harem, and pays visits with her mistress, or alone, as her vakeel or representative. A kiaya in a very great harem has her own carriage; often her separate table, where she receives the guests of secondary degree. She has two or three halaïks to attend upon her. It is usually some elderly free woman who fills this office of kiaya. The wet nurse of the hanum— the sud'na, or milk-mother (from " sud " milk and

" ana " mother)—is also a great lady, treated by her foster-child with every consideration. If she have no home ties of her own she continues to live with her as an honoured friend, and even when married out of the house, she is more often to be found in her former home on a long visit. The dada, or nurse, enjoys almost the same consideration and influence. The bash calfa is the mistress of the slaves. It is her duty to see that the women and girls perform their part in the household labours. Some establishments are admirably ordered and regulated; others are careless and slovenly, depending generally on the degree of efficiency of the bash calfa.

The preceding remarks apply to wealthy and numerous harems, not to those more modest homes where the mistress and her daughters take their active share of domestic supervision.

A slave who is unhappy and discontented can oblige her owner to sell her again. This right is not often exercised. Slaves of an imperial household are never resold, but if a sultana wishes to part with one of her women, she either makes a present of her or sends her away on a visit to some friend or dependent, in whose house she remains until they find her a husband, or she returns perhaps to the seraï.

Slaves are not often beaten by command of the master or mistress, unless for very grave offences; then the punishment is, indeed severe, and the black harem agha, usually a mild and good-natured member of the household, does not spare the strokes of his terrible courbash upon the almost uncovered form of the delinquent. But in the present day these floggings, which are not of very common occurrence, are usually due to the jealousy or tyrannical temper of a kiaya or a bash calfa, and are inflicted unknown to the heads of the house, who, when they have cause for serious displeasure, will either sell the offending halaïk or give her away.

A very great proportion of the Circassian girls die early of consumption, and a slave in a great harem whose life is despaired of is always sent out of the house to die. In this matter, little mercy or tenderness is shown, and it is then that the poor halaïk feels the full bitterness of her destiny. She is cast forth from the home where she has lived out her brief life—not unhappily—to draw her last breath amongst strangers; a burden to be shaken off as quickly as possible. There is no one whose duty or whose loving care it may be to cherish and soothe the dying girl; perhaps some one of her companions, more pitying than the rest, may devote herself to nurse and tend her, but it is most often to the simple, warm-hearted negress the motherless, forsaken halaïk turns for comfort in her dark hour of pain and trouble.

Mohammedan marriage does not imply community of property, and it follows that if a slave, the property of the hanum, should bear a child, the infant (even though the father be the master of the family) is born *her* slave, and may be sold by her at will; but the child borne by a slave to her master is legitimate and entitled to all rights and privileges equally with the children of the hanum; in both cases, however, a child's claim to paternity depends upon the acknowledgement of the father, which is sometimes withheld. It frequently happens that when the master's fancy seems to incline towards one of his wife's attendants, the halaïk is either sent out of the house under some pretext, or, if that be not practicable, the lady makes a virtue of necessity and presents the slave to her husband. They sometimes do this willingly; an instance occurs to me in the family of an imām, which consisted of an elderly lady and a younger one, the mother of two children. The elder lady, the first wife and mistress of the house, finding herself childless, had presented a Hagar to her Abraham, and she exhibited quite a grandmother's fondness for the little ones, living, they said, in great harmony with the second wife. Such harmony, however, is rather the exception than the rule. The Mussulman woman, in despite of law and custom, resents indignantly all rival claims to her husband's affection, as well as the diminution of her own children's portion of the inheritance.

If the child of a slave-mother dies, it is customary to give the woman away in marriage; she cannot be sold, as all these women become virtually, if not actually, free. They take rank from their children, and are known not by any distinctive name of their own, but as the mother of such a young bey or hanum. A halaïk is not of much account amongst her own people, not from any feeling of a lack of morality in her condition of life, but because she has no social rank. She is always mentioned with a certain degree of contempt, even by those who were themselves halaïks before some rich man's choice raised them to the position of free women and wedded wives. To be a "schéhirle" hanum (a free-born woman, literally a lady born in the city) is an acknowledged title of respectability; yet many men of rank and high station marry halaïks in order to avoid the trammels of a wife's family connections.

These Circassian women, having a remarkable power of adapting themselves to a higher position, prove quite equal to the occasion, and become as ladylike and well-mannered as the most undeniable "city-born" dames. The demeanour of an Eastern lady, particularly when receiving visitors in her own house, has much of that self-possession and repose which with us is thought to be inseparable from good birth and gentle breeding.

We have spoken hitherto of white slaves. The negresses—Nubians and Abyssinians—are on a somewhat different footing. For the white girls, the fact of being brought to Stamboul and there sold is, according to their ideas, a fulfilment of a natural destiny, which may lead them to the highest promotion, and through which they may aspire even to the imperial rank of Validé Sultana; but the poor negress has no such golden dreams to soften the bitterness of slavery. Circassians embark willingly, nay, joyfully, for the scene of their anticipated success and triumph; negroes are hunted down by the merciless slave-dealers, carried off by force, and seared and scored like sheep, to be driven in gangs, of which less than one-half survive the journey. The abominable cruelties of the African slave trade are too well known to need any comment; it is happy for those poor victims who live to reach Stamboul that a more merciful and humane treatment awaits them in the homes of the Ottoman capital. Once domiciled they are secure, with few exceptions, of a sufficiency of food and clothing, with duties and labour which are not unduly heavy; while their naturally bright and joyous natures make them quickly forget the past suffering, and many speedily gain by their gentleness and fidelity the consideration and love of the family.

The value of a black slave is considerably less

than that of a white one. Being destined exclusively for domestic service, they receive no education; they are trained as nurses and as cooks, for which they have a peculiar aptitude, and they are employed in the coarser and rougher labours of the house. As nurses they devote themselves to their infant charges with a tenderness that nothing could surpass, and it is from them that the sick or the sorrowing white girl finds sympathy, and consolation, and gentle, loving care. On the other hand, the excitable negro nature, as easily open to evil as to good impressions, makes them the chosen instruments of punishment, and sometimes even of vengeance. There is a marked difference between the Abyssinians and the women of Nubia and other parts of Africa; these last show the well-known type of broad noses, thick lips, and woolly hair, while an Abyssinian girl is frequently a model of dusky beauty: delicate featured, with small aquiline nose, long tresses of raven hair, and a figure moulded like an antique bronze. They are very delicate, however, and consequently expensive and rare, and the strong, uncomely, but good-natured-looking negress—the useful household drudge—is the sort of coloured property the most often to be met with.

Another class of slaves, the black eunuchs, called aghas or lallas (guardians), are seldom found in the present day but in houses of the first rank, where they are an indispensable part of the wealth and grandeur of the family. A lalla walking beside a carriage or seated on the raised after part of a caïque, denotes the social position of the veiled ladies whom they accompany; while a lalla who displays a strip of blue silk round the collar of his coat, proclaims the passage of members of the imperial household. These blacks, who are apt to be haughty and overbearing in public, while in charge of the harem, are gentle and good-natured enough in private life. They act as commissioners and messengers between the outer world and the inmates of the harem, and their most often-recurring duties seem to consist in conveying long and ceremonious compliments to the ladies from members of the family and friends who are not privileged to deliver their polite sentiments in person. The lallas also are especially employed as guardians of the children when walking, driving, or riding, and they submit only too indulgently to the tyranny and youthful wills of the little boys and hanums.

In the better houses there is usually a porter—an elderly man—whose special duty consists in attending to the door of the harem. He not only carefully questions and scrutinises all who pass in and out, but he must be constantly on the watch for messages from the unseen feminine population within. His attention is called by an uncouth sound of thumping on hollow wood, proceeding from a wooden receptacle inserted in the wall beside the great door; it is open on one side, and, turning on a pivot, receives various articles which are thus twisted round into the harem precincts without exposing the women to view; but their voices and unlimited requirements leave the old "kaboudji baba" little repose or kïef. The aïwass is the general useful servant of the whole house; several are employed in large families: they carry the dinners, execute commissions, and do most of the hard work. Aïwass are frequently called upon to accompany parties of the women and children who are not entitled to expect the escort of a lalla. These aïwass are mostly Armenians, free servants receiving wages; the same may be said of the greater number, if not all, the white male domestics and attendants, the blacks only being purchased slaves.

## VI.

### A WINTER IN THE SUNNY EAST.

Fancies and Facts.—A Dog's Luxury.—A Snowstorm.—The Hurricane.—Pleasure and Peril.—"Yangheun Var!" the Cry of the Night Guardian.—A Half-Buried City.—Stagnation.—The Fear of Famine.—The Black Sacks.—The Snow-clothed "Sunny East."—Great Disasters in Asia Minor.—Wild Boars and Wolves in the Suburbs.—The Fatal Snow-drifts.—Disasters at Sea.—An Impromptu "Montagne Russe."—Street Modelling.—A Thaw and a Breath of Summer.

WHEN one speaks of the "sunny" East, imagination pictures a warm and luminous country, sparkling with sunlight, pleasantly refreshed, after the great summer heats, with breezes perfumed by groves of orange and citron. The East is the enchanted land of romance, the home of poetic reverie, of luxury and pleasure. Beside this fantastic dream let us place a reality, passing in review some of the days which have just gone by in this year of grace 1874.

Until the end of January the weather had been such as is most usual at Constantinople—days of sunshine and of rain, some falls of snow, soon melted; some sudden squalls, varied by summer brightness. Such are our usual winters, but from time to time, particularly when the season in Western Europe is exceptionally mild, the hurricane and the snowstorm descend upon our Eastern land with redoubled severity.

In the first days of February a considerable fall of snow whitened the city, to the great astonishment of the wandering dogs; but as the beautiful substance rapidly spread its soft down upon their hard open-air couches, they soon found it delightful, and rolled with joy in this unusual luxury.

It snowed gently at intervals during several days, and great flights of birds were seen to quit the coast, making for the interior of the country. Every one, from this, predicted severe weather, but it was rather a benefit than otherwise; it would fill our cisterns, keep off epidemics, fertilize the country. Men put on their fur coats; the dogs, in round furry balls, slept persistently; every one was resigned. But, at last, the wind began to play its part, and then a real snow tempest, driven straight from the Russian steppes, wrapped the town as in a winding sheet. The harbour is invisible; the boats are stopped; the circulation of carriages becomes impossible. Now and then a foot passenger, braving the tempest, climbs with difficulty the street exposed to the northern blasts; the daylight fades; the pale and flickering street-lamps are extinguished by the hurricane, each instant more violent, more sinister.

There is a ball to-night at the palace of the Austrian Embassy. The robust Armenians who carry the sedan-chairs will hardly consent to take charge of their usual burdens; the service is dangerous along the steep and slippery streets, but a pleasure-loving public cannot forego its amusements; fabulous prices are offered, and the ball-room is partly filled. There is dancing! gaiety! and the storm rages wildly around. The wind falls on our house like a discharge of cannon; snow, hail, and wind mingle in wild whistling shrieks; then, suddenly, nothing! not a breath—an ominous, sinister hush. They are dancing, there below! there, where the lights tremble feebly across the wild darkness; they are dancing amidst flowers and perfumes; and from the Black Sea comes a low rolling sound—the gathered power of the tempest. It swells, it roars, it bursts in a thousand thunders! Ah! merciful Heaven! have pity on the unhappy souls that struggle with the terrors of that fatal shore!

A loud cry, and the stifled sound of a club striking the snow. It is the club of the night guardian, who gives warning of fire. It burns with fearful violence on the neighbouring hill-top, and those who remember the terrible catastrophe of 1870 tremble with anxiety; but here the thick snow renders good service; the sparks fall, hissing, and are extinguished. In spite of the wind, the fire is soon mastered.

The next day, the tempest continuing, the town is half buried. It is scarcely distinguishable through the frozen panes; the neighbouring street, usually so animated at this hour, shows us one man—more courageous than his fellows—who climbs the steep slope, slowly and painfully, crying out "Milk" in a stifled voice. "Soudji, soudji," the cry reaches us, sad and mournful, like the cry of a perishing soul.

That day the life of the city stops. The telegraph is silent, the railway, the tramcar, the omnibus, the street cab! Nothing moves; the Exchange is closed, as well as the banks and offices of Galata. Some shops, open for a short while, are quickly shut again, and in the midst of this sad perplexity there are serious fears of the failure of provisions and firing. No stores are made here against a season of exceptional severity. One lives from day to day; and if these tempests should endure yet a short while, famine and the last degree of misery would be at our doors. The municipality is aroused; they discover that the charcoal merchants are hiding their fuel to raise the price, and an order is issued. It is resisted at first, but soon afterwards—perhaps in submission to authority, perhaps through fear of an early cessation of the cold—the point is yielded, and the sad whiteness of the street is spotted all day by an irregular procession of black sacks carried up slowly by the labouring " hamals."

Some days later sad news comes in from the environs, and, above all, from the provinces. The snow tempest, which passed lightly over Southern Russia, has descended with overwhelming violence on Asia Minor, Greece, and even Syria. Athens, the classic mountains, the Parthenon, all are draped in snow. Jerusalem witnesses the rare spectacle of its streets spread with this unexpected substance; but it is on Anatolia that the heaviest calamities have fallen. The post expected from Koniah does not arrive, and it is feared that the caravan, sometimes numbering forty men, with their horses, must be lost in the snowdrifts; the flocks in all that part of the country have perished by thousands, and, to complete the misery, the wild boars and the wolves, driven from the forests by hunger, have ventured even to the environs of Pera and Stamboul. Every hour some tragedy is related, and (all allowance made for exaggeration) enough remains to fill one with the deepest pity.

It is said that some milk-carriers, crossing at early dawn a ravine that nearly touches the last houses of our outskirts, were attacked and devoured by the wolves that on these rare occasions come down from the forest of Belgrade and from the Balkans. In the environs, sportsmen, shepherds with their flocks, workmen on the railways, have met with the same fate. Many persons also—in one case a whole family of twelve—have been found dead in the snow without food or fuel.

The same terrible news reaches us from the Archipelago, and especially from Crete, where several mountain villages have been suddenly cut off from communication with the outer world. The long list of misfortunes seems never full.

Accounts from the sea are, if possible, more distressing. The wrecks are innumerable. During the night of the great tempest, the finest steamer in the Russian service broke down at the mouth of the Bosphorus—happily without loss of life, as all were brought to land by the men of the admirable rocket and lifeboat service under Mr. Palmer; but many smaller boats went down far from all possibility of help, and the number of those victims must ever remain unknown.

The storm has exhausted its fury; the wind has fallen, but the snow remains, and the steep streets of Pera are enlivened by a slipping and sliding crowd. A narrow and rugged pathway before our house shows the comic side of this strange winter scene, with many variations. Now it is a group of children, in wild spirits, who rush down the slope on wooden frames, that they usually keep for the delights of slippery mud; then it is a Turkish woman, or perhaps a negress carrying some heavy bundle. After patient but vain attempts at the usual method of descent, she avoids the risk of falling by bravely subsiding on to a corner of her cloak, and in an instant is down the slide in safety. Some Europeans plant the feet firmly, and descend with an air of calm majesty. The Oriental, incapable of so bold a deportment, hesitates, clings to the rough stones, wavers, and often reaches the bottom unexpectedly, and rather upside down.

At Stamboul and at Pera the great heaps of snow have developed in the population a new taste for modelling. Every open bit of ground is ornamented by a lion or some other beast of unknown form and species, while snowballs are flying about, though not always well received by the unaccustomed native.

Some days later. The wind is blowing from the south, the sun shines, the air is heavy; there is a rapid thaw. Much white is yet seen on the opposite mountains and plains of Asia; much yet remains even in Constantinople; but such is the inequality of temperature here, that the weather is hot, stifling. People begin to talk of their summer arrangements and to seek for country houses. During a month or two we shall have some rain and much mud; then, without transition, the summer, the radiant summer of the Bosphorus; and of all this deluge of snow with which Turkey has been visited, there will only remain, as a souvenir, some patches of eternal whiteness on the distant summits of Olympus above the beautiful range of mountains that borders the Gulf of Nicomedia.

# VII.

## THE ART OF LIVING, ACCORDING TO GREEK FOLK-LORE.

A Baleful Day.—How to Dismiss a Visitor Politely.—The use of Salt in a Slipper.—Further Value of Slippers.—"Na! Na!"—Giving and Taking.—Spilt Salt must be Peppered.—The Danger of a Half-open Door.—Sad Consequences of Sitting on a Box.—Unwinding a Spell.—The Risk of Tying up a Destiny.—How Vinegar becomes Musty.—An Easy Way of Ensuring Custom.—How to Mend a Broken Head.—Great Dangers connected with the "Wash" of a Household. Three-legged Trivets have Grave Responsibilities.—Awful Result of Open Scissors.—The Three Cloves.—The Danger of Hasty Compliments.—The Evil Eye.

During the many years in which I have been living in contact with the unlettered classes of this country, I have found frequent amusement in gleaning such items of their folk-lore as came in my path. Some of these are very quaint, as the following samples, collected chiefly from Greek sources, will show.

Tuesday is considered a most unfortunate day on which to begin any kind of work; from the cutting out of a dress to the sailing of a ship, all must go wrong: the dress will not fit, the sweetmeats will ferment, the house will be weak in its foundations, the ship will most certainly be wrecked. One hour out of the twenty-four is so especially baneful, that a child beginning life at that time is sure to grow up vicious and unmanageable. No one, however, knows exactly which is the fatal period, and all Tuesday-born children may enjoy the benefit of the doubt, until their perversity betrays the malignant influence that overshadowed their birth.

If you wish to dismiss a visitor without incurring the painful necessity of hinting that the visit is unwelcome, let some one quietly slip a pinch of salt into his goloshes, left outside the door, and immediately the unconscious guest resolves to depart. You may then with safety entreat him to prolong the pleasure of his society: nothing can withstand the subtle power that compels him to leave.

In many counties the howling of a dog is taken as a sign of death in the neighbourhood. Here nothing is easier than to avert the omen. Again, it is only a little salt that is required; put it in the toe of a slipper, which you turn gently over, and you may rest in peace.

A slipper is a strangely useful article; there should always be one at hand for emergencies. Terribly bad luck will befall a family if one of its members is allowed, unchecked, to grind the teeth when asleep; quickly strike the mouth of the offender with a slipper three times and the family misfortunes are avoided.

The mysterious influences that hover round our beds are moved to evil by other grievances besides the gnashing of teeth. A black handkerchief on the head of a sleeper is an abomination. Woe to the woman who may have thoughtlessly so bound up her brows; her good destiny peeping in at the door and seeing the sombre headdress, will cast off all interest in the sleeping sinner, and with the gesture "Na! Na!" take flight for evermore.

There is great danger in giving and taking incautiously. During twelve days before Christmas, carefully avoid giving anything to any one, or harm will come of it; and at all times and seasons, remember never to give either salt or ashes: let people take what they need of those homely substances, but if you give them, your house will inevitably be burned down.

Never take a piece of soap from a friend's hand; let the giver lay it down, and you may take it up with safety, and thus avoid the bitter quarrel which would surely follow the neglect of this trifling precaution.

To spill either oil or spirits is most unfortunate; but if wine is spilt by a genuine accident, you may fairly rejoice in the happy prognostic.

If salt is spilt unintentionally, it is sufficient to scatter a little pepper upon it to arrest the evil consequences which would otherwise follow.

A half-open door may occasion serious misfortunes. If the door of the house is standing open when a corpse is carried past, it must be shut in all haste, or the uneasy spirit that has so lately left its earthly tenement will glide in to take up its abode where it is not desired. On the doorstep of the house from which the poor body has been so hastily removed, a vase or bottle of wine must be thrown down and broken, that it may not, at least, seek to re-enter its lost home.

If the door of a cupboard is left partially open, a visitor may happen to glance unconsciously at the worldly goods stored up within; but the most disastrous results will follow the innocent glance, as the property will gradually but surely slip out of the possession of that family by the fatal power of the "evil eye."

A person who sits down to rest upon a box filled with clothing may, quite unwittingly, hinder the happy marriage of the young girl whose belongings are packed up there: adverse influences will certainly prevent the old woman, whose business it is to negotiate marriages, from coming to *that* family to seek for a bride.

Again, any one who sits on the ground in the way of those passing in and out of a room, occasions much needless trouble; for the unthinking person who may have hurriedly stepped across the obstruction must—in spite of haste—instantly return, to step over a second time, and so unwind the spell; otherwise the one stepped over will, ere long, shrivel up and perish.

You may be tired, or reflective, or perhaps in a defiant mood, nevertheless carefully abstain from standing with the arms crossed; to do so is to tie up all good fortune in your destiny.

Be sure to buy vinegar before the sun is down, if sold afterwards it will become musty; but it is not easy to procure it at that time, as the bakals are aware of this necessary precaution.

The first money taken by a dealer in the morning should be rubbed all over the face, to ensure a good amount of custom for the rest of the day.

A child falls and cuts its head on a rough stone. Is it the first care of the mother to wash and bind up the wound? That is an after consideration. She must first find the exact spot where the accident occurred, and, turning her head away, pour on it, over her shoulder, a libation of wine or sugared water, then go quickly away without looking round. By this wise measure all bad consequences will be avoided, and the hurt can be looked to at leisure.

The careful Eastern housewife enjoys the guidance of many rules of which others are deprived by ignorance and want of faith. She is especially attentive to the phenomena that affect the bougatha, or great wash of the household linen, carefully taking out the pieces of half-burnt wood from beneath the copper when all is finished, and placing them aside to die out gradually. If, from a fatal idea of economy, she is rash enough to extinguish them in water, the house and family will infallibly decay from that time.

A fine display of cleanly washed and snowy linen is a cheering sight after all the labour bestowed; but beware of the false friend who, coming in, treacherously admires it. "How beautifully the bougatha has succeeded! how spotless! how white!" Can anything be more cruel? Soon afterwards the unfortunate washerwoman feels a sharp pain in her finger. She has been struck by the "evil eye," and there is but one remedy; to cut off some part of the neighbour's dress—some frayed tatter of her well-worn jacket—burn it in the candle, and apply it to the aching finger.

Cooks have a responsibility connected with the three-legged iron trivet on which they set their saucepans over the charcoal stove: when no longer wanted, they must be careful not to leave them standing, but to place them with the feet horizontally, otherwise any relation likely to pay the family a visit will be prevented from coming.

When a pair of scissors is left gaping on a table,

it is said that the Archangel Michael's mouth is open, ready to take the soul of some one member of the family.

There is a simple and easy method of overcoming the malignity of the "evil eye"; the remedy is valuable in proportion to the injury inflicted by the unconscious glance. Take three fine cloves, stick them solemnly on a pin, burn them a moment in the flame of the candle and wave them about in the air. If one of the cloves bursts, the effect is attained; if not, take another three and recommence. The bad influences must be indeed tenacious (or the spice box unusually damp) that can prevent the desired explosion of the clove, always provided the trial be made with the needful patience and with unwavering faith in its efficacy.

A person invited to two marriages taking place on the same day, must only accept one of the invitations. To attend both weddings would bring misfortune on the second couple.

Do not be too eager to compliment a mother on the birth of an infant, but remain at least half an hour in the house before entering her room, lest rejoicing should turn to lamentation.

Such and similar superstitions, of which the number is infinite, trivial as they may seem in themselves, possess a certain interest, some in their evident derivation from sources of the highest antiquity, others in their connection with like beliefs amongst the peasantry throughout Europe, everywhere modified and shaped by local circumstances, but all springing from the same dread of unknown and mysterious influences, of which the most potent and the most universally feared is the power of the "evil eye."

# VIII.

## BROUSSA.

Broussa, which is, after Smyrna, the most important city of Asia Minor, has been, from very early times, celebrated for its mineral waters, and, subsequently, for its production of silk and silk fabrics. The city is beautifully situated on the northern slopes of Mount Olympus, that rises 6,400 feet from the plain. The highest peaks, clothed with snow during the greater part of the year, are clearly visible at Constantinople, about seventy miles distant.

On the bold spur of rock rising at the entrance to the city, may be seen some remains of the citadel, the site of the ancient town; the walls, a double line on the southern side towards the mountain, strengthened by towers and a broad moat, are of Greek construction, of the thirteenth century, but some blocks of masonry both on the east and west of the plateau seem to show a much earlier date.

Of the ancient city of Prusa, founded about two centuries before the Christian era, and, according to some historians, at the suggestion of Hannibal, by

Prusias, King of Bithynia, with whom the celebrated Carthagenian general had taken refuge, there remains to-day scarcely any vestige; repeated sieges, fire, and earthquake have done their work of ruin effectually; they could not, however, destroy the legendary interest in the surrounding country that goes back to mythological times, for the noble mountain summit that enters into all the finest points of view, rising from the opposite limit of the plain, and now called the Mount Katirli, answers to Strabo's description of the Arganthonios, where Hylas, the friend of Hercules and one of the crew of the Argo, was carried off by the Nereïds. At the foot of Katirli, the town, on the shore of the Gulf of Ghemlek, stands on the site of Cius, founded by another of the Argonauts.

Towards the end of the first century of our era, Bithynia became a Roman province, and in 103 A.D. the Emperor Trajan appointed as governor of the united provinces of Bithynia and Pontus, Pliny the Younger, whose celebrated letters to his imperial master prove his solicitude for the welfare of the country under his care, and the untiring zeal with which he promoted every useful public enterprise.

Writing from "my apartment at Prusa, at the foot of Olympus," he obtains for the "Prusenses" the permission to build a new bath on a site contained within the quarter now called Hissar. Pliny has much anxious thought also on the subject of the Christians, already very numerous in his province of Bithynia. He cannot see the justice of the accusations of their enemies, and his long letter to Trajan on this topic is esteemed by the Church as a strong testimony in favour of the oppressed community.

From the tenth to the fifteenth century, Broussa was several times besieged, taken, pillaged, and abandoned; the city was attacked in vain by the Latins in the eleventh century, and at length, in 1327, after a ten years' siege, opened its gates to the Ottoman Turks, under Osman and his son Orkhan. In the beginning of the fifteenth century, Broussa was once more sacked and burnt by the Tartars under Tamerlane, but again, after an interval of civil war, arose from its ruins, and it was the Sultan Mehemed Tchelebi, son and successor of the unhappy Bajazet, who endowed his native city with its most beautiful and interesting monuments.

For the Ottoman Turk, Broussa is almost a holy city: the cradle of their empire, and the last resting place of their most celebrated men, of whom more than five hundred lie under the shadow of Olympus: sultans, vezirs, saints and enthusiasts, legislators, poets, musicians and doctors, renowned for their learning and their piety. The older parts of the city are crowded with picturesque buildings, erected as pious, learned, or charitable institutions —now mostly fallen into decay; and many a legend clings about these crumbling stones, adding a poetic halo to the picturesque beauty of this most charming spot.

The majestic slopes and wooded gorges also of Olympus were peopled with historical personages; wild enthusiasts, santons, abdals, dervishes, poets, and philosophers, the successors in their cells and hermitages of the Christian martyrs and recluses, whose memory survives in the Turkish name still given to the mountain—Keschich-Daghy, the Mountain of the Monks.

Many celebrated works on theology, law, and medicine were written in the deep repose of those solemn groves, and thence issued strange fantastic beings in times of struggle and crisis in the troubled city below. We read of Abdal-Murad, who, summoned by Orkhan to the siege of Broussa, performed prodigies of valour with a wooden sword of fabulous dimensions, with which he destroyed monstrous serpents that infested the country. His cell and tomb are seen high up upon one of the boldest spurs of the mountain.

There is the legend of a venerable dervish of Constantinople, who finding himself unable to meditate calmly in the turmoil of a great city, transported himself each evening to the solitudes of the holy mountain, never failing, however, to be found at his téké before the early morning prayer.

Then again there is Gheikli-Baba (the Father with the Deer), issuing from his peaceful hermitage, at the call of Orkhan, mounted on a stag and wielding a sword weighing a hundred and fifty pounds.

The greater number of the old monuments of Broussa are connected with this period—the foundation of the Ottoman Power—and with the illustrious persons who flourished during the first century and a half of its existence; a glance backwards, therefore, may have some interest. It will suffice to show the modest origin of the Ottoman dynasty, the pastoral and half-savage manner of life of the predecessors of Osman, and the rapidity with which he founded and enlarged a kingdom by his valour, and consolidated it by his wisdom. In referring to the life of Osman, I do not intend (to borrow the words of the quaint old author Knolles), "with a long and faigned pedigree to set him out of Noah his arke; but only so far as shall be pertinent unto our purpose." Turkish tradition, indeed, goes back to the time of Abraham, and claims Oghuz Khan as the founder of Turkish power and civilisation. According to this legend, he lived at Yassa, at that time the capital of Turkestan, and it goes on to say that some of the later inhabitants, Usbegs, penetrated into Moldavia, where they formed a settlement, and gave to the capital of the new country the name of their native city.

In the twelfth century we begin to read of the Seljuk Sultans of Roum, the largest principality of Asia Minor, having Iconium (now Koniah) as its capital. Ala-eddin I. appears as a benefactor to his country; notwithstanding his wars with Djenghiz Khan, he found time to establish many useful and charitable institutions in the various towns of his small kingdom, and he solicited for them the talisman of an inscription from the hand of the most venerated of Oriental mystic poets and saints: Mewlana Djellaleddin of Boukhara, founder of the order of Mewlevi dervishes.

This Sultan of Iconium (who used the crescent as an emblem before the time of the Ottoman dynasty) gave shelter to a crowd of learned men flying from the East before the ravages of Djenghiz Khan, bringing with them to the extreme west of Asia the literature, science, and arts of Turkestan and Persia.

The same scourge was the remote cause of the foundation, not long afterwards, of the Ottoman Empire, for, disturbed also in his distant home near Mahan, on the frontiers of Khorassan, by the same Djenghiz Khan, Soliman Shah, a descendant of Oghuz and chief of a Turcoman tribe, wandered westwards, "his people," says Knolles, "with their wives and children, after the manner of the Tartar nomads, their ancestors, following him in poore tents and carts, covered with a very coarse kinde of cloth, being indeed nothing else but a very rude kinde of sturdie herdsmen."

This Soliman, at the head of the little clan Kaï—forming part of the great tribe Kaïsak—wandered for some time in the plains of Anatolia, but at length, unable to endure this exile from his country, he decided, at the death of Djenghiz Khan, on returning whence he came, and was drowned whilst attempting the passage of the Euphrates at Djaber. His tribe dispersed; some pushed forward to their Eastern homes; some went into Syria and parts of Asia Minor, where their descendants may be seen to this day following precisely the nomad, pastoral manner of life of their ancestors; their black tents are even now often met with about Smyrna and the Dardanelles, in the plains of the Troad, and among the rugged slopes and valleys of Mount Ida. They are known as Turcomans or Uruks (nomads).

Ertoghrul, one of the sons of Soliman Shah, with four hundred families, his immediate adherents, made his way slowly back once more towards the north-western coast, where he finally obtained a settlement on the borders of Phrygia and Bithynia, at Suguet, on the banks of the river Sakharia, and at the foot of the western branch of the range of Mount Olympus.

This concession was made to him in return for warlike service rendered to the Sultan of Iconium. Here he dwelt in peace, surrounded by the tents of his pastoral tribe, and we read that so far from seeking to enlarge his borders he, with "patience, taking the world as it came, and making a virtue of necessity, and contenting himself with little, bare himself kindly towards all men," and so, peacefully, he died A.D. 1289. His tomb, in the neighbourhood of Suguet, is much visited by Mussulman pilgrims.

Othman or Osman, one of the three sons of Ertoghrul, displayed a much more adventurous spirit. He was by no means inclined to "take the world as it came," his energetic spirit sought a vaster field of action than the modest colony of herdsmen. Long before the death of his father, being elected by common acclamation to the command of the small clan, he had commenced a series of successful exploits in the adjacent provinces of the weak and tottering Byzantine Empire; to repulse the inroads of the Greeks on peaceful bordering cities, he began by a battle, in which he vanquished a certain captain of Eïnegheul, who was in the habit of harassing the flocks and herds of his tribe on their way between their summer pastures on the mountains and their winter quarters on the banks of the Sakharia. Having obtained for them a peaceful enjoyment of their rights, he turned his attention to another small neighbouring castle, surprised it by night, burnt it, and put to the sword all the Christians he found there. This naturally roused the anger of the neighbours, who, joining together, complained to the captain of Kara-Hissar, that those "Turks, who not many years before had been from pity received as poor herdsmen into the country, were now beginning to take violent possession of the ancient lands of the Christians." They besought him, therefore, to join with others "to expulse those unthankful, encroaching, and merciless strangers out of their countries." The unfortunate people little knew that from this very small beginning and encroachment the power of these same poor Turcoman herdsmen would strengthen and increase with such amazing rapidity that a century and a half later would see the descendant of Osman on the throne of the Cæsars, absolute master of the Empire of the East.

The onward progress of Osman was not to be checked. Aided by his suzerain lord, the Sultan of Iconium, he took possession of several strong castles, after which, having inspired his neighbours with a wholesome fear of his prowess, he concluded that it was now wiser to enter into friendly alliance with them. Osman proceeded, therefore, to set the affairs of his little dominion in order, building mosques, establishing independent courts of justice (the first at Kara-Hissar), and opening markets in the great towns, to which he attracted trade and supplies by the equity and moderation with which he treated alike both Mussulman and Christian.

Nicea was the first city of great importance which fell before the resolute sword of Osman. The treasures found there he distributed amongst his warriors, receiving for himself, from his suzerain, Ala-eddin II., every possible mark of approval and honour; but the modesty of Osman prevented him from appropriating the full rights of a sovereign (which some of these honours conferred) until after the death of Ala-eddin, the last of the Seldjuk Sultans of Roum. He then for the first time (about the year 1300), caused prayers to be made in his name in the mosque of Kara-Hissar, and money to be coined with his symbol. This event is considered by many authorities as the act of foundation of the Ottoman Empire, although some prefer to date it from the nomination of Osman, some years earlier, to the dignity of Bey or Commander of Provinces, when this new dignity was proclaimed with banner, *kettle*, and drum, in the towns of Kutayia, Balik-hissar, Aïdin, Sivas, Sinopé, and Kastamouni.

Osman continued to enlarge his borders, extending them even as far as the castles of Anatoly and the shores of the Black Sea, sometimes, however, hindered by the gout; sometimes pausing to busy himself zealously about his subjects' welfare, establishing such a quiet and wise government that people flocked to him to live under his rule; then, bursting out again into fresh conquests, until, in his old age, the pursuit of a Prince of Bithynia led him to Broussa.

Being unable to take the city by assault, Osman ordered two large forts to be built on the principal approaches to it (one of these was at Eski Kaplidja, the other on the spot now occupied by the Italian Consulate), and after a resistance of ten years, Broussa was reduced by famine to open its gates to the Mohammedan conquerors led by Orkhan, a son of Osman, in the year 1327; but the aged chieftain was then on his death-bed. By his own wish his remains were conveyed to Broussa and buried under the dome of the principal building there—the cathedral, afterwards called Daoul Monastir.

The name of Osman Ghazi is venerated by all true Ottomans as a type of chivalrous heroism, justice, and moderation. It is observed of his extraordinary career, that his great moral power was no less remarkable than his rapid and unvarying military success; for the beauty of his character was so universally acknowledged, that although only possessing a tenth part of the territory of some neighbouring princes, he held the highest place amongst them. His charity was unbounded: he never omitted to succour the orphans and widows amongst his subjects, and in his palace tables were spread for the poor, whom he often assisted to relieve, serving them himself with the greatest kindness.

The founder of the Ottoman dynasty bequeathed to his successors a great name and a sovereignty extending over the greater part of Asia Minor, with an army which, composed originally of only four hundred and sixteen horsemen, had increased to the number of six thousand warriors. Of personal property he left wonderfully little. It is curious to read the simple catalogue of his possessions: "He left neither gold nor silver, only a spoon, a salt-cellar, an embroidered caftan, and a new turban; some flags in red muslin, a stable full of excellent horses, some yoke of oxen for the labours of the field, and choice flocks of sheep," the ancestors of the imperial flocks which feed at this present time in the rich pastures at the foot of Mount Olympus.

The name of Orkhan is more intimately connected with Broussa than that of his father, as he conducted the ten years' siege; it was at Bounar Bashi that he planted his victorious banner. Orkhan founded numerous mosques and public edifices throughout the kingdom, and revived the ancient custom of ornamenting these buildings with poetical inscriptions. It was Orkhan also who established the first Medresseh, or College, in the Ottoman Empire; he founded at Nicea the first imaret, or soup-kitchen, for the poor. In every district there exist, even to the present day, villages known by the name of Orkhanlar, which were established by him for the benefit of refugees.

Orkhan died at the age of seventy-five, and we find it recorded that his long reign of thirty-five years was unsullied by barbarity or violence, and that his wise measures and political institutions gained for him the title of the Numa of the Ottomans.

The four immediate successors of Osman were also interred at Broussa: Mourad I. in the mausoleum of the fine mosque founded by him at Tchekirghé; he fell at Kossova, and his remains were brought back to his native place and capital. Bajazet (Yilderim), the son of Mourad, as celebrated for his magnificence and prodigality as for his heroic but disastrous struggle with Tamerlane (Timour Lenk, or the lame Timour), died a prisoner of the victorious Tartar, and his body, brought back by his son Musa, was buried in the beautiful but half-ruined turbé that bears his name.

Mohammed I., surnamed Tchelebi, on account of his love of the arts of peace, lies in the mausoleum attached to the most beautiful of the monuments of Broussa, the celebrated Yeshil Djami.

Mourad II., father of Mehemmed Ghazi, the conqueror of Constantinople, was the last whose resting-place is found in this, the cradle of his empire and of his dynasty.

Amongst the illustrious persons buried at Broussa, and who flourished during the first period of the Ottoman power, we must remark Alla-eddin, the eldest son of Osman. He yielded his right of succession to his brother Orkhan, but none the less was he actively employed in the organisation of the infant State. He regulated the coinage, and many other matters of importance, and, together with Orkhan, realised the project of a standing army, the most notable element of which was the troop composed of young Christian captives: the great dervish Hadji Bektasch bestowing his benediction on them, named this military body Yeni Shery (the new troops). They are known to us by the familiar name of Janissaries.

The memory of Soliman, a son of Orkhan, is held in great veneration by the Osmanlis. He was the first to establish a footing in Europe, by the conquest of some strongholds in the neighbourhood of Sestos. His tomb is at Boulaïr, not far from the town of Gallipoli.

Broussa contains the tombs of some princesses noted in history for the munificence with which they enriched the city and the province with important monuments and charitable institutions. Niloufer Khatoun, the first wife of Sultan Orkhan, deserves especial mention as the foundress of one hundred and eleven of these beneficent works; many of them are in Broussa, but the town of Nicea owes to this princess one of the finest mosques in the Ottoman Empire. It was in the castle of that city that Niloufer Khatoun passed the latter years of her life in peaceful retirement, and she was there visited by the celebrated traveller, Ibn Batoutah, who speaks of her as a " pious and excellent princess."

Broussa in the present time is a city restored and renovated. Those only who knew it in its former desolate condition can fully appreciate all that it owes to the energetic governor of the province, Ahmet Vefyk Pasha. By the terrible earthquake of 1855, Broussa was shaken to its foundations: the mosques and minarets half thrown down, large spinning factories destroyed, even the course of the mineral springs disturbed; the city was impoverished and ruined. At that time, no better means of conveyance existed than miserable talikas on an almost impassable track, and one hotel sufficed for the small number of adventurous travellers. The Broussa of to-day has arisen from its ruins. Gradually, the fine remains of monuments that once adorned this cradle of the empire have been repaired with the utmost taste and skill, while the welfare of the modern city has been studied with equal solicitude. A good carriage road from Mondania is continued through the entire length of Broussa; excellent carriages are in constant use; several hotels have been opened in different quarters, to suit the convenience of the tourist, the invalid, or the commercial traveller. But the most important work has been the drying up of the marshes by the suppression of the rice-fields, that caused the fever and ague from which the inhabitants formerly suffered severely. Scarcely less valuable to the country has been the recent introduction of the rose culture. The greater number of the refugees of the last war are from the districts most celebrated for the rose perfumes; they find the climate and soil around Broussa in every respect suitable to this sort of cultivation, and in consequence several thousand rose-trees have been planted within the past two years. Seven colonies of refugees have been located on every available open ground; each has its little mosque, its fountain, and its school. By the same wise care a supply of water, which by its peculiar quality enhances the value of the silk, has been brought from a source high up on the mountain to the spinning factories in the western suburb of the city. The market is now much better provisioned than formerly, and the new road to the interior, when completed, will still further develop the resources of those fertile but hitherto almost inaccessible regions. It is impossible to mention all the improvements due to the indefatigable exertions of Ahmet Vefyk Pasha, but we must not forget to note with gratitude the fact that the Christian schools and orphanage at Broussa have always been steadily protected and encouraged by him, and that all those who need it, the widow and orphan, without distinction of creed or race, never fail to meet with prompt and certain help. We may also add that this vigilant governor, the terror of brigands and malefactors, has endowed this beautiful spot with a degree of peace and safety quite unknown in the great metropolis of the empire.

Broussa contains one hundred and five mosques, of which twenty-five are in ruins.

There are fifty-four spinning factories, that employ from two thousand to three thousand women and girls. The beautiful Broussa silks and gauzes so much esteemed for their delicacy and strength, are woven, as are also the towel stuffs, in private houses on hand-looms of the most primitive kind. Many of these may be seen at work in the neighbourhood of the bazaars, behind the great mosque Olou Djami.

## IX.

## THE BATHS OF BROUSSA.

### NO. I.

Contrasting Beauties of Broussa and the Bosphorus.—Getting on Board.—Travellers and their Bags.—The Harem of the Boat.—Our Small Party.—The Princes' Islands.—The Gulf of Nicomedia.—The Open Marmora.—Dislocated Perspective.—Collapse.—The "Talika."—Winding Roads and Leafy Lanes.—The "Durbend."—Luxuriant Vegetation.—Beautiful View from the Bridge.—"Tchekirghé."—The Baths.—"Hotel du Mont Olympe."—Giovanni.—A String of Camels.—Fine View from the Hotel.—Exploring Adventures.—The Jews' Quarter.—The Ruined "Fabrica."—In the Bazaars.—Kutaya Pottery.—Sketching under Difficulties.—Cream Ices.—The Heavenly Valley.—View from the Mills.

ALMOST at the very gates of Constantinople, within an easy summer-day's journey of that much-visited capital, lies a region of sylvan beauty, so exquisitely endowed with all the charms of the most perfect combination of mountain, wood, and water (which people frequently travel so far to seek and to enjoy), that one is struck with wonder at the general ignorance concerning this sweet spot—Broussa, on the north coast of Asia Minor—until it is remembered that, with the contradiction inherent in human nature, blessings easily attained are lightly esteemed, and that a place which may be visited any day is rarely visited at all. It is not, perhaps, astonishing that the people of this country care little for a retreat where elaborate toilettes, formal promenades, and incessant visiting cannot be the order of the day; that they prefer to seek out the gay, gambling mineral baths of Western Europe—leaving the healing waters which nature here offers to them almost unnoticed; but it is greatly to be regretted that intelligent tourists should so often leave Constantinople without seeing this neighbouring city, the cradle of the Ottoman Empire, rich in those rural attractions which are most wanting in the far-famed actual capital of the East. The charms of the one do not, however, suffer by comparison with the claims of the other: they are widely different. The shores of the Bosphorus are bright, sparkling, and graceful; the clear blue water reflecting the fairy-like palaces and "yalis" which overhang its depths, the blooming and highly cultivated gardens revealed through every opening, the softly swelling hills, the glancing caïques, have all a brilliant beauty of their own; but people are apt to feel disappointed at the low proportions of the background to this picture, and, above all, at the general want of wood and foliage. Broussa, spread out at the foot of Mount Olympus, and nestling among the hanging woods of its lower slopes, can boast of the grandeur and sublimity of the wildest forests and mountain scenery, with such a luxuriance of vegetation, such bowery nooks and grassy dells, such tumbling rushing waters, such gushing fountains, such giant trees and wonderful creepers draping the sides of the dark gorges of the mountain, as I have never seen surpassed.

Broussa also is infinitely more Oriental in character than Constantinople. Here the grand type of the genuine Asiatic Turk, comparatively so rare on the European shore, is constantly met with; the lofty swelling turban flourishes, while the modern fez is the exception; wild beings from the interior of Asia conduct long strings of camels laden with the raw produce of those remote districts, and the very plants by the wayside indicate what I have heard called a semi-tropical region.

*May 8th.*—Off at last! The steamer for Broussa being advertised to start at eight in the morning, my husband and myself had hurried considerably on our road to the bridge, and threading our way along the narrow lane which is the principal thoroughfare in this quarter, we avoided as best we could the heavily-laden animals and the dangerous contact of the flour sacks, and of huge blocks of firewood bound to the sides of staggering horses, who seem to pervade this particular street; then, turning the corner by the little Turkish confectioner's (where they make such excellent rahatlokoum), we wound ourselves through the crowd of Circassians (most of them slave-dealers) hanging about the neighbourhood of the Tophaneh market-place, and so along the bustling highway to that part of it called by the unpoetical name of Box Street. Here the open shops on each side are occupied by the workers in cypress wood, which they use chiefly for rough-looking square boxes. These are considered as an infallible preventive to moth, and the pungent aromatic smell of the wood on entering this neighbourhood is so strong as to be at times quite sickening; but to-day we did not perceive it. We hastened on to the bridge to find that the Broussa boat, which usually starts from thence, was standing some way out in the harbour. A caïque, however, soon took us alongside, and, clambering up the narrow ladder of the steamer (an Austrian, and the best of the two boats on the line), we have struggled through all the inevitable bustle and confusion of the moment of departure towards the quarter-deck. There are no seats of any kind as yet, but my husband, aided by our Greek manservant, has made the best possible arrangement for my comfort, and they have left in haste, as the bell has ceased to ring, and I am to start on my journey alone.

Now the anchor is up. The machine palpitates and wakes to life with a shudder; the great wheels begin slowly to revolve, and yet there are loiterers still clinging to the lowered steps of the companion-ladder. The boatmen scream and gesticulate in their frantic efforts to regain possession of their passengers returning to land. The heavy Maltese boat pushes its clumsy form amongst the frail caïques, like a porpoise amid a flock of sea-gulls, scattering them on every side. The water tumbles, leaps, dances, or laps around the sides of the steamer. There are movement and agitation all around.

The travellers begin to settle themselves and their property. Amongst them there are some, perhaps, leaning over the side of the vessel, who perceive nothing of the confusion around them. In all the moving picture they see but one small black spot, dancing on the waves and fast disappearing in the distance. They watch it with tearful gaze: with the heart rather than the eye they see the waving signal of farewell; and the sad unspoken adieu—at once a blessing and a sigh—follows that tiny speck until it passes out of sight. But there are few of these saddened travellers on board the Broussa boat. There is no room for sentiment, for the quarter-deck is crowded with most practical-looking heaps of boxes and bundles, osier baskets, covered with a stout, reddish-brown leather, or even with the untanned cow's-hide, and travelling-bags of every possible description, from the well-appointed bag in black leather, strapped, buckled, and locked, belonging to the experienced tourist, down to the native sack, in coarse striped cloth of goats' or camels' hair, which displays by its gaping mouth the heterogeneous nature of its contents, such as a loaf of black bread, a paper of tobacco, some cheese, a candle, a pipe-stem, a water-melon, a bunch of raw onions, and a few other light and elegant necessaries for the voyage. Lying around, also, are several birdcages, a dog in a basket, with its puppies, a miniature garden of shrubs in cases, a good many corpulent umbrellas, and plenty of ropes and cords everywhere.

The native women are spreading out their mattresses on the flooring of the deck; children, water-jars, pipes, and provisions being placed about them conveniently. An Oriental family is soon comfortably installed.

I am in the harem division of the boat, but the distinction is not strictly kept up, as some gentlemen are seated near the entrance without opposition. My nearest neighbour on the right hand, who shares with me the advantage of leaning against the large heap of bedding covered with a crimson rug, is a Nubian, dressed in the costume of Egypt, with which every one is now familiar—a large white calico cloak covering the head and figure, and the long, thick calico veil falling straight from below the eyes, supported by a stiffened, narrow stripe down the middle of the forehead. Her dress is scrupulously clean, and her only discernible feature, the dark, soft eyes, look pleasant and good humoured; but she sits very silent, for I think she hardly understands the Turkish spoken around her: her familiar tongue is the Arabic. A poor woman is crouched on the deck close by. In the intervals of conversation she begs a little, evidently just to keep her hand in, for she soon turns to another subject, or caresses her child, a very pretty but sadly dirty little Ottoman, from whose dangerous vicinity I shrink as much as circumstances will permit. Several other women and children are grouped about, and have already composed themselves to sleep on the mattresses spread on the boards. There is an independent youth also, belonging to a party established near, who takes intense pleasure in answering his mamma's repeated calls with precipitate haste, in order to brush aggressively past me; but they are all quiet and friendly on the whole, and the lad's manœuvres are infinitely amusing.

Another party of Mussulman women has just emerged from the cabin. Their appearance excites attention, for three of them are young, and therefore supposed to be good-looking. Stools are placed for them, and in a moment they are as thoroughly composed as though they had been here for years.

I am still alone, the captain of the steamer having

consented to call for my friends off Moda Bournou; and now, as the vessel begins to deviate from the direct course, I hear all the people around me wondering where we can be going. It is needless to attempt explanation, as the distance is very short; in fact, we are now nearing the point, and there are the caïques shooting from the little stone scala. I see turbaned huts; we stop; they dart rapidly alongside, and I discover that the large party I had expected to join has melted to four—Aunt Sally, Uncle Ben, Colonel G——, and Fanny. Poor Uncle Ben has lately met with a severe fall, spraining his ankle and dislocating his arm; so that he is helped up into the steamer with some difficulty. He is going to Broussa to complete his cure by the use of the sulphur baths.

We are altogether a little party of five, besides Uncle Ben's Armenian servant Joseph. Many regrets for the absentees are exchanged as we meet, but yet we make up our minds to enjoy our trip thoroughly, and I think we may fairly expect " good times." I know that Aunt Sally is a delightful travelling companion, and our two gentlemen are both proverbial for their good temper, a special blessing on a journey. Poor Uncle Ben, patient as a lamb under his misfortune, never dims our spirits by complaint, but takes things as they come, and sits in a state of quiet enjoyment of the passing scenery; while Colonel G——, bright, cheerful, and active, an indefatigable and clever sketcher, a universal referee, full of information and anecdote, ever on the alert to perform some act of kindness and to promote the pleasure of those around him, is the life and soul of our party.

Now we start again: they put on the steam, and as we begin to enter the open Marmora the heavy rain-clouds roll away, the water becomes azure and transparent. I see the great blue palamède fish, in shape resembling mackerel, but as large as salmon, running races with the steamer; the porpoises are rolling about, the people are all chatting cheerily on deck, savoury odours and sounds of preparation arise from the cabin, the steward has brought up the camp-stools: I am faithful to my travelling bag and heap of bedding; and we all feel ourselves thoroughly in "k'ief."

We are passing the Princes Islands on our left: Prinkipo, the most distant of the group; then Antigone, bare and uninteresting; and nearer still the jagged cliffs of Proti, of flaming red and rich ochre-coloured earth. We pass sufficiently close to distinguish the buildings on Platé, now known amongst the English as Bulwer's Island; and, last of the beautiful cluster, the bold wild granite peak of Oxeïa towers from the water, desolate, rarely visited by man, the home of cormorants and sea-gulls, who are circling now in hundreds round its crest.

We have been called to luncheon in the cabin, but

returned on deck as soon as possible. We turn our attention to the long line of noble mountains bordering the Gulf of Nicomedia, which are, apparently, passing before us in a slowly moving panorama. These majestic and beautifully formed heights, which serve as a dreamy background to all the views from Constantinople southwards, lose nothing of their grandeur on a nearer approach. But for the rare spots of soft green which came into view, a few goats, a tiny wreath of curling smoke, a desolate tchiftlik or two, one might conclude that the whole of this vast tract of neglected land is utterly abandoned to nature. There is a scattered hamlet at the entrance to a gorge which might be glorious if the swelling uplands were clothed with trees; now it is all desolation. Soon we are rounding "Armout Bournou" (Pear-tree Point), named from a solitary pear-tree on its summit, and then the scenery appears more smiling and attractive; the aspect changes—we enter, as it were, another region, not discernible from Stamboul—we are passing before the northern slope of the mountains, their sides become cultivated, then fertile and luxuriant; but we forget to notice this feature of the landscape any longer. On the opposite shore of the Gulf of Mondania, the summit of Olympus, in all the solemn majesty of its snowy coronal of peaks, towers before us to the sky. I observe, although we are yet many miles distant, that the range of lower mountains, rising immediately behind Mondania, is rich to luxuriance, abundantly clothed with wood, in which the soft tint of olive groves is distinctly visible, broken by the sharp dark point of an occasional cypress; and——the wind has freshened considerably, as we are passing the roughest part of the gulf, and I begin to perceive that the scenery is not nearly so interesting as I had fancied it. I find that I prefer to gaze on the straight boards of the deck; they are not picturesque, but they at least seem steady, while all other lines of perspective have become frightfully dislocated. The trees and houses on the coast, viewed in connection with the masts and cordage of the steamer, are rolling about in the wildest manner. Olympus, too, may be all very well, but I am sadly afraid it bores me. I feel an utter conviction that "there's nothing new, nothing true, and it doesn't signify," and I think—I think—I would rather not think about it, or about anything whatever any more.

I am sitting at length in a talika, in a narrow village street, under the glaring reflection of a long white wall. We have landed at the wooden scala of Mondania (the steamer continuing her course to Ghemlik, at the head of the gulf); we have passed through the large shed which serves as custom-house, and after some trouble have succeeded in obtaining three talikas and two pack-horses, but we are not off at once by any means. Uncle Ben has been heaved, poked, pushed, and pulled with difficulty into his vehicle, but when Aunt Sally endeavoured to follow the floor gave way, and she stepped through quietly on to the ground: as she said, laughing, "If it weren't for the honour of the thing one might as well walk." The driver—a merry, good-humoured ragamuffin, with twinkling blue eyes, a mouth in a perpetual grin, and about sixteen years old—took the occurrence as quite a matter of course; he got a large stone and knocked the boards in again; then we thought we should start, but no, there is a certain amount of shouting to be got through before the baggage is settled on the packs. One heap is formed, and then it tumbles to pieces again; while it is being readjusted, some heavily-laden bullock arabas come lumbering along; they must pass through the thick of the confusion, for this narrow passage is the high road, so horses, packs, and baggage are quickly huddled aside to make room, and the building up of our property begins all over again. It is good to bear in mind a French proverb, "Tout vient à point, à qui sait attendre;" the business *is* settled at length, and we leave this burning spot, where I am sure a thermometer would have marked 100° at the very least.

Uncle Ben's carriage leads the procession, F—— and myself are in the second, and Colonel G—— in the third. Our way lies at first along the shore, where the cool breeze comes most refreshingly across the crested waves, and I return to the conviction that Olympus is really very beautiful after all, crowning the curve of the lovely bay with the snowy summit which we shall soon lose sight of, for I know that half way across the plain the topmost point disappears behind the peaks which constitute the second region of the mountain; so I gaze at the beautiful picture to the utmost, with great regret that I should have been unable to make even a slight sketch. The colour of the sea on our left hand is an intense lapis lazuli, while on our right rises a high hill covered with rich vineyards, mulberry groves, and olive gardens. Soon we turn at a sharp angle, and leaving the sea-shore, plunge into this verdure, winding through a leafy lane, reminding us of Devonshire, till we are brought back to the East by glimpses of a party of Turkish women, in yashmak and feràdjé, riding astride, taking a short cut through the fields; and by the wayside fountains, where children are waiting with cups of pure fresh water, and with little bunches of wild flowers, which they throw into the carriages, of course in expectation of backshish.

Somewhere amongst the vines and olive groves, to the right of the road, and at a short distance behind Mondania, we are told that ruins of the ancient town of Apamea may still be discerned, but the luxuriant foliage around us, the tall Indian corn, the waving vines, and leafy mulberry trees prevented our seeing anything of them from the carriage.

We go very merrily on—the air is full of song (in which the nightingale takes a distinguished part), and fragrant with the breath of the wild flowers, and also, perhaps, with the blossom of some early vines, than which I know no sweeter scent; the talikas do not shake us more than we expected, and if the bottom of Uncle Ben's conveyance occasionally falls through, there are plenty of stones at hand, and his merry young driver considers it a capital joke to have to settle it again in its place. This youth has a peculiar fashion of driving, for though we are going along at a good pace, he rarely looks at his two skinny little ponies, but sits persistently with his back to them, turning round to laugh and jeer at the driver of our carriage, which is now directly behind. It is wonderful that we meet with no catastrophe. I have inward unconfessed tremors at many points of the road, but nothing worse has happened than dislocation to our parcels, and we are all drawn up to rest for a few moments at the Durbend, the small station of rural police on the summit of the pass, about two hours distant from Mondania. They bring us little cups of coffee, which are passed to us quite handily through a large hole in the window, and while we are sipping it a party of Turkish travellers gallops up and stops. It is the Pasha's harem, our fellow-travellers on the steamer, and there is the young hanum herself, mounted on a handsome grey horse and on a European saddle. This is a most unusual sight, and confirms my impression that she is not of Mussulman origin. She makes her horse fret and curvet for awhile at a little distance on the soft turf, then goes off at a graceful canter down the road in front. We resume our jolting progress, and begin to descend the other slope of the mountain towards the great plain of Broussa, which spreads out before us rich in wood and water and groves and park-like clumps of trees. We are all in a state of exclamation and delight at the sight of this luxuriant foliage, these leafy trees with their lower branches sweeping the ground, so very refreshing to our English eyes, wearied with the barren burnt-up hills in the neighbourhood of the capital.

We have just reached a second very old stone bridge, and paused to enjoy the distant view of Broussa nestling at the foot of the purple mountain, partly bathed in its shadow, partly touched with golden and ruby light, flashing from dome and minaret, from bath and kiosk, then softening to a rosy haze as it reaches the plain, and melting away in the soft vapours that cling about the distant mountain ridges. I can faintly trace the castle heights overhanging the clustering buildings of the city, and the minarets of the Olou Djami catching a sparkle of brightness from out the solemn shadow of the mountain; deep in this shadow a pale bluish tinge, winding and disappearing into its depths, reveals the opening of Gueuk-dereh (the Heavenly Valley). Beyond the shadow, far from the clustering dwellings, the sun's rays linger caressingly and sadly on the desolate mosque and tomb of the unhappy Bajazet, and farther still towards the north a spark of fire flashes from the gilded crescent on the dome of Emir Sultan Djamissy. The snowy crest of Olympus has long been lost to us, but some patches of dazzling white linger about the highest visible peaks, and as we advance, and the distant city sinks into grey shadow, these peaks still glow and sparkle in all the glorious effulgence of an Eastern sunset.

The bridge near which we have halted is the one built by Niloufar, the beautiful Greek wife of Orkhan, whose name is given to this day to the river which passes beneath it from out the gorge of Missikeny, and spreads its silver windings across the landscape.

We continue our way, and soon, on the right hand, rising considerably above the level of the plain, we can distinguish the village of Tchekirghé (the Grasshopper), the first of the line of mineral baths, with its immense khan for the accommodation of patients. Our plans have been changed, and instead of proceeding to the inferior hotel at this village, it has been agreed that we are to go to Loschi's, in the Muradyieh suburb of Broussa, where rooms had been previously engaged; but the hanum and her party, who had kept near us for the most part of the journey, turn off to the right, taking a lane leading upwards, and we lose sight of her graceful figure and flowing draperies under a leafy canopy of hanging boughs.

We pass the baths of Eski-Kaplidja, Kukutlu, Yeni-Kaplidja, and others of smaller pretension. We know that we shall see them again, so we take small note of them now, or of the marble fountains by the roadside, framed in the natural setting of leaves and wild flowers. Avoiding the picturesque but ill-paved street of the Muradyieh, and passing smoothly for a short while under the arching boughs of walnut, elm, and beech trees, we turn to the right, and see perched high above us, on the edge of a grey line of jagged rock, our place of rest, a modest-looking rose-coloured house, bearing on the signboard, "Hôtel du Mont Olympe, tenu par Joseph Loschi." We reach it very tired and weary, and as we alight at the door of this unpretending "locanda," we are welcomed by the present mistress of the house, Marietta, and by our old friend the waiter, Giovanni Gillardi.

We were soon installed in some of the best rooms; everything seems so familiar to me from my happy visit here four years ago; all is quite the same as then—the same scanty but clean furniture, the same simplicity about the arrangements, the same people, with just a touch of those four years about them; for Marietta is a trifle more buxom and more florid than formerly; and Giovanni, the head-waiter, manager, purveyor, and factotum of the establishment, civil, patient, and active as ever, has a plainer mixture of grey in his dark hair as he stands there in the sala in his best black satin waistcoat, a flaring candle in his right hand, his feet in the first position, bowing, "Mesdames, la soupe est sur la table," for dinner bells and gongs are several steps in advance of the Arcadian simplicity of the Hôtel Loschi.

Besides the table, some straw chairs and a chintz divan compose all the furniture of the dining-hall on the first floor, but the table-d'hôte dinner is excellent, for Loschi himself was a noted "artiste" in the culinary department, and his traditions remain, although he has quitted the house.

*May 9th.*—A brisk tinkling of many bells, dying softly away in the distance, awoke me this morning: I hastened to the window to see a long string of camels slowly progressing down the winding road in front of the hotel. There may have been about forty of these ungainly but picturesque animals, with their heaving walk, their awkward feet, humps, red tassels, and uncouth, wild-looking cameleers. They were bringing sacks of corn to be ground at the mill, which stands quite near us on the right hand.

Each camel, as it came up to the great gateway of the building, knelt down to be unloaded, then rising to make room for a successor, knelt down once more a little farther off, ranged in a row, to rest, until a certain number having been relieved of their burdens, they rose, slowly filed off, and disappeared down the road across the little rustic bridge, in the direction of the plain, the music of their bells mingling with the song of hundreds of nightingales, long after the drooping branches had hidden them from our sight. I was glad to see a string of camels once more; they give such a thoroughly Oriental character to a place. On my first arrival in Constantinople, one used often to meet the huge animals laden with charcoal from the forest of Belgrade, heaving their ungainly forms along the high street of Pera, to the terror of the horses and, I must confess, the great inconvenience of the foot passengers; but they have almost disappeared from thence, and are, even now, scarce in Stamboul; their presence here at Broussa is quite in harmony with this thoroughly Asiatic locality.

What a lovely view of the Castle hill from the right-hand window of our room! In the foreground, the great French flour-mill is the prominent object, square and gaunt-looking, still bearing traces of the battering which it received by the masses of rock hurled against it from the mountain-side during the great earthquake of 1855. On the farther side of the building we can see part of the gigantic black wheel, turned by one of the numerous torrents which rush impetuously from the gorges of Olympus; and beyond this mill the road, winding by a mosque and turbé, disappears in the grey shadow of a small Turkish cemetery, and comes to view again in the warm sunshine of the hillside, bright figures dotting it with cloak, and caftan, and feràdjé of every possible tint. A school of small children is straggling along under the guidance of two mollahs in grey and green caftans and snowy turbans; next a party of mounted zebeks, gorgeous as macaws; then quiet traders and loitering, listless women, trailing their canary-coloured slippers along the dust.

The road branches off after leaving the suburb of the Muradyieh, the main thoroughfare entering the town under the castle heights, which rise abruptly, a confusion of grey rock and profuse vegetation; half way up, a long-deserted silk factory, propped by powerful beams, is another evidence of the force of the earthquake. Near this tottering building we see some natural caverns amongst the underwood, and on the summit of the cliff stands the unpretending wooden konak of the Pasha, beside the ruined square tower of the old castle.

The principal portion of Broussa is hidden from us by the gentle slope from the foot of the Castle hill: we see only a part of the Jewish quarter, an irregular mass of houses buried in trees. Behind this rise the noble forms of Olympus, the peaked summits changing in aspect with every changing cloud—now shrouded in vapour, now flashing out golden or ruby-coloured, now a deep purple or a pale lilac, and now a rugged crest of the faintest dove colour, with some touches of dazzling snow lingering in the deep fissures and amongst the dark pine-trees of the second region.

Breakfast over, we are impatient to set out upon our rambles, and so, while waiting for Colonel G——, who had business in the town, Aunt Sarah, F——, and myself determined to employ the time in exploring those tempting-looking caves on the hillside, to which we fancy we can trace a little pathway. We start therefore under the guidance of an old Jew hanger-on of the house, or rather attended by him, for we soon discover that he knows nothing of any proper way, and that we must organise a kind of steeplechase for ourselves. Turning upwards from the broad path leading into the town, we get at first into a plantation of young mulberry-trees. Here we wandered for a time amongst the slender boughs, admiring the gigantic periwinkles which carpeted the ground with dark-blue stars, and yet with an uncomfortable feeling that we must certainly be trespassing, and that the old Jew is resigned under protest. But those caves had to be reached, so, coming to the brink of a very steep little path, promising to lead in the right direction, Aunt Sarah in advance, we found that we had to adopt a primitive and perfectly safe method of descent, for to go down on our feet was impossible. The hillside echoed our laughter as we sat down, and grasping firmly at the masses of periwinkles on either side, steered our way one after another to the small grassy platform below; the old Jew behind was coming down in the same manner, with the look of a patient martyr. "Are we not déli Frangs" (mad Franks) said I, to call a smile upon the poor pale face. "Zarar yok, Madama" (It is of no consequence), said he, with grave resignation.

After all our trouble, having previously been too much above, we found ourselves now equally below, the entrance to the cave; we never reached it, and after straying into the private garden of an Armenian house, frightening and being frightened by a large watch-dog, and disturbing a party of people placidly seated in a rose-covered arbour, we quietly turned homewards by the shortest way we could discover, consoling ourselves with the handfuls of lovely wild flowers and fragments of glittering stalactites.

After a little rest we started once more, the Jew

carrying the sketching blocks. We left poor Uncle Ben patiently seated at the window to watch our departure, and preparing to beguile his captivity by taking a sketch of the Castle hill. Another day, when he may be able to move so far, we shall place him in the jessamine arbour beneath, from which he will have a good view of turbaned Moslems, and other attractive "subjects," passing along, while enjoying the cool plashing of a tiny fountain in the little hotel garden. We wave our handkerchiefs and parasols at the last point visible from the window, and disappear into the Jewish suburb. Here the remarkable cleanliness and brilliancy of the windows of all the houses would have revealed to me the class of the inhabitants, had other evidence been wanting, for I have always observed in Turkish towns that, whatever may be their shortcomings in the matter of cleanliness in other respects, the dwellings of the Israelites may always be known by the wonderful brightness of their window panes. Several women looked out at us from these windows, their headdresses, a gauze or painted handkerchief, ornamented with a flower drooping near the ear. The men wear long straight dresses of cotton, very short in the waist, and a shawl girdle; they mostly adopt the fez, which they bind round the brows with a painted handkerchief.

At the end of the Jews' quarter, and before entering that part of Broussa inhabited by the Greeks, and immediately beneath the Castle hill, you come upon an open space on the right of the road, where the tangling creepers and rubbish are varied by masses of fallen masonry and crumbling brickwork. This spot is one vast grave, for it was here that a large spinning factory stood on the slope of the hill, and was utterly destroyed by the great earthquake, partly shaken to the ground and partly overwhelmed by the huge crags detached from the overhanging cliffs: fifty or sixty young women were at work there; every one of them perished, and the bodies have never been disinterred. The factory was happily at the time on half work, or more than a hundred persons would have been buried in its fall.

Leaving this sad spot, we pass for some distance along a raised pathway, covered by the projecting first-floors of the wooden houses, supported by high wooden posts. The precaution of raising the pathway is probably taken on account of the heavy floods of water which at times rush tearing down the middle of the street, particularly at the season of the melting snows.

We turn to the left, and are at the entrance of the bazaars. Here we come to a halt, for all are simultaneously struck with a most effective "bit" of bazaar scenery—the low shops right and left with their stores of brightly coloured vegetables, heaps of fresh spinach, pale green " coloketheas," glowing tomatos, and bundles of gigantic leeks; then the cooks' shops, with well burnished pans and bubbling jets of water in the middle of the paved floor; a saddler's, with a great display of ornamental frontlets for buffaloes, richly embossed with gaudy-coloured beads, and high-peaked saddles bound and mounted in brass; the turbaned vendors are lazily sitting on their counters, or lounging in easy conversation with their neighbours. All these things are in the soft shadow thrown by the high raftered roof; but a few yards farther is a break where the roof ceases, with a downward flap of half-broken boarding (picturesque to the last degree, with its garlands of vine branches), and a golden stream of joyous sunshine pours on a marble fountain, the trunk of a twisted elm-tree, the drooping thread-like streamers of a weeping willow, and the brightly-dressed figures about the primitive *al fresco* establishment of an old coffee seller. This charming bit of light is brought out in strong relief by the gloom of the farther streets of the bazaars stretching away from that point in several directions.

Such a subject was not to be lost, and Colonel G——, planting himself firmly in the right spot, utterly regardless—as such a bold sketcher should be—of wondering eyes and gaping mouths, commenced work; while Aunt Sally, F——, and myself, attended by Joseph, wandered away to see what was to be seen, and, after a few turnings, came upon some shops of coarse native earthenware. This ware is made at Kutaya, and although exceedingly rough in execution, is not without merit in the form and harmony in the colouring; the prevailing tint is a bluish-green, with the pattern picked out in black. We bought for a few paras a-piece, mugs, ink-bottles, saltcellars, and some ingenious little toys for children; after this, we made a descent upon the pipe-shops, where the long jessamine and cherry-wood stems are set up in bundles against the wall, and the smaller wooden pipes, more or less ornamented with amber and glass mouthpieces and wooden "lulés," repose in the glass cases. Some of these wooden pipes are very prettily adorned with a barbaric sort of traced pattern in colours.

Our shopping over, including some strings of cornelian charms purchased for a few pence, we wended our way back towards the weeping willow, a landmark where five or six roads meet. We discovered the Colonel, still sketching vigorously, surrounded by an admiring and appreciative crowd of natives. I stationed myself beside him to take one or two of the figures. The people behaved very well. It is true they leaned oppressively close to my shoulder, and I could not doubt that they made free use of the leeks and onions which grow here to such perfection; but they were so good-tempered that I endured the infliction with the best grace possible, and it was quite amusing to see how anxious each man was that his neighbour should not impede our view. One ragged individual constituted himself master of the ceremonies, lamentably frustrating our efforts to seize the effect of the quiet dignity of some genuine old Asiatic Turk, or the lounging swagger of a passing zebek, by announcing the fact to the victim in triumphant haste: "Now, oh Mustafa, the tchelebi is making your picture; stand still!" or, "Ibrahim, my soul! the Cocona is doing your right eye; look round that she may see it well;" the effect of which, of course, was that the Ibrahims and the Mustafas immediately lost the position which we were trying to perpetuate, dropped their arms straight down, turned out their toes, and looked intensely sheepish. But we struggled on, resigned to the inevitable; and when we shut up our books and resumed our progress through the bazaars, we had the satisfaction of feeling that we had furnished the good folks of that quarter with an interesting topic of conversation over their pipes and coffee for the next day or two.

I had undertaken to pioneer my friends towards the Gueuk-dereh (the Heavenly Valley), the most beautiful of the gorges of Olympus. The way for some distance is not interesting; you follow an interminable street of private houses, or rather of their garden walls, varied only by the police station, with a group of brilliantly bedecked zebeks and zaptiehs lounging round the gate, and by an occasional fountain. At one of these, Colonel G—— paused to take a sketch, his attendant Jew holding the umbrella over his head. The contrast between the firm attitude of the free-born Briton, and the bending, timid air of the patient Jew, was irresistible. I took a note of it in my sketch-book; after which, seated on the stone ledge round the base of a small mosque, we stopped an ice-man who was passing, with his ice-pail swathed in flannel, and his gay-looking stand covered with tiny saucers and arrow-shaped spoons, and decked with little bunches of flowers. His ices proved to be the "Caïmacli doudourma," or cream ice—a delicious compound of sweet cream, salep, sugar, and rose-water, which he served out liberally heaped up in the gold and blue saucers, at the rate of one penny each.

We reached the valley at last, after many a turn and winding, following the course of a rill of clear water which was tumbling and bubbling down the centre of the wonderfully uneven pavement. The gorge is fringed on both sides for some distance by the houses of the Armenian quarter; but hastening to leave human habitations behind us, and passing beyond a little wooden bridge thrown lightly over the ravine, turned upwards on the right-hand bank along a lovely mountain path (reminding me strongly of a similar pathway in the Desert of the Grande Chartreuse) until we reached the neighbourhood of the mills. They are rough-looking flour-mills, worked by a small but impetuous torrent which is guided in its course by a succession of dilapidated and wildly picturesque troughs, mounted on high wooden piles, and, as it were, dripping leaves, sparkling with falling drops all over the neglected decaying structure. We stop, but the path goes winding upwards far away among blossoming shrubs and blushing rose-bushes, round threatening granite crags, and blocks of the purest white marble, till it passes out of sight in the vapoury chasms of the noble mountain.

The view from the mills of Gueuk-dereh (at the point where the rugged path turns abruptly round the trunk of a large walnut-tree) is one of the most beautiful about Broussa. The foreground is the deep leafy ravine, clothed with every variety of foliage, from the great elm, and walnut, and mountain-ash, whose topmost branches are almost beneath our feet, to the soft blossoming elder, the wild vine, the hop, the broad-leaved rhubarb, the rich green masses of the wild angelica, the thyme, the mint, which spring luxuriantly all around. The opposite side of the gorge rises dark, and stern, and gloomy; on a small plateau, capping a projecting mass of granite rock, an immense cypress shoots upwards, tall and straight, casting a long blue shadow over a few irregular tombstones, which cluster round the grey trunk, and over a party of bright little Turkish children, flickering in and out of the sunshine. A noisy stream of water comes tumbling down from the upper regions of the mountain; far below us, it rushes through the solemn gloom of the deep chasm; as it passes beneath the light wooden bridge, it catches some sparkles of brightness from between the dense masses of boughs and creepers, then loses itself in the darkness of a ruined stone arch. Beyond this, some of the buildings of the city appear, embosomed in trees, among which white minarets, pink, blue, yellow, and dove-coloured houses, peep out here and there; and we can distinguish the domes and minarets of the Yeshil Djami. Then there is a broad space of shimmering tints of purple, and rose, and gold-colour, in which we make out the rich plain of Broussa, with villages and mulberry groves, sleeping in the evening sunlight; the panorama finishes with a range of lilac-tinted mountains. It is a scene to look·upon and to store in one's memory for ever.

I made a somewhat hasty retreat from this well-named "Heavenly Valley," for being seized with a spirit of investigation, I undertook to explore the bottom of the ravine. I was getting on pretty well, with the assistance of Joseph, when, crossing a small dyke, I contrived to step, not across, but into the pool, so that on rejoining our party, with my enthusiasm for the moment considerably damped, it was decided to return at once to the hotel, a distance of two or three miles.

On our road back through the Jews' quarter, we observed the women in groups outside their doors, working. They were mostly making silk buttons, and one and all were busily employed. One delicate, pale young Jewess was sitting on a couch near her window, hard at work; there was a tiny baby, whose hammock-cradle, suspended in the doorway, was being swung vigorously backwards and forwards—no one apparently setting it in motion. We found that the industrious young mother, in order to leave her hands at liberty, was moving the cradle by a string fastened to one of her feet. I think these much-abused people cannot at any rate be accused of idleness.

## X.

## THE BATHS OF BROUSSA.

### NO. II.—TCHEKIRGHÉ.

Mountain Trout.—The View and the Passers-by.—The Trysting Tree.—A Sober Traveller.—A Wild Zebek.—A Santon.—Hawks and Storks.—A Start.—The Mouradiyeh Suburb.—The Mosque and its Surroundings.—An Aggressive Umbrella.—Rustic Fountains.—The "Kïef."—Bademli Bagtché. —Yeni Kaplidja Hammam. — Cypresses. — Tchekirghé. —Eski Kaplidja Hammam.—The Mosque of Mourad I.—A Fountain of Hot and Cold Water.—The Sultan's "Tonghra." —Interior of the Mosque.—The Ruined "Turbé."—A Flowery Lane.—A Rustic Resting-place.—The Mineral Waters of Eski-Kaplidja.

WE are very merry at our breakfast table, talking over our excursion of the previous day, and laying out our plans for making the most of the coming hours. We are interrupted for a moment by Giovanni, who has just brought up for our inspection a pail full of lively trout, taken from a small lake near the summit of Mount Olympus. Some Armenians have the monopoly of this supply, and I imagine there are not many of the inhabitants who would wish to infringe their right of fetching them from almost inaccessible altitudes. I may as well mention that oil extracted from the trout is considered here an infallible remedy in cases of rheumatism and stiff joints; it is used at the baths, and is sold at a high price.

Well, the trout dismissed to the lower regions of the house, whence they will emerge at dinner-time considerably sobered, we begin once more to discuss our plans. We weigh the comparative merits of horses and donkeys, with a decided leaning towards the former; but, on inquiry, finding they are not to be had easily—the greater number having been sent off to fetch the travellers from Mondania—we resign ourselves to the humbler style of locomotion, and, while waiting the convenience of the very independent donkey boys, we turn for a moment to that lovely scene of wonderful fertility, which induced one author to remark that "the Moors, when exiled from Andalusia, which they still call the terrestrial Paradise—and the Jewish tribes who, later, shared their fate, and came to seek a refuge under the Ottoman sultans—thought they had found a new Grenada in this rich and beautiful country."

The weather is delightful; bright and breezy, with soft fleeting clouds which throw cool patches of purple tone across the landscape. We watch them as they float slowly, first over the broad expanse of woodland and mulberry grove, with walnut, chestnut, and plane-tree, waving poplar and stately cypress, which, beginning at the foot of the crag under our windows, stretches away to half the width of the plain; then the shade softens for an instant the glowing brilliancy of the rich cultivation beyond, dimming as it passes the silvery sparkle of the winding Niloufar; but soon the little river flashes out, bright and joyous in the sunshine, and the purple shadow is creeping away gently up the noble mountain range which bounds the view—the Mount Katarli (*Arganthonios*). Sometimes, as these shadows of the clouds flit over the rock-bound gorges, or the light vapours rest on the summit of the mountain, it looks all sombre, solemn, and majestic; then, as the sun again, touching up the points, gradually bathes it in a soft radiance, bright patches of cultivation spring into view, climbing high up to the foot of the granite crags, nestling even in the little dips and dells between them, with here and there a winding horse-track, a scattered hamlet, or a solitary tchiflik; around the base are hedgerows and patches of rich red and yellow earth; above, in the distance, rise, blue and shadowy, the peaks and summits of Mount Samanli, on the farther shore of the Gulf of Mondania.

The northern end of the Katarli range is pointed by two high fantastic masses of granite rock, overhanging the Greek village of Fillardar, and below it many other villages, half buried in their mulberry groves and vineyards—the principal among which is Demirdesch, celebrated for its silk—help to give life to the landscape. To the south, the mountains, still bounding the fertile luxuriant plain, rise and fall with exquisite variety of outline, until they melt away in the blue distance towards Kutaya, Yeni-Shehir, and the wild regions of the interior of Asia Minor.

But our attention is soon attracted from the rather dreamy contemplation of primeval hills to the living and breathing beings who enliven the foreground of our picture. The hotel stands on the highroad to the baths; behind the house, the grey rock rises so abruptly that the ground floor of our next-door neighbour's wooden tenement projects its supporting beams close under the corner of our roof, while in front the narrow stony road, with its low parapet, quite overhangs a large dilapidated flour-mill. On the other side of the low wall a pomegranate in full blossom, a myrtle-bush, and a fig-tree covered with its young fruit, just raise their topmost branches into sight; then the grey rock falls straight down, draped and festooned with creepers of every form and colour, to a small platform of neglected ground all ablaze with scarlet poppies; it dips again, to nearly the level of the plain, very abruptly—so much so, indeed, that without raising our eyes we can almost distinguish the soft fur of the little squirrel who is gracefully winding about the topmost branches of a lofty poplar on the other side of the road.

Directly in front of the entrance to this broad turning road, which seems to plunge into a wilderness of leafy shade, a hundred yards or so farther on is a halting-point for those who " welcome the coming," or " speed the parting guest." Some stop here in the shelter of a large chestnut-tree to the right, to take leave of the friends whom they have escorted thus far from the town; others, to wait for those who may come into sight from under the green canopy of the overhanging boughs. We watch the people as they pass either way. A Greek party has arrived and stopped: there are three horses well laden with baggage, bedding, and carpets, with large panniers for the children, who are already installed; several men and women are on foot—they pause and say a few last words; the horses' girths are examined, the baggage readjusted, the soft carpets folded more commodiously on the top of the heap; then there is a little leave-taking, two women are hoisted up into their places on the carpeting, half astride between the panniers, a man gets into a similar position above the third horse, two or three more follow on foot, and the small procession moves slowly onwards: the friends watch them from the corner till they disappear behind the drooping boughs of an enormous walnut-tree.

Now other figures pass across the space, emerging from under those same walnut boughs; a stately venerable Turk, wearing an ample bright green turban and a dove-coloured cloak, with wide hanging sleeves. He rides a sleek donkey, with plenty of red tassels and a general air of comfort about him, and is followed by his servant on another donkey, carrying his master's long pipe in his hand, and his small travelling pack on the back of the saddle. They are jogging on with imperturbable steadiness, and it is well that the road is very broad at this part, for there comes now, rushing helter-skelter past them, a wild-looking individual, who is urging his fiery Arab with his shovel stirrups; his head is covered with the brilliant crimson and gold-coloured Syrian haïk, its long fringes floating over his breast and shoulders; the coils of his shawl-girdle cover one-third of his body, his belt bristles with sword, yataghan, pistols, and many other weapons, and in his right hand he grasps a formidable matchlock. He is a zaptieh, or policeman, sometimes here called a zebek, a kind of half-tamed brigand.

Something else comes slowly and totteringly forward into the patch of sunshine; it is a huge mass of mulberry boughs for the silkworms, and we at length make out the motive power, in the tiny hoofs of a feeble little donkey. It has a head somewhere among the leaves, but undiscernible; a dirty boy with bare legs and a new red fez, which bobs about like a gigantic poppy among the green leaves, is poking the animal on from behind. Next, three talikas rattle by full of Turkish women, and accompanied by two shabbily-dressed mounted servants; it is the harem of a small Pasha, come from Constantinople for the bathing season. Then follow some Turkish women in thick white yashmaks, worn outside the ferádjé, according to Broussa fashion; they sit astride, with a child's head peeping contentedly above the edge of the pannier on each side of the horse. Behind them, a heavy bullock-cart is moving ponderously along, with a pleasant jingle of bells from the animals' heads, and a deep bass accompaniment of ghastly groans from the creaking, suffering wheels. This is followed at a short distance by some camels, who have bells also, but which ring a different tune, and their footfall is noiseless.

Presently comes an old Greek priest, on foot; he has a long snow-white beard and a high black hat without a brim; then a party of Mussulman dervishes, with tall caps equally brimless, but made of yellowish felt, and looking like inverted unbaked flower-pots; with them is a wild-looking Santon, who has a face like mahogany and streaming black hair. He is clothed in a wondrous mass of tatters, which must take him a full month to adjust, and, once hung together, they are never afterwards disturbed. At a short distance behind the Santon, who is hobbling forward, proffering occasionally his begging-dish, resembling a small antediluvian canoe suspended from chains, there passes down the road the other way a restive and very vicious-looking donkey, carrying a Greek lady to the baths. She is astride like the Turkish women, but *plus* the crinoline, which must account for the animal's capers—perhaps he objects to being, in any way, put into a cage. We are deep in this profound speculation when we suddenly perceive that the space that we have so long been watching is empty for a moment, and we have time to note that, in addition to the cool sound of the rushing mill-stream, the song of the nightingales is unceasing; it rises all around us, mingling with the voices of many other feathered choristers.

There is a great twittering of the swallows also, who are building their nests in the corners of our windows, but just now they seem disturbed, and are wheeling round and round in a confused, purposeless kind of way. Ah! there is the cause: a brown speck is swooping swiftly towards us; now it passes close, and we see a large hawk with its strong hooked beak, and vicious-looking claws drawn tightly up under its breast, ready to pounce upon the first unhappy little victim. He has of course, nothing to say to the fine stone eagle, soaring loftily and solemnly towards the rock-crowned summit of Mount Katarli, nor will he venture an encounter with that ungainly stork who comes sailing heavily along, his thin neck stretched out, and his long legs hanging helplessly downwards, intent on reaching the dwelling which he has erected on the broken top of the ruined turbé, close to the mosque of Mourad II. The stork's flight reminds us that we are going in the same direction ourselves, for the donkeys are at the door, and the time is too precious to be wasted.

There is a little difficulty at first about the starting, as here thick-padded cushions only are used, and the animals object to our English saddles; they do not fit them, and the donkey-boys never manage to fasten the girths properly. But we are off at length, after much laughing; and, with a feeling that one is decidedly too large for one's conveyance, and must inevitably topple over, we start on our visit to Tchekirghé, the village of the iron baths; Colonel G—— having taken care, as he said, to charter a Jew for the proper conveyance of the sketching blocks.

Turning to the left from the door of the hotel, our small cavalcade winds, stumbling along, over the rough, uneven road, through a part of the village, or rather suburb, called the Mouradiyeh, from the mosque of Sultan Mourad II., which stands at the northern extremity. We came to it soon after passing the ruined tomb of a saint, supporting the house of our friend the stork.

I have rarely seen anything more thoroughly

Oriental than this old mosque with its surroundings, and the figures lounging and grouped about the open space in front. The mosque itself is not large, but it has a fine colonnade, the architrave ornamented by various fantastic patterns in brickwork. During the late restorations, it has undergone an amount of whitewashing which has not improved it. I liked it better formerly, with the green, yellow, and red tints painted by time on its neglected surface.

All about it is delightfully in keeping. To the left of the mosque, at the entrance of the street, is a little old café, frequented by wild zebeks, bending under the weight of their warlike belts, dervishes with their hideous felt hats, and venerable mollahs and imāms, who sat smoking long pipes and nodding their enormous turbans at each other as we passed. An old Turk was pounding his corn in the public mortar in the centre of the green.

In one corner of the court of the mosque there is a most remarkable group of cypress-trees; they are of gigantic height, and bend a little forwards over the road, some of the large branches being gnarled and twisted in an incredible manner.

On the right side of the open square stand some antique Turkish houses painted a pale green, with small pointed windows; and beyond them, on a line with the principal building, is the massive brickwork entrance to the enclosure containing the tombs of Mourad and his family. Farther on, another building, also of fine brickwork, is a part of the original foundation, which included, besides the mausoleum, a school, a khan, and a kitchen for the poor.

The bright masses of crimson roses seen through the grated openings of the wall of the enclosure, the deep cool shade of the lofty plane-trees, the faint murmur of a plashing fountain, almost tempted us to dismount and visit this interesting burial-place. But we resisted the fascination for to-day, and, pushing forwards towards Tchekirghé, were soon in a lovely winding lane—lovely, indeed, in everything except the pavement; *that* seems as if large formless stones had been flung down by some giant hand, and left to settle themselves as best they might. Some people will tell you that these roads were formed by Hannibal, by way of beguiling his exile; and as they have, doubtless, received little or no care since that remote period, their present state is quite in the natural order of things. In spite, however, of the condition of the ground beneath our feet, which, after all, concerns the donkeys more than their riders, we thoroughly enjoy our progress.

Colonel G—— leads the van. Strong in the possession of those sketching blocks, he presses gallantly on, prepared to commit the whole country to paper, if need be, inch by inch; but the conscious dignity of the advance is sadly dimmed by the unruly conduct of a large old umbrella (spread open for the sun), which absolutely refuses to do duty otherwise than inside out, shooting up at the same time offensive and aggressive points, which entangle in all the bushes by the wayside.

We pass some rustic marble fountains nestled in the luxuriant vegetation by the roadside. Close to one of these, of rather higher pretensions, a small police station has been established, outside of which they have erected a kïef, or place of repose. The arrangements are quite primitive. Some leafy boughs rudely bound together, and supported on slight poles, form the roof; a few squares of matting are spread on the earth, and a cafedjie has formed, in a hollow of the bank, a miniature fireplace of stones, where he boils his tiny pot of coffee; he has also hollowed out a shelf in this bank, and ranged his painted waiter, his little cups, and even a narghilé or two upon it, with perfect order. His pincers for taking the live coal to the smokers are pendent from a nail in the trunk of a tree; a tchibouk is leaning against it, and a clean soft towel droops from one of the lower branches.

Three of the policemen, picturesque personages, with fierce moustaches and formidably armed, with very much of the brigand about them, are enjoying a smoke and a quiet chat as they lounge upon the matting; but a few low stools are standing about for the benefit of such customers as pretend to ultra refinement, and they really look so inviting under the flickering green shadow of the kïef, that we determine to rest there for a few minutes, the more especially as a peasant has just come up with a basket full of splendid cherries; so we take possession of the stools and eat cherries, while the cafedjie bustles about with the excitement of distinguished visitors. The awful-looking brigands have proved benignant neighbours. I gained the good graces of one of them by bestowing some of my cherries on his funny little dog, who ate the fruit and put out the stones quite like—I was going to say a human being, but I must rather say much better than the human beings of these parts; for here every one, down to the smallest baby, eats cherries, stones and all, with perfect unconcern, which proves that the air of Broussa is wonderful for the digestion.

Soon after leaving this pleasant kïef, the tall hedge on the right-hand side of the road ceases, and a beautiful view of the fertile plain opens out at some distance below. In the foreground there is a broad terrace of greensward, upon which stands a dismantled Turkish house. This spot is known as Bademli Bagtché (the garden of the almond-trees). It gives its name to the mineral springs which supply the sulphur baths clustered together a little below the grassy plateau, the largest and most important of which is the Yeni Kaplidja Hammam; you look down upon its massive buildings, its noble domes, and solid stone walls. Still lower you can just perceive the roof of the Kara Mustafa Hammam, reserved for the exclusive use of women.

Resuming our way along the high road, we passed two other sulphur baths, neither of them remarkable from an architectural point of view, but much esteemed for the quality of the springs. The large octagonal building, painted of a pale green, which stands near the gate of one of them, is the tomb of Fatma Sultana, a daughter of Mehemet Ghazi.

After passing this group of baths, our road dipped for a while under a canopy of over-arching boughs, then into the denser shadow of a grove of splendid cypress-trees : such cypresses!—lofty, spreading, graceful, and majestic. They are not unlike a certain kind of cedar. I have met with nothing to equal them in Constantinople. A few trees of this sort, but very inferior, may be seen in the Turkish burial-ground near the Oc-meïdan.

The grove is a cemetery : turbaned tombstones, mostly in the form of columns, and the yet more ancient square, upright blocks of rough-hewn granite, all grey and mossy with age, lean about in every stage of neglected decay over the soft, fresh turf, or prop themselves against the knotted trunks of the trees. The gay flowers have ceased to glow in this spot, where everything has a tinge of gentle melancholy, which might be all too sober without the bright occasional glimpses of the distant plain, gleaming here and there through the grey foreground, like flashes of golden and azure light.

The earth here, as in many parts about Broussa, but more especially in this neighbourhood, is of a deep red colour, varied with patches of bright yellow and orange, betraying the buried mineral wealth which lies, alas! unheeded and unsought for by the careless masters of the land.

Emerging from the gloom of the little cypress grove, we came out once more upon the open hillside, and dismounted on a grassy knoll fragrant with thyme and bespangled with daisies. The village of Tchekirghé rose before us, crowning a steep hill and embosomed in trees. The graceful mosque of Mourad I., with its tapering minarets, points the summit of the slope; then pink and red and blue and pale-green houses, half-buried among clustering vines and swelling plane-trees; and at the foot of the hill, the fine collection of buildings called the Eski Kaplidja Hammam, with two cupolas and a basement of solid antique masonry.

The view was too beautiful to be passed by; so, in defiance of the burning sun, we settled ourselves to work, Colonel G—— under the memorable umbrella, reduced to order, and meekly held over his head by the patient Jew. We remained until we had made careful sketches of the spot, after which, and before entering the village, and at the foot of the hill, we observed two large blocks of wrought stone, one on each side of the road, looking like the foundations of a large portal. Perhaps these may be some remains of the strong tower built by Orkhan, as historians tell us, at Eski Kaplidja, for the reduction of Broussa.

We reached the mosque I have already mentioned —that built by Mourad or Amurath I., the son and successor of Orkhan. It is a majestic pile. On one side of the principal façade stand some of the finest Oriental plane-trees that I have ever met with, rivalling the lofty building in their height, and spreading their giant arms across the broad terrace in front, which commands an admirable panoramic view of the fertile champagne country, covered with groves, orchards, and vineyards, stretching away to the foot of the purple mountains.

A covered kïef has been erected at the extremity of this terrace. Several Turkish ladies were lounging there on our arrival, enjoying the charming prospect and the fresh breezes which sweep across the plain; their feràdjés, of every hue of the rainbow, greatly enhancing the exquisite beauty of the whole picture.

Adjoining this kïef, and directly in front of the principal entrance to the mosque, a circular marble basin, with a jet of water in the centre, adds its pleasant drowsy murmur, although on a close examination I cannot say that the waters have a cooling effect, for this particular fountain has the remarkable attribute (not considered meritorious among human beings) of "blowing hot and cold with the same breath." The water flowing in the basin is steaming, while that bubbling up in the centre is cold and pure as crystal.

We turned to visit the mosque, seeing the guardian, key in hand, waiting to conduct us, on condition that we slipped off our shoes before passing the threshold. We all did this accordingly, and after crossing a lofty colonnade and through a handsome arched doorway, we stepped upon the rich soft carpets which covered the whole floor of the edifice.

This beautiful mosque was built by the orders of Amurath during an interval of repose at Broussa, after the conquest of Adrianople, Philippopolis, and Apollonia. The architect was a prisoner of war of the Ottoman fleet—a Greek or Frank Christian; and this accounts doubtless for the peculiar plan of the building, in the form of a cross, which has led some persons to believe it to have been originally a Christian church. Around the base of the dome he constructed sixteen small rooms, to serve as a school for students.

In the same year (1365) which saw the beginning of this fine work was commenced that wonderful seraï or palace of Amurath, at Adrianople, which still exists, though in the last stage of dilapidation and decay. Amurath also completed and enlarged the buildings of the ancient Greek bath, near the foot of the hill of Tcherkirghé. He built another small mosque in the "Heavenly Valley," besides schools and hospitals.

This apparent favour towards pious and learned institutions did not prevent Amurath from being profoundly ignorant. He could not sign his name, and when called upon to affix his signature to a commercial treaty concluded with the merchants of Ragusa, he adopted the simple expedient of plunging his hand into the ink, and dabbing it down at the top of the paper, with the three middle fingers united, the thumb and little finger stretched out. This infantine mode of placing "Amurath, his mark," originated the toghra, or imperial sign-manual. The form was adopted from that day forward, as intended to signify the name of the reigning monarch; a scribe, styled Nischandji Baschi, or secretary of state for the signature of the sultan, being appointed to write beneath, in legible characters, the actual signification for the time being.

It may still be traced at the present day, rendered elegant by flourishes and various delicate caligraphic conceits.

The interior of the mosque at Tchekirghé, with the exception of its peculiar form, is very much like that of any other mosque, in its quiet, hushed aspect: the small "mimber," or pulpit, with its straight little staircase; the monstrous wax-light at the farther end, on either side of the "mirhab," or niche in which the Koran is deposited; and the gigantic Arabic letters round the walls, forming the names most venerated by the Mohammedan worshippers. These massive characters have a very imposing effect, particularly when contrasted with the delicate coronals of slender glass lamps which hang glittering and trembling from the lofty cupolas of the roof.

The imām who acted as our guide was very civil and obliging. Indeed, the civility and good-humour of the inhabitants of Broussa generally, as well as the apparent absence of fanaticism, and the ease with which all religious establishments may be visited, is a subject of universal remark by travellers to this city. It greatly enhances the pleasure of our little excursions, to feel that we may expect pleasant looks and kindly words, rather than the rough repulse which often meets one in rambles about Constantinople, although even there there is much less difficulty of the kind than casual travellers are apt to imagine.

After our examination of the ground floor of the mosque, which was soon terminated, as the whole building may be seen at a glance, our guide conducted us up a very dirty, rough-looking staircase to the long suite of prison-like rooms situated around the dome. There are sixteen of these dismal cells, with low doors and heavily grated windows. We just peeped into the cells, rendered yet blacker and more repulsive by the occupation of the Circassian refugees who spent some time here a few years ago, and we were all right glad to escape from them and to breathe once more in the happy sunshine streaming over the broad stone terrace above the portico. The narrow staircase leading up the minaret, which opens from one corner of this terrace, tempted us to ask if we could be permitted to ascend to the exterior gallery, but the guide declared it to be impossible for any one not well accustomed to climb like a cat. The minaret has been so severely injured by the great earthquake, that whenever the wind is rather violent it rocks and threatens to fall over. The staircase is consequently much dislocated, and he himself, he declared, could only ascend it with stockinged feet and at the risk of his life; so the idea of ascending a minaret had to be abandoned, and we left the mosque to visit the tomb of the founder, on the opposite side of the road. Here, again, the terrible earthquake had been at work; the interior of the handsome turbé is a ruin, blocked up with scaffolding, lumbered with masses of fallen marble—a general scene of dust and desolation.

The handsome porphyry and verde-antique columns, which formerly supported the roof, are some of them standing, it is true, but having been shaken to pieces, they have been patched up again, bound with hoops of iron to keep them together, and covered with plaster.

Formerly, they say, the sword of Amurath was preserved suspended over his tomb, together with the cuirass which was dyed with his life-blood at the great battle of Cossova, in his war against Lazarus, King of Servia. In the heat of the engagement, as some relate, and before victory was declared for either party, a Servian noble, Milosch, starting up suddenly from a heap of dead and dying, pretended that he had a secret to confide to the Ottoman leader. Amurath leaned eagerly forward to listen, and fell, mortally wounded by the Servian's dagger. The dying Emir[*] had strength enough left to give orders which decided the victory in his favour.

[*] It was not until the reign of Bajazet, the son of Amurath, that the title of Sultan was adopted.

The death of Amurath originated another peculiar usage of the Ottoman Court: it became, from that time, an established custom that all persons about to be favoured with an audience of the sultan should be divested of their weapons, and led into the presence securely held on each side by the chamberlains, whose office it is to introduce strangers.

We gazed into the half-ruined turbé from the entrance door, wondering which might be the last resting-place of the grizzly conqueror, or which, if either, the tomb of his slaughtered son, Sandschi Bey, who was at one time governor here at Broussa during his father's warlike campaigns. He afterwards joined with the young Greek Prince Andronicus in an attempt at revolt.

It was in this turbé of Tchekirghé that the remains of the founder's grandson Musa were deposited: he had perished miserably in a marsh, flying, grievously wounded, from an ineffectual struggle with the partisans of his more powerful brother Mohammed. The arrival of this funeral train at Broussa produced a startling effect upon the Prince of Caramania, then engaged in the burning and destruction of the outskirts of the town, and more especially in a sacrilegious outrage on the tomb of Bajazet, the father of the dead prince. It seemed to the Caramanian to be a direct warning of divine vengeance, and he fled in abject terror; nothing softened, however, for one of his faithful followers observing that, if he thus took flight before a dead Ottoman, he could scarcely expect to resist the living, the trembling savage had him instantly strangled on the spot.

We are mounted again, and having turned to the left, after leaving the turbé, we have paused at the meeting of two roads, to select the one which may take us the quickest out upon the mountain's side. Before us is the large entrance gate of part of an hotel which has been lately opened at Tchekirghé—the other half of the establishment lies on the other side of the road. Round the doorway of this latter building a group of European loungers is watching the proceedings of a party of Turkish women who inhabit the other half for the bathing season, and are now getting under weigh, with much difficulty and some little screaming, for an excursion on horseback. One lady is sitting in European fashion; she keeps her beautiful grey horse a little apart from the rest. It is the young hanum—looking even more graceful than when we saw her before—in a pale blue feràdjé and gossamer veil. She continues at a short distance until her party is ready to start, then dashes forward at a canter, and takes the lead. Her women follow, with a brigand-looking cavass or two, and we, concluding from their manner that they quite know the way (which we do not), and that the scene of their promenade cannot fail to be a pretty spot, determine to bring up the rear, at least until we are fairly out of the straggling village, and can see our road before us.

We were not deceived: a few windings brought us to the entrance of a beautiful shady lane; but here our donkey-boys showed symptoms of mutiny, declaring that having been engaged to bring us to Tchekirghé, they would go no farther. We knew that the excursion was well within the powers of all concerned, biped and quadruped, so we stoutly persevered, tugged our animals into single file, and went merrily on, along a little mazy, heathery pathway, arched over with trees and shrubs. We struggle past rose-bushes, and long branches of honeysuckle; here again the elder and sweet-scented privet strew their snows upon our head, and we crush the bright blue periwinkles beneath our donkeys' feet. Up and down went the little path; up and down, up and down, and finally upwards, by a sharp scramble, until we came to a stop at a rustic kïef, called the Kadi Kiosk.

Once before (it was years ago) I came riding along this little pathway; then (for it was earlier in the year) these rose-bushes were heavy with swaying pink clusters, the air was truly " lilac-scented," as these beautiful bushes formed a leafy wall on either side, entangled with honeysuckle and jessamine, of which any garden might be proud; the large highly perfumed bunches of blossom were there in perfection. One can hardly give too high an idea of the exceeding floral beauty of this spot, which cannot, I think, be surpassed on this side of the tropics. The last fortnight in April and the first week in May is perhaps the best period for seeing the wild flowers in perfection.

Below us the slope of the mountain is clothed with mulberry, walnut, chestnut, and fruit-trees, varied with rich vineyards and occasional patches of Indian wheat, till it reaches the plain, where the silvery Niloufar flows swiftly and silently on towards the antique stone bridge. Near the banks are piles of timber which have been floated down from the dense forests of Mount Olympus, and are waiting to be carried off at the proper season. Beyond the river the plain is grassy for a while, then wooded again, until it breaks into a gorge of wondrous beauty, entering the very heart of the mountain. Within this gorge lies the village of Missikeny, near which the Niloufar takes its rise. Olympus continues to spring upwards on the left hand in all the majesty of rock and forest scenery, while far away in front, somewhere in the blue vapoury distance, lie the lake and town of Apollonia. We are not yet sufficiently high up upon the mountain to distinguish them.

I think it difficult for any person more thoroughly to appreciate the simple comfort of chicken, ham, and Palmer's biscuits, with the addition of mohalibé, ices, and coffee, bought on the spot of itinerant vendors, than did our small party, as we reposed in the rustic shed, with the beautiful picture before us, and refreshed by the music of a tiny fountain, which bubbled up within the kïef from amongst tufts of soft grass, bright daisies, and other wild flowers. The mohalibedjie and the iceman had wandered up to this favourite halting-place, in hopes of a stray customer or two; the coffee was furnished by the turbaned proprietor of the shed, who sat on a mat smoking a narghilé, after supplying our wants, or washed his little cups in the running water of the spring. All was very primitive, very peaceful. After a long rest we left it with some regret and a strong determination to return. By-the-bye, how often do travellers express a positive and unalterable intention to revisit this or that lovely spot, and how very, very rarely is the intention carried out! But we certainly *will* return to the Kadi Kiosk, for we cannot leave Broussa without a visit to the cave of Inkaya, higher up the mountain side.

We took a different road homewards; avoiding the village altogether, we struck into a shady lane on a lower slope of the hill, but here our enjoyment was damped, not to say annihilated, by the atrociously bad pavement, varied with mudholes, which made the progress something between a stumble and a flounder, until we landed once more in the usual highway, just a degree less bad, near the great iron bath of Eski Kaplidja.

A beautiful blue bird, very large, and of a kind unknown to us, was clinging to a projection of the grey stonework; his mate flew in and out the heavy draperies of green ivy, covering a part of the lower wall. The cupolas have been lately defaced (admiring natives deem them ornamented) by a coarse blue design on whitewash—a sad eyesore on that part of the building.

The mineral waters and baths of Eski Kaplidja were celebrated in very early times; the domes and much of the superstructure were built by Amurath, or, as he is really called here, Mourad I., but the foundations and basement story, as well as the bath itself, are old Greek work of wonderful solidity.

Passing downwards below the level of the wooden rooms for patients, which cling to the east front of the building, and are further supported on high wooden piles (which, by the way, give the whole thing a most picturesque effect from a distance), we came upon a white marble gateway, ornamented with small columns and other signs of former care and adornment about it. This led us into a large vaulted chamber filled with steam rising from a seething rivulet which rushes tumultuously through a narrow channel in the ground, whence, tumbling down the hillside, it is lost in a wilderness of trees and shrubs. The ground of this open vault is formed of solid layers of mineral deposit, which has raised it considerably above the original level, and a conical mass of the same substance, issuing from the inner wall of the building, looks like a petrified cataract; the round aperture is completely blocked up by it, and the water now finds its escape from within a second vaulted chamber. We were drawn there by the roaring sound of the torrent, but the heat and thick steam made it impossible to take more than a rapid survey. The waters of Tchekirghé have at times quite an inky tinge. My donkey had a particular objection to crossing it as it bubbled down the road, however small or insignificant the rill might be.

On our way back towards the entrance to the village, Aunt Sarah stopped to take from the grey wall of the bath some tufts of exquisite maidenhair fern, which grows there in profusion. A lover of ferneries may find great treasures here; Aunt Sarah's collection, as well as her book of wild flowers, is rapidly becoming valuable: some of the specimens are extremely rare.

Our return from Tchekirghé was marked by no greater incident than that a group of pretty little girls at play in the open ground before the mosque of Mourad II., saluted our passage with stones. One sweet little dot, grasping a muddy old shoe nearly as long as herself, was calmly preparing to wipe it down F——'s dress, when I prevented her, raising my parasol in pretended anger; the little creature shrank back, but the moment I was at a safe distance a sharp stone flew past me with great force, considering the tiny hand from which it came; it cut my own hand slightly. Such a blow on the face might have been unpleasant. But these incidents are matters of course at Broussa, where all the little children are pretty, and all throw stones at strangers, particularly at Franks, most especially at ladies, the youthful population being, I am sorry to say, as notoriously rude and ill-mannered as their elders are civil, good-humoured, and obliging.

# XI.

## BROUSSA SILK.

### NO. I.

Eastern Method of Rearing Silkworms.—Difficulties of Investigation.—Sensitiveness of the Worm.—Value of Mulberry-leaves, and of Silkworm Seed.—Great Care Needed.—The First Sleep.—A Healthy Appetite.—The Second Sleep.—The Third Sleep.—Voracity.—Repose and Work.—The Miniature Grove.—A Fairy Hamac.—The Cocoon.—Silk-rearing Establishment at Demirdesch.—Frames used in Removal.—The Moths.—The "Graineurs."—The Riches of a Peasant that "Make themselves Wings."—The Public Ovens.—The Quality of the Water used in Washing the Silk.

THE method of rearing silkworms in this country does not essentially differ from that in use in the south of France, yet the silk produced at Broussa and throughout Asia Minor being in great request at some of the largest manufactories at Lyons, an examination of the Eastern system may discover some details of interest.

It must be observed, however, that such examination is by no means an easy matter; the silkworms are mostly raised by the peasants who, with their superstitious dread of the evil eye, seek by every possible means to guard their precious nurslings from the noxious glance of strangers; but into one or two large establishments at Demirdesch, a few miles from Broussa—the property of more enlightened masters—visitors are sometimes admitted without reserve.

The silkworm's eggs, called, in trade, silkworm seed, are produced on sheets of paper or squares of linen cloth. The seed brought from Japan is always on coarse linen, upon which the moth has fixed its eggs so closely and firmly, that it may be washed several times without risk of detaching them.

The extreme delicacy of the silkworm, its sensitiveness to all outward influences, renders the rearing of this creature difficult and uncertain: all atmospheric changes, noise, bad odours, damp, oppressive weather, or great heat make it suffer; a storm is particularly injurious; it takes fright, and if preparing to spin, it will refuse to climb up into the branches, and quickly perishes.

During the first six weeks of summer it is curious to note the anxiety which weighs upon the public mind at Broussa. At this time the precious worm is passing through the stages of its nervous and fragile existence. Every one discusses the weather in the most serious tone; no other conversation is possible. An overcast sky brings a corresponding cloud on the brow; great heat unstrings the nerves of the heartiest man, and a threatened storm or a slight roll of thunder produces general consternation. Many merchants risk heavy sums in the purchase of the seed, and one hour of tempestuous weather may be sufficient to ruin them.

There are few large establishments for silkworm rearing, such as the one visited at Demirdesch; it is more customary for the merchant to speculate in the purchase of seed, which he distributes to the peasants, who raise the worms in their cottages, and receive in payment a proportion of the cocoons. If the peasant does not own a mulberry plantation, the merchant provides the leaves, which, from the enormous quantity devoured by the worms before they reach maturity, cost a very considerable sum of money.

The mulberry-leaves are sold either by the plantation or by the load. The price varies greatly, according to circumstances; the load of leaves has been known to sell for as much as £1 T., while they have an almost nominal value if the eggs are hatching badly. The price of the silkworm seed is calculated not only according to quality, but according to the prospects of the season. It varies from 800 francs to 2,000 francs the ocque (rather more than $2\tfrac{3}{4}$ lbs.)

At Broussa it is commonly said that the nourishment of the worm does not affect the colour of the silk, which depends entirely upon its species. When there is a scarcity of mulberry-leaves, they give lettuce to the young worms, but this sort of food must not be long continued; it makes the silk weak and valueless. Some people use the very tender oak-leaves even in preference to the mulberry.

The best kind of mulberry-tree was brought from Italy and grown at Broussa by the late Mr. Sandison, who was the first English consul in this city.

Silkworms just hatched require the most minute and constant care, with a gentle and even heat. A good workman sets the eggs to hatch in a chamber heated to a given temperature. The little black worms, scarcely larger than ants, are then carried into a room slightly cooler; they give them the youngest and tenderest leaves chopped as finely as possible. Two or three times a day the food is renewed by sprinkling it lightly; the worms, already very voracious, climb quickly up into the fresh green.

At the end of eight days the young worm, which has grown rapidly, while its colour has become lighter, makes its first sleep, during which it casts its skin and comes forth, at the expiration of the term—from twenty-four to thirty hours—invigorated and embellished, to feed again with renewed appetite. It now devours the leaves whole, and they are supplied more frequently. A healthy worm has extraordinary feeding powers. During the period of sleep the worms have a strong mark on the forehead.

Another sleep, with a fresh change of skin, takes place at the end of a second interval of eight days, and the worms issue from it more hungry than ever. After the third sleep, leaves no longer suffice; small branches are placed upon the trays and rapidly stripped. Some species of the silkworm sleep three, others four times; after the last sleep the worm eats no more, but prepares for work in earnest.

In a chamber set apart for the cocoons a miniature grove of little branches and twigs of dry oak has been prepared, by fixing them around the walls and upon light frames all over the floor. The trays are carried in, and the worms lose no time in installing themselves. They climb all about, select their resting-place, and begin by making a tiny fairy hamac, in which they gradually disappear, enveloped in the beautiful tissue of the cocoon, which is white, straw-colour, gold, or amber. Sometimes they are found of a pale lilac or of a bluish tinge; the white is the most esteemed.

Forty days is the period usually required for rearing the silkworm till it begins to spin, and a capable workman will take care that it shall have consumed in that time a given quantity of food. If the insect does not eat sufficiently, the quality of the silk is weak. When the worm is idle and delays the spinning time until the hot days of July, the silk becomes almost worthless. Twenty-two degrees (R.) of heat will make the worm sicken.

Amongst the numerous dangers to which these frail and precious little workers are exposed, the ant may be reckoned as the most formidable, and it requires minute attention to preserve them from the sting of their enemy, which is fatal.

In the great silk-rearing establishments at Demirdesch we found vast chambers perfectly aired, but sheltered from draught, and the temperature would have been agreeable but for the sickening odour of millions of little worms, who were making up for lost time after their second sleep.

The building was of wood, considered preferable to stone, as less liable to absorb and retain damp; it had the appearance of a large barn. Most of the rooms were carpeted with trays about a yard long, and rather narrow, upon which a multitude of worms were devouring the freshly spread leaves, vigorously and noisily; for the noise produced by this innumerable collection of tiny jaws, all working at once, is almost inconceivable. Every two or three days the trays are emptied and cleaned.

In order to remove the worms they use here long bands of netting strained upon open frames; these are spread with fresh food and placed lightly above the worms, who thus easily transfer themselves to their new bed of leaves. This is an excellent plan, as it avoids the necessity of touching the little creatures. Many worms are destroyed when they are removed by hand, or even by an instrument, however carefully used.

The amount of work required in a great silkworm rearing establishment may be estimated by the calculation that the produce of one ocque of eggs (2¾ lbs.) needs the unremitting attention of forty persons, in order that the worms may be regularly and equally fed, and also (no less important) kept scrupulously clean.

In ordinary years the cocoons are ready to be collected in the early part of June. A small quantity is reserved for the eggs, and, in due time, the moth pierces its beautiful prison-house, flutters away its short life, and dies, leaving on the square of paper or linen hundreds of eggs, fastened in close and perfectly symmetrical rows, looking like minute seed pearls.

The moths chosen for this end are selected with the greatest care. Each one is taken lightly, and the head and eyes examined; only those that show every sign of perfect health are allowed to finish their career in peace.

When the silkworms are beginning to spin, some amongst them refuse to work, and remain behind, inactive: these are ill and will soon die.

The remains of dead worms are eaten with avidity by fowls, but this sort of nourishment gives a bad flavour both to the poultry and to their eggs.

Immediately after the cocoon harvest, all the roads and byways of Asia Minor as well as the southern parts of European Turkey, are overrun by busy travellers. A stranger will ask who are these men, hastening from village to village? Simple tourists? Certainly not. Pedlars? Still less, for they have no pack and little baggage, and yet in the more dangerous parts of the country they have a strong escort, heavily armed, which still does not prevent frequent mishaps, for the brigand who disdains to molest a modest traveller in search of the picturesque, keeps a keen look-out for these mysterious wayfarers. They are called in French "les graineurs," men whose business it is to buy up the fresh silkworm seed. The peasants with whom they trade understand nothing of cheques, and the purchaser must carry all his fortune in solid coin, which makes him a valuable prey.

The cocoons intended for the spinning wheels must be exposed for a few minutes to a strong heat, either to the sun or in ovens constructed for the purpose, in order to kill the grub before it becomes a moth. In some of these ovens a jet of hot vapour is thrown upon the cocoons; in others, dry heat is used. Any delay in destroying the grub causes the loss of the cocoon, which once pierced, is cast aside as useful only for the most inferior tissues.

Formerly, in the province of Broussa, as throughout Anatolia, the necessity for a rapid and forced sale of their cocoons caused great loss to the poorer peasants; all the ovens being in the spinning factories, a high charge was made for their use. What could the poor man do, whose whole fortune consisted of a few bushels of cocoons, and hope? He filled his baskets in hot haste, packed them on the mule or little donkey, and set off for the nearest town, along a road ablaze with hot sunshine. It not unfrequently happened that the great heat hastened the development of the unlucky moth, which issued joyfully from its silken tomb to revel in newborn freedom, while the unfortunate countryman, waking perhaps from a nap under a shady tree, sees his baskets crowned by a fluttering white haze which thickens and increases as he pushes forward in frantic haste—his riches, which have literally made themselves wings.

Some years ago, this difficulty was overcome by the establishment of public ovens built along the high roads of the province of Broussa. The initiative of this beneficent and useful scheme is due to the untiring energy of Ahmed Vefyk Pasha, to whom Broussa is indebted for many valuable and philanthropic works. These public ovens are the property of the village schools, and the small charge made for the use of them (about a farthing per kilogramme of cocoons), is within the means of the smallest purse, while by the immense quantity of cocoons brought, a small income is derived for the benefit of the schools.

The first cocoons are preferred. Four oques of cocoons should yield one oque of good silk, but this proportion is uncertain.

The quality of the water used in washing the silk has an effect on its value: the spring which flows from the heights of Sultan Selim, on the side of Mount Olympus, and is brought to the quarter called Hamsa Bey, is the finest for the purpose. Silk washed in this water gains 20 per cent. in the market. This stream is so heavily charged with mineral substances, that the pipes through which it flows down the mountain are quickly filled with incrustation, although the incline is extremely rapid.

## XII.

### BROUSSA SILK.

#### NO. II.—THE SPINNING FACTORIES.

A Spinning "Fabrika."—Unpleasant Odour from the Boiling Cocoons.—Native Workgirls.—Their Pay.—Clever Workers.—The Finished Hank.—Broussa Gauze.—Handkerchiefs.—Towelling.—The Bath Burnous.—" Burundjik."

STRANGERS visiting Broussa naturally conclude, from the name "fabrika" given to the lofty many-windowed buildings grouped together at the two extremities of the city, that the beautiful gauze for which this place is celebrated is manufactured in these workshops. It is not so, however; the fabrikas are exclusively spinning factories; the silk is woven in private houses, principally by women.

Let us enter a large Armenian fabrika that is situated behind the Mouradiyeh suburb. Near the great entrance-door many groups of women and girls are lounging in the shade of noble chestnut-trees that overhang a neglected courtyard. Some are crouched on the grass, eating a scanty breakfast of bread and hard white cheese; others, leaning on the grey mossy stones of a ruined wall, are laughing and whispering as they take note of the strangers who are gazing at them. It is "païdos," the hour of rest, and we must wait until the clash of a great gong recalls the workwomen to their duties. We quickly follow them into a vast room, running the whole length of the building.

The noise of the wheels is deafening, and it requires at first some resolution to withstand the unpleasant influences of the sickening smell and heavy vapour from the boiling cocoons. This gallery contains a hundred wheels, fifty on each side, worked by steam, but half of them only are in use. As the new silk has not yet come in, they are winding last year's cocoons.

The girls are mostly Greeks, with three or four Turkish girls amongst them, wearing an apology for a yashmak. There is a factory in another quarter of the city which is worked entirely by Turkish women. The Mussulman women of Broussa are very industrious; they do a great deal of heavy work in the fields and amongst the mulberry plantations; they weave a great proportion of the silk and cotton stuffs, and you may frequently see an energetic countrywoman bringing her dairy produce in from her distant homestead, or bearing a heavy load of leaves for the silkworms, for sale in the market.

Working hours in the factories are from sunrise to sunset; consequently, the pay is higher in summer than in winter. It ranges from three to eight piastres a day (6d. to 1s. 4d.).

Each girl sits before a square trough of boiling water, kept at 50° Réaumur by means of steam injected into it from time to time. A provision of cocoons hangs in a bag before each trough; a bunch is taken out and beaten lightly with a whisk in a basin of boiling water—this work is given to the children. It is done in order to detach the ends of the gossamer threads, after which the cocoons are thrown into the great trough. The spinner collects a cluster of the threads, and separating the required number—generally four—rolls these for a moment together between her palms, and passing them, doubled, through two small porcelain buttons in front, they join, and are carried over two wire hooks above her head, then again over two other hooks, and the spinner pressing it with her finger on a large canvas cylinder which is revolving rapidly, it catches the delicate silken thread, and the skein, once begun, continues without break until the required weight is obtained. The fine thread is perfectly even and regular. The talent of a good spinner consists in the adroit placing of new threads as each cocoon is exhausted. The machinery is so arranged that each cylinder winds two skeins at once, the worker using at the same time the cylinders to the right and left.

A strict superintendence is maintained in these factories; overseers, both men and women, are constantly passing up and down before the wheels, to remove instantly the finished hank. It requires considerable ability and experience to do this exactly at the right moment, as they must judge by the eye of the weight of silk wound into a skein before removing it. The skeins are then carried into another part of the building, where they are weighed, essayed, classed, and finally twisted into the beautiful hanks, in which form they are ready for the silk bazaar and the weaving looms.

After the real silk threads have been wound off the cocoon, there remains the interior covering of the grub, colourless and uneven in texture. This is made use of as "spun silk," and for articles of inferior quality.

The attitude of the silk-spinner is graceful. The girls, as is the case with most Eastern women, have delicate and well-formed hands, and their arms much adorned with bangle bracelets, worthless but picturesque; but they suffer terribly from the boiling water in which their fingers are constantly plunged, and to relieve them in some degree they have a basin of cold water always ready. In the evening they bathe their fingers with vitriol.

The beautiful silk gauze, which is now so well known throughout Europe, is woven in rough hand-looms in private houses. The genuine Turkish article is very narrow, and it requires a considerable number of yards to make a dress. The cost at Broussa is about six or seven piastres the pic, equivalent to 1s. 4d. to 1s. 6d. a yard. In Stamboul the price is higher.

In spite of its light and diaphanous texture, the Broussa gauze is extremely strong. When washed, the material, while losing its evenness, acquires a silkiness and softness much preferred by many people. The prettiest gauzes are those with white or maize-coloured stripes, as the silk has always a yellowish tinge; blue and pink stripes are never so clear and true in colour. Black gauzes, striped with black or white, are also very successful, and from the durability of the material are less expensive than most of the light fabrics of English or French manufacture.

Very good handkerchiefs, also, are made at Broussa, not unlike our India-silk handkerchiefs, as well as a mixture of silk and cotton, cool and strong, much used for light summer clothing for men.

Passing from the silk trade to the cotton manufactures, we must especially notice the celebrated towel stuff. The soft fluffy Broussa towel is made in the rudest and most primitive-looking looms, scattered about in the cottages, but principally in a low quarter of the bazaars. We visited a mean-looking dwelling, where, in a rough room on the ground floor, seven looms had been set up. Five of them were being worked by three men and two boys, who threw the shuttle with marvellous dexterity, while another boy was busy winding spools of coloured silk, ready to be woven into the borderings. These towels, when of a superior kind, are expensive, even at Broussa, costing as much as thirty piastres, or about 5s. the pair—they are always sold in pairs—but the quality is immeasurably superior to any of the imitations made in England, which utterly fail in the soft, spongy, absorbent texture that forms the great charm of the genuine fabric.

The bath burnous, in the same downy material, is too well known to need description. It is a modern innovation; the old-fashioned bath takim, or set, consists of one immense towel or wrapper about two yards long, and wide in proportion; of another a yard long, to envelop the shoulders, and a third, rather smaller, for the head.

The burundjik, a beautiful material used for the best sort of caïkdjis shirts, looks like a very thick cream-coloured crape with silky stripes. It is largely woven at Broussa, as also throughout all this part of Asia Minor.

## XIII.

### THE MINERAL BATH.

The Yeni-Kaplidja Hammam. — A Shifting Crowd. — The Djamékian, or Robing-room. — The Hammamdji. — The Sookluk.—Screened Compartments and Dwelling-rooms.—Great Heat of the Springs.—Picturesque Scene in the Djamékian.—Swing Cradles.—Youth and Age.—A Betrothal Party.—Two Brides Elect.—Ceremonious "Sela'ams."—A Handsome Swimming-bath.—Mosaics and Coloured Tiles.—A Beautiful Bather.—Touching Solicitude for an Aged Negress.

THE Yeni-Kaplidja Hammam, the largest and handsomest of the Broussa baths, was embellished by the Sultana Mirhimah, a daughter of Soliman the Magnificent and wife of his grand vizier, Rustem Pasha: her name is also celebrated as the foundress of the fine mosque near the Adrianople Gate of Stamboul. In our own day the perfect restoration of Yeni-Kaplidja is due to the indefatigable zeal and labours of Ahmed Vefyk Pasha. This bath is situated on the west side of the city, about a quarter of a mile beyond the last houses of the Mouradiyeh suburb, and below a projecting bluff of the mountain known as the Bademli Bagtché (the almond garden). From the edge of this plateau you look down upon the domes of the large building covered with thick glass bubbles, serving as windows, which give the effect of a violent eruption on the metal surface, produced (it might be fancied) by the intensity of the heat beneath.

The entrance is through a shabby wooden portico; from this, by a very short passage, you find yourself in the presence of a moving, shifting, talking crowd of women and girls, and indeed some very small boys also, in every stage of decomposition in the matter of dress. One is a little uncomfortable just at first, feeling that many of them may not quite like to be gazed at by strangers, but as no one seems to mind it in the least, it is needless to be over-considerate.

We had come—a small party of ladies—with the intention of trying the effect of the baths; but the first glance into the djamékian, or robing-room, was enough. The heat, the unpleasant odour (arising principally from the mineral waters), the sloppy, dirty state of the floor, but, above all, the very unattractive crowd with whom we must have mingled in such close communion, was too much for our spirit of enterprise, and we sought for some quiet corner where we might rest a moment and look around, quite abandoning all idea of becoming sharers in the delights of the place.

A bath consists of three principal divisions: the

djamékian, the sookluk, and the hammam. In some there is a fourth chamber of intense heat, for vapour baths, which is reached from the Hammam: it is called yarakan (sudatorium).

The djamékian is furnished all round with a wooden platform, raised about two feet from the ground; there is a marble fountain of cold water in the centre of the hall. In this first chamber, the bathers rest on their arrival, and they return to it, wrapped up in towels, after leaving the water. When the bath is used by men, the platform is neatly furnished with little mattresses covered with the striped sheets of the country. The bathers lie down for a time, smoking and sipping coffee, until the effect of the great heat of the hammam shall have passed off, when they can dress and encounter the outer air with safety; but at such times as the bath is given over to the women, everything of the kind is carefully removed, as the ladies make a day of it; from early morning the place is crowded. They bring their babies and their dinners, and create such an amount of litter and dirt that the hammamdji does wisely in leaving them nothing but the bare boards, on which they spread their own mattresses and carpets. It must be observed that we are speaking of women of the humbler classes.

The sookluk is an intermediary chamber, through which you pass into the hammam.

The djamékian is lighted by small windows, placed very high up towards the roof. The sookluk and the hammam receive a subdued light from the glassy bubbles before mentioned.

The hammamdji, or mistress of the bath, occupies, on the left of the entry, a raised platform, from which she commands a view of the hall. She receives the entrance money as the bathers arrive, and superintends from her elevation the order and general working of the establishment. Several bath-women are employed under her.

Looking about for a resting-place, we discovered a small unappropriated space on the edge of the platform, near the little hearth where the coffee was being prepared; and, encouraged by a good-natured-looking negress, who seemed to hold partial possession, we installed ourselves and began to examine the novel scene.

At the farther end of the vast hall some high wooden partitions enclosed rooms let out for the use of persons of a superior rank, and near us, on each side of the entrance door, the platform—raised higher and screened from the public by cafesses—was occupied in a similar manner. There are also built round outside the bath several apartments, which may be hired for the bathing season. They command most exquisite views of the surrounding country, and are exceedingly cool and airy.

For wealthy families the bath is sometimes hired for a fortnight or more at a time. Ladies of rank seldom if ever frequent the public hammam. At Constantinople every house of importance contains a private bath, occasionally more than one. At Broussa the better class of ladies either go to the mineral bath at an hour when they can secure it to themselves, or the water is brought to the houses in great closed barrels, the heat of some of the springs being so great that the water brought in the course of the evening is not of a proper temperature for use before the following morning.

The scene we gazed upon in the djamékian of Yeni-Kaplidja was strange and decidedly picturesque. The price of admission being very trifling, Turkish women, Greeks, Armenians, negresses, and even gipsies, crowd the place, and we could not but remark that, considering the very motley nature of the assembly and the low class of the greater number of the bathers, there was much less to offend one's sense of propriety than might have been expected under the circumstances.

The places in this great robing-hall were all occupied. From long beams stretching round the room, at a height of six feet above the platform, and from those running into the wall, hung feràdjés and draperies of all sorts and colours. Little hammock-cradles were fastened about in every direction wherever a cord could be conveniently fixed, and the poor babies were being violently swung backwards and forwards. I never before saw infants so ruthlessly tossed. Some set the little beds in motion with the hand, some with the foot; and if a little one happened by chance to get a moment's rest, a passer-by thought it her neighbourly duty to send it again upon its travels, and away went the hammock more furiously than before. A very pretty young Turkish woman near us had her baby in one of these vibrating couches; a very tastefully embroidered silk coverlet was thrown across its feet; a broad band, worked in gold and ingeniously secured by bits of wood, served to keep the infant from falling, while its tiny face was guarded from the flies by a gaily ornamented gauze handkerchief.

Around us the parties of women on the platforms were eating, drinking, smoking, sleeping, dressing or undressing, according to fancy. At the handsome white marble fountain in the centre some bathers, just returned from the hotter rooms, were bathing their heads and faces in the cold water, or drinking from the metal bowl attached by a chain to the basin. Others eat ices, standing round a female ice-vendor, who is crouched on the floor at the foot of the fountain. The dripping forms of the bathing women clattered by on high wooden "naëlin" to and from the hammam, poising on their heads a dry bundle of the soft Turkish towels, or perhaps the soap in the metal "tass" or bowl. Some women returning from the water were enveloped in the burnous, or in the bathing takim or "set," consisting of a large wrap folded round the waist and falling below the knees, a smaller one covering the shoulders, and a third winding round the head like a fantastic turban. Those who intended returning to the plunging-bath wore only the large wrapper, which being of silk or cotton, according to the means of the wearer, is always striped, most usually in broad bands of red and orange, which greatly increases the picturesque effect of the clinging draperies. Most of the girls were adorned with necklaces of rough cornelian charms, and wore bangle-like bracelets.

Some small children walked airily about, very simply and neatly dressed in a couple of gourds tied to the waist as floats; and one sweet little fairy of two or three years old—left alone for a moment by its nurse—stood carefully wrapping a towel about its head and shoulders, displaying the prettiest little pink and white form imaginable.

On the whole, there was not much beauty to be remarked. Some few of the young women were fair, and attractive enough as they lounged with careless grace chatting with their friends. But then, the old ladies! No, it is impossible to describe them. Anything more apish, more shrivelled, more mummylike than some of those ancient matrons, with their scanty, straggling locks, partly grey and partly a pinkish scarlet, it would be difficult to imagine; they are only equalled, if not surpassed, by the stout specimens; *they* were a sight not to be forgotten. If "a thing of beauty is a joy for ever," what must be the result of gazing upon a fat, elderly woman of the East in her bathing costume?

Opposite to the spot from which we were able—ourselves almost unnoticed—to make our quiet observations, a Turkish bridal party had taken up its station for the day. It consisted of two young betrothed girls about to be married, with several relations and some slaves.

One of the brides, though scarcely pretty, was bright and rosy-cheeked; the other not remarkable in any way. They sat for some time after their arrival, resting and conversing, as if their sole object were to display their toilettes, for they were handsomely dressed, and seemed to belong to a respectable class of society; but at length they began to prepare for the bath. The slaves extended two feràdjés, which served as a perfect screen, until the brides emerged from the shelter carefully enveloped in handsome striped silk wrappers, which passing over the bosom and close under the arms, and falling nearly to the ankles, formed a very modest and sufficient covering; the hair fell over the shoulders in long plaits. The improvised curtains just mentioned were held up by their slaves for most of the women of a respectable standing. In almost every case the robing and unrobing were managed with great decorum.

When the two brides were fully ready, they proceeded to salute their immediate relations, kissing their hands and putting them to the forehead; then they slipped from the platform into their "naëlin" (clogs) which were quite new and richly inlaid with mother-of-pearl. On these they clattered across the hall, and went through the same ceremonies of respectful salutation with two groups of women seated near us, and whom we supposed to be the families of the bridegrooms elect. After the performance of these duties, the young girls, attended by their slaves, went off through the sookluk to the hammam.

In about half an hour, flushed and panting from the heat of the steaming pool, they returned to the djamékian, went through the salutations once more all round, spent some time in eating ices and other dainties, and again disappeared into the hammam. Eastern women are not content with a moderate use of the water, but go in and out for hours, eating between whiles; the old ladies solace themselves with smoking. The bathers begin to retire about an hour or two before sunset.

We passed into the sookluk, a large hall, provided, like the djamékian, with a marble fountain in the centre. There is an oblong tank to the right of the doorway, especially destined for the use of sick animals. People were lounging and walking about here, waiting a few minutes before encountering the cooler air of the robing-room. The temperature, charged with sulphurous vapours, is said to be from 28° to 30° R. It was suffocating; and on passing through the low doorway into the great bath-room, it required some resolution to induce us to remain a sufficient time to take in the features of the scene, as the floor was deluged with hot water, women were crowding in and out, and the odour of the heavy vapour was sickening. The temperature can be lowered when desired, by taking away a few of the glass bubbles in the roof.

The hammam of Eski-Kaplidja deserves minute notice. It is exceedingly handsome, of an octagonal form, and having a vast basin or swimming-bath in the centre, in which three circular steps lead down into the water. The floor of the hall is composed of a mosaic of exquisite coloured marbles, and the walls, to a certain height, are lined with beautiful porcelain tiles from Nicea, coloured and gilt, while all above is of the purest white marble.

Facing the principal entrance, a large entablature of even richer coloured and gold tiling, surrounds a delicate white marble fountain set in the wall, while each of the eight sides is so formed as to enclose a small chamber provided with a fountain and jet of water between the clusters of colonnettes supporting the open archway; and again, between these chambers, at each of the angles, there is a jet of water and marble basin for ablutions.

The hot springs that supply Yeni-Kaplidja issue from a mass of incrustation of carbonate of lime, at a few yards distant from the building. The spring is stated to mark 68° R.

The great bath is emptied every evening, cleaned out and refilled, so that bathers who are the first to arrive on the following morning, have the benefit of perfectly pure and clean water.

As we entered the hammam, the marble lake was full of women and girls floating about, some of them supported by gourds. They looked picturesque enough, seen by the half light from the mysterious little windows in the lofty cupola. Some were splashing about, their long hair streaming behind them, while others sat on the margin wringing their dripping tresses. One handsome girl was lying at full length on the burning marble pavement in an attitude of such exquisite grace that we stopped in admiration. The charm of the picture was wonderfully heightened by the broad stripes of her wet silk wrapper, her cornelian necklace, and bright blue bangles, as, with one slender hand slightly supporting her head, her dark hair fell back in a stream of glistening ripples.

But we could endure no longer stay in that atmosphere; and hastening through the sookluk into the djamékian, took up our old station near the coffee-stand. Whilst waiting to become sufficiently cool to risk once more the outer air, we were much interested in watching the proceedings of a party on the opposite side of the hall. A poor old negress, hideously ugly and very feeble, was being tenderly led along from the inner rooms by two white girls; when they reached the part of the platform occupied by their family, all the women rose, and the poor invalid was helped on to the mattress which had been prepared for her with as much gentle care as if she had been a pasha's lady. Most likely she was the nurse who had brought up the hanum or her daughters. The little incident was quite touching in its simple evidence of loving and kindly feeling towards the humble, unattractive black slave.

# XIV.

## THE PEARL OF THE EASTERN ARCHIPELAGO.

Mythology and Legend.—The Home of Erinna.—Genoese Castles.—An Open Roadstead.—Fine View from the Promontory.—A Prosperous Island.—Careful Cultivation of the Olive.—Lesbian Wine.—The Harbours.—Fine Harbour of Hïera.—Valuable Hot Springs.—The Tomb of Kiatib Oglon.—His Fate.—A Ruined Téké and Cemetery.—Curious Epitaphs.—Bâhhl Genghizz Khan, the Last Prince of the Crimea.—Beauty of the Myteliniotes.—The Daughters and their Fortunate Destiny.—Unequal Laws.—Custom stronger than Law.

Issa, Pelasgia, Lesbos, Macaria, Mytilene! how many celebrated names for an island measuring but eighty-one miles in length and forty-eight in width! And yet, might we venture to add one more to this list—venerable from its great antiquity—it would be named "The Pearl of the Eastern Archipelago," the brightest jewel in the graceful chaplet of islands sprinkled on the blue waters that bound the shores of Asia Minor.

To the island of Lesbos, the rival of Athens, mythology owes some of its most poetical legends. It was on these shores, dear to Apollo, that the head and the lyre of Orpheus, driven by the currents to the neighbourhood of Antissa, were piously placed in the same tomb, from which the head continued to utter oracles, while the mysterious tones of the enchanted lyre had power to influence even the stern and rugged rocks of the island.

Was it not to Lesbos that Arion, floating on his dolphin, returned to his native land and raised a statue in the temple of Apollo? The remains of that famous temple are still visible, and ancient coins, with the impress of Arion on the fabulous dolphin, are not rare at Mytilene; but the accents of the mysterious lyre have been silent for long centuries, and the nightingales, no longer subjugated by the powerful charm, sing to please themselves, without care for legend or fable.

Lesbos was renowned in ancient times for the beauty of its women, their wit, their delicate needlework, and their easy morality. It is the land of poetry. At Lesbos was born Sappho, six centuries before the Christian era; and there her pupil, the gentle Erinna, died at the age of nineteen, leaving to posterity the three hundred lines of her poem, "The Distaff," * composed while spinning in the

* This poem has not been preserved, but it is mentioned and highly praised by several of the poets whose lines form the Greek anthology; the following extract, translated by a friend, is a specimen of one of these sonnets:—

"There is a little sweet Lesbian way of Erinna's, but it is all mixed with honey from the Muses; her three hundred lines are equal to Homer's, and she a maiden of nineteen years; a worshipper humble cottage of her mother, who disapproved of her gifted child's poetic fancies. She submitted; breathed out her soul to the movement of her spindle, and passed away in the dawn of her genius and renown.

Alceus, and divers poets, philosophers, and writers of renown; Lesbonay, a sage in the time of Augustus, and Potamon, his son, who held a class of rhetoric at Rome, and was the cherished friend of Tiberius, have all contributed to the glory of their native isle.

It was at Lesbos that the last emperor of Constantinople was married to the daughter of the Genoese Prince Gateluzzi, who was the last Christian prince of Mytilene. The island passed under the yoke of Persia soon after the fall of the Greek Empire.

The Genoese occupation of Mytilene has left numerous and important traces in remains of castles and forts, of which local historians state the incredible number at thirteen thousand. But the great fortress that overhangs the principal town of the island, and gives it its name of Castro, would alone suffice to bear testimony to the past grandeur of its Genoese princes. It is a majestic pile, covering the high promontory with immense towers and bastions, within two lines of high crenellated walls. This

of the Muses, she was touching the distaff in fear of her mother, who stood at the web. Erinna is as far above Sappho in hexameters, as Sappho is above Erinna in lyric verses."

imposing mass, half ruined at the present time, closes one side of the harbour. Viewed from the sea, the effect is admirable, and travellers have only too good an opportunity of enjoying it, as the harbour, that should give hospitality to ships of the largest size, is now, through neglect, so much filled up that only the lightest vessels of local traffic can find a refuge there. The fine steamers of the Austrian Lloyd's and of the Egyptian line do not attempt to enter; they remain in the open roadstead, to the great discomfort of their passengers and the serious detriment of the cargo to be discharged. It happens even sometimes in the winter, that it is found impossible to disembark, and the steamer continues its route towards Smyrna. Occasionally in stormy weather the vessel slackens speed without casting anchor. The boatmen of the great lighters, forced to brave every danger, and accustomed from childhood to this perilous service, display an almost incredible amount of strength and daring.

A few years since I arrived in this roadstead, under the shadow of the fine Genoese castle. We had stopped at Gallipoli, at the Dardanelles, and at Tenedos—a small island renowned for its wine, but offering no attraction to the traveller in the picture of its burnt and arid slopes, its poor fortress, and its eight sad-looking windmills. Farther, on the right hand, Imbros and the pale majestic silhouette of

Samothrace melting into the soft evening haze; then the picturesque and rugged coast of Mytilene is followed, until at sunset the steamer casts anchor before the city.

The arrival of the Austrian mail steamer is the event of the week, and all the society of the place meet on the summit of the rocky crag that overhangs the harbour. At the same time, if so inclined, a lover of scenery may enjoy one of the most graceful pictures imaginable. The town of Mytilene, that covers the isthmus at the foot of the hill on which the castle stands, stretches southwards to the first slopes of a fine range of mountains. The sides, clothed with luxuriant vegetation, show, amidst the dark green of orange groves, or the pale foliage of the olive, white villages, church steeples, pretty villas, hamlets, and farms; then woods of chestnut, beech, and plane; vineyards, meadows, and upland pastures. One is almost reminded of the bay of Naples and of the rich slopes of Pansilippo.

Seen from the port, the town wears an aspect of prosperity that is rarely met with in the East. A closer examination does not destroy this first impression. The island of Mytilene rivals the neighbouring island of Schio for richness and fertility, and surpasses it in the industry and energy of the fine race, of Grecian origin, that inhabits it almost exclusively. In a population of 100,000 souls,

20,000 only are Mussulmans. In this estimate of 80,000 Greeks, 300 may be considered as foreigners. They are, with few exceptions, natives of the Ionian Islands.

The inhabitants of Mytilene are for the most part landowners. There are few large estates; but, on the other hand, extreme poverty is unknown in the island. The property of the Baltazzi family is the most important, owing to the extreme care with which it is cultivated and the labour bestowed on the olive groves that form its principal wealth. In many places, particularly on stiff mountain slopes, the olive-trees require expensive and difficult management. Each tree, separated from its neighbours, must have a wall on the lower side to maintain the earth around the roots. In fields less well cultivated the olive-roots may often be seen above ground, but the crop suffers in proportion. To give some idea of the importance of the olive in Mytilene, it may be stated that some years since the exportation of oil amounted to 300,000 quintals.

Oranges and lemons are also much grown, although this culture is less practised than in the neighbouring island of Schio. Mulberry-trees—for the use of the silkworm, formerly so abundant that 100,000 ocques of cocoons could be exported—now serve merely to add a shade of tender green to the rich foliage of the island. The commerce in silk has ceased through a malady of the worms, and little use is now made of this branch of industry.

The wine of Lesbos, so celebrated in ancient times, is far from meriting at the present day its old renown. The unfortunate custom of adding elderberries for colouring, and of rubbing the inside of barrels with resinous plants, in the hope of preserving the wine, give it an acrid and disagreeable flavour that only natives appreciate.

The island of Mytilene possesses natural advantages which might, under a wise administration, go far to restore its ancient importance. There are three harbours; the largest is called the harbour of Kalonīa; that of Sigri is found on the west coast; but the large inlet, known as the Harbour of the Olives, or Hïera, distant only four miles from the principal town, is regarded as one of the most important in the Archipelago. This arm of the sea, sheltered by high mountains, runs fifteen miles into the land: the largest fleets of Europe might lie there at ease.

The abundance of running water and of mineral springs, the pine-forests that crown the heights, the fresh sea breezes perfumed by the aromatic plants that clothe all the uncultivated land, render the climate of Mytilene one of the healthiest in the East. The natural hot baths are at present only used by the inhabitants, as the total want of proper accommodation makes a residence there impossible for strangers; but the mineral springs have lost nothing of their old healing virtues, and the erection of a simple but well-organised bathing establishment could not fail to be a successful speculation. One of these springs, known as Polichnito, from which the water gushes at 100°, is used by the neighbouring peasants for cooking their food. They simply plunge their caldrons into the stream, and the dinner is quickly ready.

Mytilene counts sixty-four towns and villages, divided amongst three districts—Castro, Molivo, and Kalonia.

Castro is the capital of the island, and the residence of the Governor and of the consuls. A Turkish garrison occupies the great castle, but no complaint is made of this neighbourhood. At Mytilene the Mussulmans live in peace with the Christian population, and the military band of the regiment is highly appreciated by the loungers in the elegant café and garden at the base of the fortress.

Near to this spot, and on the edge of the high road that crosses the isthmus, may be seen a Mussulman tomb surrounded by a gilt railing and shaded by a fine cypress. This tomb recalls the tragic fate of a local celebrity. Kiatib Oglon was the last Dereh-Bey of Smyrna, where his good looks, agreeable manners, and immense fortune procured him a degree of popularity that gave umbrage to the Sultan Mahmoud II. Perhaps the sovereign, whose hand was not light, had serious cause for displeasure. The exact reason is not known, but one fine morning the admiral of the fleet, having received a hint on his departure from Constantinople, cast anchor before Smyrna. The Governor and the Admiral exchanged visits, and Kiatib Oglon accepted with pleasure an invitation to dine on board. It is said that on the eve of the day named for the festivity a mysterious friend sent to the Dereh-Bey three presents—a horse, a gun, and a waist-scarf. To the Oriental mind the interpretation was, "Fly, or you will meet a tragic death!" Kiatib Oglon either did not understand, or scorned the mysterious advice. He went on board; dined sumptuously, and after many compliments and salutations, descended into his boat; but he sees with amazement that, during the progress of the feast, the great ship has quietly glided away from the shore, and that Smyrna is in the far distance; they are nearing Mytilene. The rowers draw once more towards the vessel, and urge the Dereh-Bey to regain the deck by the companion ladder used by the sailors. The unfortunate man then fully comprehends his fate. Without a word he resigns himself to it, and the cord has soon accomplished the terrible will of Sultan Mahmoud.

They built him a beautiful tomb, turning, according to custom, the inscription inwards, as a sign that the death was a violent one by superior authority.

On a hill that overhangs the town towards the south, we find an old cemetery shaded by some cypress-trees. A small téké existed here, raised in honour of a direct descendant of the Prophet, named Ebul-Hassan-Ben-Hassan. He was at one time "chériff" of Mecca, and died in exile at Mytilene. The téké is now in ruins, and the handsome headstones—their marble and the gilt inscriptions still fresh owing to the purity of the air—lean to right and left, disjointed and broken, half buried in rampant weeds and nettles, in the sad-looking enclosure. And what sombre and sanguinary histories are revealed by these epitaphs! It is to Kemal Bey, one of the most learned literary authorities in Turkey, that the discovery of most of these inscriptions is due. They fill up an important void in the national history.

Some of these records are before me. The first narrates the fate of an exile who died by poison at Mytilene. The second is the epitaph of a personage who, four times Grand Vizier under three sultans, strangled the heir to the throne to gain favour with Osman III., and himself perished in exile in the same manner. One only on the list attests a natural death. The subject of the epitaph had a remarkable name, "The man who eats no onions." The last inscription deserves notice; it speaks of Bâhhl Genghizz Khan, the last reigning prince of that family in the Crimea, who was named Khan of Bessarabia, after the Russian invasion. He was afterwards exiled to Mytilene, where he died of grief in the early part of this century.

The natives of Mytilene are a fine race, the men tall, well made, and vigorous; the women, on a more delicate model, have expressive features, with dark, wavy hair, long dark lashes shading fine eyes of a bluish-grey; they have a majestic carriage, and seem convinced of a fortunate destiny. And such is the case, for Mytilene is the paradise of young girls. From the moment of her birth, the marriage and future prospects of a daughter are the subjects of highest interest to the entire family. The eldest daughter is particularly favoured. They begin at once to spin, weave, and work, in order to provide for her trousseau and her household. The mother begins upon immense pieces of linen and cotton stuffs; she makes vast lengths of woollen material; she embroiders the garments; she prepares everything. As the sisters gradually grow up, they also assist at the spinning-wheel, the distaff, and the loom. All work for the eldest, but on each piece of finished stuff some lengths are reserved for the younger daughters. It is, however, always the eldest who receives the larger portion; it is she who inherits the family mansion; and the anxiety for the prosperous future of a daughter is even carried so far, that it not unfrequently happens that parents will give up their home and its comfortable ease, in order that their child, on her marriage, may at once be established there, going themselves to end their days in some mean lodging. When a man is sufficiently rich to encounter the outlay, he will build a house for each of his daughters, preparing and furnishing it entirely.

At the death of a father, it is the eldest brother who is expected to support his sisters and to provide their dowry. He must not think of marriage for himself until these sisters have been suitably established. When there is neither father nor brother, the uncles even consider it their duty to provide for their female relations as far as their means will allow.

These usages, that give advantages to the daughters, to the prejudice of the sons of a family, although they may be found in a lesser degree in the manners and customs of the Greeks, are far more stringent at Mytilene than elsewhere. Attempts have been made in vain to obtain some modification that may work with more justice for all. Old habits are too strong, and very little improvement has been effected. The traditions of the island date the origin of these peculiar customs from the time of the conquest of Mytilene by the Turks, when all the men were dispersed or perished. The women and children alone remained, and the arrival of a man—a protector, a support for the desolate home, who might be also a husband for the daughter, was the aim and object of their prayers. What emotions, what rivalries, agitated all this feminine population when a boat from Schio or from the mainland was discerned on the horizon! It might bring husbands of their religion and of their race. Each family hastened to endow the eldest daughter with all the finery that could be procured. She was dressed in her gayest garments; jewellery was borrowed on all sides; and they led her to the shore, anxious to present to the view of the new arrivals the most beautiful and attractive of those expectant brides.

## XV.

### ROUMANIAN MONASTERIES.

#### NO. I.

IN these days of eager exploration it would seem incredible, but is nevertheless perfectly true, that a beautiful region of civilised Europe remains as yet unknown and unvisited by the ubiquitous English traveller. A country rich in attractions for the artistic and intelligent tourist; a land of mountain and stream, of forest-clad heights, and valleys of luxuriant fertility, inhabited by a simple and hospitable race, in whose language, manners, and superstitions the traditions of their Roman origin can be clearly traced.

This new "playground" may be reached, from London, in three days, and the cost of a few weeks' wanderings is less than would be neeeded for any other tour. I allude to the eastern slopes of the Carpathian Mountains, where a month was lately spent by a small party of English in visiting principally the monasteries and convents of Moldavia.

The language of the Roumanians would prove a

subject of deep interest to many, being mainly derived from the Roman colonists settled in Dacia by Trajan in the beginning of the second century. They introduced "a Latin which was no longer that of Rome, but a primitive and already corrupt dialect . . . . there are words belonging to the ancient Doric, to that popular idiom that had ceased to be used in Rome in the time of Virgil and Cicero."[*]

The curious salt mines at Okna and elsewhere, the numerous mineral springs, and the great mineral wealth of the country, might prove attractive to many; while for the artist, the botanist, the lover of nature, there is inexhaustible enjoyment in the grandeur of mountain summits and mysterious depth of wooded gorge, in virgin forests of almost unknown extent, in lovely valleys and woodland glades of exquisite softness and beauty, and in the amazing wealth of blossoms that carpet the soil of one of the most fertile countries in Europe; and, lastly, the striking and beautiful costumes worn by the Wallachian peasantry form an additional attraction in this scheme of a novel holiday excursion.

To the traveller who can cheerfully submit to some inconvenience—and no traveller is worthy of the name who cannot do so—a visit to the mountain monasteries of the Carpathians may be accomplished with the greatest ease. There is no necessity to

[*] Ubicini.

engage rooms beforehand, no heavy reckoning to damp the enjoyment of your short stay. In a country where hotels exist only in the cities and great towns near the line of railway, the wanderer into the interior seeks his shelter in the monastery, both men's and women's convents being equally prepared to receive guests. You simply drive up, in a vehicle drawn by four horses harnessed abreast, to the great entrance gateway; you are at once received without question, installed in the guesthouse, and hospitably entertained for three days, an allowance being made by the State for the reception of travellers. No remuneration is exacted, but a liberal present to the hospital, the church, the schools, or the poor is thankfully received.

The writer, with two friends and an interpreter, were, with one or two exceptions, the first English people to visit these monasteries and to explore the beautiful wilderness in which they are mostly situated; but very soon the extending lines of branch railways will open up the country and destroy much of its native and simple beauty. Those who wish to see Roumania while the "glamour" of past centuries of picturesque costume and antique usages still lingers, must not long delay their visit.

The usual method of travelling, after leaving the railway station, is, as we have already mentioned, a carriage drawn by four horses harnessed abreast.

Saddle horses may doubtless be procured, but ladies should in that case take their own saddles. The carriages are of all sorts, generally light four-wheeled hooded chaises, with sufficient room for two persons, with a servant beside the driver. A third traveller may occupy a small movable seat in front, but this seat is usually ill-placed and fatiguing. On some excursions it is necessary to employ bullock waggons, and it is very customary to descend the river Bistritza on a raft.

The carriages cost from 17 francs to 20 francs a day, with a present to the driver. An arrangement may be made when the carriage is engaged for several days. The driver is supposed to feed his own horses. It was estimated by our party of three that three francs *a day* for *each* person produced what might be considered in those parts as a quite satisfactory present to the monastic charities. It is not usual to exceed the term of the third day. Most of the native excursionists, and they are numerous, come on the Saturday to spend the Sunday with their relations and friends in the monastery, and take their departure on the Monday. For a lengthened stay, furnished cottages in the precincts of some of the monasteries may be rented at a very low charge.

Two or three ladies travelling alone, with a thoroughly trustworthy servant as interpreter, may visit all parts of the country with perfect ease and safety. The climate among the mountains is delightfully cool, and waterproof coverings are indispensable.

The currency is very easily mastered, being the same as the French decimal system—gold twenty-franc pieces, francs, and bani.

The entire cost of one month's travelling divided amongst three persons amounted for *each* person to about £16. During this time eleven monasteries were visited, and more than a week was spent in hotels at Bucharest, Jassy, Folticheni, Baltateshti, Curtea d'Aghish, and Piatra.

When time is an object it may be useful to remark that the "Orient Express" reaches Bucharest in three days, having sleeping carriages and an excellent "restaurant" in the train. All railway fares between London and Bucharest may be easily ascertained. Those in Roumania may be roughly estimated at two francs an hour, second class (very comfortable carriages) and the ordinary train; three francs an hour the "accéléré," or fast train.

# XVI.

## ROUMANIAN MONASTERIES.

### NO. II.—ADAM, JASSY.

From Bucharest to Berlad.—Jewish Coachmen.—A "Fool-woman." —Monastery of Adam.—The "Fundarik."—The Maïca.—The Maïca Staritza.—The Call to Service by the "Bar and Mallet."—Interior of the Church and Costume of the Nuns. —Church Ornaments.—Comfortable Homes of the Maïcas, their Confectionery, their Industry, and their Dress.—The New Monastic Regulations.—In the Staritza's Garden.—The Procession and the Prayers for Rain.—A worthy Lady Superior.—An Early Drive.—An inevitable "Difficulty."— Soothing Scenery.—At Jassy.—Great Jewish Population. —Beautiful Old Church, Treï Sfetitili.—St. Nicholas.

We left Bucharest in June, 1884, by a night train, losing nothing, as the country in this direction is flat and uninteresting. In the course of the night we change at Marachesti and at Tekutch, to arrive at Berlad at eight o'clock. We had picked up, at one of the stations, the interpreter, whose services were kindly lent by a friend, on the understanding that his care of us should in no way interfere with the business for which he usually travels in these provinces. The aim of our wanderings being, not the highways, but the byways of Roumania, an interpreter was indispensable. The bargaining with Jewish coachmen would alone have worn out all travelling enthusiasm had we been left to our own unaided resources, and we shall always remember with gratitude this worthy man's exertions on our behalf; but I regret to say that in the general hurry of progress we had irreverently shortened his name, Barnescu, to Bar, and as such he has since remained in my notes and memories.

We leave the railway at Berlad, the end of an eastward branch from the main line running northward through Moldavia, and, passing across the shabby little station, are quickly made the centre of a lively contest between all the tattered Jew drivers of the cranky chaises and dilapidated barouches waiting to be hired. Rattling up to the centre of interest, each shambling carriage adds its proportion of dust and vociferous offers, until an agreement is made with a crafty-looking coachman, the owner of the most roomy vehicle; but it is not without much disputing, feints to drive away with disdain, return, and further parleys, that the sum of 25 francs has been settled. It is a shabby old carriage, with its four little horses harnessed abreast; but, after seeing the baggage strapped up, or hung about wherever there is a convenient projection, we enter it with a sigh of relief that the clamour is over. Not at all! Our Jew, having driven on for about five minutes, deposits us at the door of a small inn, where some refreshment may be obtained. It is set out in a rustic parlour, pretty enough with its row of bright geraniums in the little windows, but presently poor Bar arrives with a troubled countenance. The driver, having secured his victims, now demands 35 francs to continue the journey. He has been joined by another of his race more crafty than himself. They make a great show of unstrapping the lullage to deposit it in the muddy road. The other vehicles have all disappeared, so there is no help for it; we must bend to the inevitable—make a fresh bargain and start again with the hope of reaching our destination in peace. This exasperating bargaining and the bad faith of the Jewish coachmen was the only infliction in our happy journey, and they were repeated more or less every time we had to engage a fresh carriage.

The Jews in Roumania are a great and serious evil, the "leprosy" of the country, as they are often called. Their injurious influence is most felt by the peasantry, whose land by slow, but sure, degrees they get into their power by means of mortgages and bad debts, luring them to drink and every sort of vice and degradation. Almost all the trade of Roumania is in the hands of the Jews, and, although the Government is doing its utmost to modify the evil, it is difficult to overcome a subtle power that has been growing for centuries.

Our coachman, an expert driver, was also a typical specimen of the race in these parts, dressed in a long greasy black gaberdine, with a tall hat, and straggling ringlets on either side of his crafty face.

The road after leaving the outskirts of Berlad had nothing to recommend it except an abundance of beautiful wild flowers. We noticed with pity several great herds of cattle, pent in open enclosures on the bare hillside, utterly without shelter from the burning sun.

More than half-way to our destination, we stop under the shade of the first spreading plane-tree that we have met with; it overshadows a swing-well for watering the horses. A cart filled with trusses of hay has also paused at the same spot; it is under the charge of a soldier, and is returning from conveying what our worthy Bar calls a "fool-woman" to the hospital for lunatics in the Monastery of Adam, which place is reached after a drive of three hours and a half, the latter part over a more undulated country, with pretty patches of woodland scenery. A child holds open the gate of the rude enclosure of a poor-looking village, and the carriage, turning to the left, climbs the summit of the hill on which the monastery is situated. An arched gateway under a massive tower leads to a large quadrangle. As in most similar establishments, the principal church occupies the centre; the monastic dwellings surround it on three sides, and on the fourth, adjoining the entrance tower, we find the "fundarik," or guest-house, for the reception of travellers.

It looks very clean and very pretty, with tiny gardens on either side of the short flight of steps leading to the broad verandah that runs round three sides of the building, the projecting roof supported on white columns. The monastic cottages have also their verandahs, their white columns, and their little garden plots, while some are much ornamented. We see lace curtains and bright flowers; through the open windows handsome rugs, photographs, and many little adornments supposed to be inconsistent with severe monastic rules; but these good ladies, who are all long past their youth, are not at all cloistered. The community reminded one strongly of the "Béguinage" at Ghent. Men, principally peasants coming on business, walk about freely in the enclosure; and several of the "maïcas" inhabit cottages outside the quadrangle, but within the outer boundary wall.

We have sent no notice of our approach; we have simply driven through the archway and stopped near the door of the fundarik; but a kindly reception seemed quite a matter of course, and the Maïca Fundaria comes forward beaming a welcome; quickly instals us in the best rooms, brings "dulces" and coffee, and, not long afterwards, serves up dinner in another apartment; part of this consists of curds and cream.

Our cheerful, obliging hostess, now called Katinka, was baptised as Caliope. On entering the "religious life" it is customary to take another name. This, our maïca for the time being, is a brisk, energetic old lady, very anxious to make us comfortable. She has a barefooted servant, and they bustle about, bringing in great heaps of padded quilts and pillows, which are quickly spread on the broad divans; and the very clean, comfortable beds are most welcome after the fatiguing journey from Bucharest. Before, however, wishing us the "Buoné nocté," she carries into the room a large tray of dulces and fresh water for our solace during the night.

Our first visit was paid to the Maïca Staritza, the Superior of the monastery, the Reverend Mother Xenia Manóu, a very small, elderly lady, related to the Stourdza and Mourousi families, a most gentle, winning, and ladylike person, looking delicate and fragile, but with a calm dignity of manner that is remarkable, considering the seclusion in which her life has been passed; for she was brought to the monastery when little more than an infant. She lives in very pretty, comfortably furnished rooms, led up to by a small garden. The dwelling is all on one flat.

There is the call to afternoon service in the church —the bar struck by the mallet. The sound is as penetrating as a bell, and seems in its quaint simplicity to harmonise with the rustic-looking cottages of the enclosure. The interior of the church is handsome, and the screen gorgeous; but the heat, increased by many tapers, was stifling, and the long standing very exhaustive. One or two priests were officiating, but the maïca and two of her ladies took some part in the service—the Psalms or lessons probably.

The costume of the nuns on these occasions is dignified and graceful—a long black cloak worn over the usual dress of brown serge; it falls in plaited folds from the shoulders, and being very long, the effect is exceedingly good. Round the head they drape a thin black veil over a cap of serge or velvet, according to the circumstances of the wearer. One end of the veil is thrown over the left shoulder.

The service appeared to consist of alternations of chanting and intoned reading. The late arrival, the "fool-woman," was there, looking not at all "fool," but immensely profuse in bowings, crossings, and prostrations, afterwards kissing all the faces, hands and feet of all the pictures round the screen, crossing herself incessantly; and having utterly exhausted these aids to devotion (an arduous undertaking), she suddenly, with a defiant air, marched out of the church.

We were shown the vestments and church ornaments in a chamber behind the sanctuary: a magnificent cross in wrought gold set with jewels, several splendid vestments embroidered in gold and brilliant colours, two mitres, and some large bands of velvet covered with offerings of jewellery, bracelets, necklaces, rings, for the adornment of the priestly vestments on occasions of great ceremony.

After this rather wearying exhibition we went for a round of visits amongst the maïcas, beginning with a very bright, energetic lady, the Maïca Yustina Filébéiu, one of the heads of the community. I think she is the Maïca Ecônoma, treasurer and superintendent of the financial and worldly interests.

Up some steps, and crossing the verandah, you enter a very neat and well-arranged dwelling. On either side of a little entry, which ends in a bright vista of garden and orchard, you find the drawing-room and dining-room, with two good rooms at back; behind these again a kitchen with several outhouses, and a room where Maïca Yustina's hand-loom is set up. A piece of brown cloth is in course of manufacture.

The ladies in Roumanian convents are celebrated for their confectionery, particularly in the matter of dulces, the sweetmeats to be taken before the glass of water and the cup of coffee, a universal Eastern custom; and Maïca Yustina's sweets were in no wise behind the monastic reputation. Most of the articles worn by herself or decorating her rooms were also the work of her industrious hands: the long black veil, of the finest and softest grenadine; the wide-sleeved cloth pelisse, her usual attire; some strips of bright-coloured carpet, as well as the handsome covering thrown over the divan. Many of these ladies rear silkworms, and spin, weave, and work up the material.

The next cottage under the verandah belongs to a very attractive and particularly sprightly maïca, Natàlia Vralùi. She is rich and wears a handsome velvet cloak over the serge dress. Her round monastic toque is also of black velvet. The elegant veil draping her head and shoulders is wonderfully becoming to the beautiful complexion and bright dark eyes of this lady, whose dwelling is furnished with lace curtains to the windows and rich stuffs on the soft divans. The floor is handsomely carpeted, the glasses for water beautifully cut, the spoons for the "dulces" in heavy wrought silver. One or two side-tables and "étagères" display, amongst other elegant trifles, a large collection of photographs.

Considering that these ladies can obtain permission to visit their relatives and friends in the various monasteries and convents almost as often as their means will allow of the expenditure, one must conclude that conventual life in Roumania is not an existence very hard to endure.

One of the sweets offered with the water in this house was of a rather uncommon sort—a delicious preserve of very small, unformed walnuts flavoured with vanilla; elsewhere we found pieces of angelica cut like large nuts and floating in syrup.

Our sprightly entertainer, after giving the recipe for the walnut "dulce"—we blundered through the explanation by the help of Maïca Yustina's few words of French—brings out for admiration some hanks of silk of her rearing and spinning, a most exquisitely delicate work, intended for a grenadine veil.

Each of these ladies has a servant received into the convent on this condition: the State allows them 148 francs a year: the richer members of the community have their own property. Most of the community at Adam, as in similar monasteries, were received as very little children, and have known no other life, but since the new regulations came into force in 1864 it is forbidden to accept any fresh member under forty years of age; men must be sixty before they can take the monastic vows. These rules tend, of course, to the rapid decrease, and eventual extinction, of monastic life throughout Roumania.

There are fifteen houses in the quadrangle at Adam, comprising a village school. The community counts about one hundred and fifty women, both those in the enclosure and in the surrounding cottages.

After the conclusion of our visits, the energetic Yustina, with one of her companions, conduct us to the Staritza's garden on the slope of the hill, a somewhat wild and neglected domain, where we sit on a bench overlooking the neighbouring tree-clad heights besprinkled with cottages, and are amused by their reminiscences of an English family from Galatz that spent some time (fifteen or twenty years ago) in this peaceful retreat, seeking relief from the intolerable sultriness of the Lower Danube. The maïcas had a vivid recollection of every member of this little party, and asked after them by name or by description, which I clearly recognised. This was almost the solitary instance in which we could discover any trace of the passage of English travellers in the monasteries and places that we visited during a five-weeks' sojourn in Moldavia; and I may fairly claim for our little party that it should be regarded in the light of a modest pioneering enterprise.

The bell, or the bar, was sounding at intervals

throughout the night. Early on Sunday morning all the bells seemed jangling together, and presently a procession was seen to issue from the church to pray in the fields for rain, that was much needed. (N.B.—The clouds were promising a convenient downpour at any moment.) The procession wound over the grass. First a nun carrying a long wooden bar, which she strikes with a mallet in a jaunty kind of measure, bells ringing all the time from the tower above the gateway; then follow strong maïcas or soras, some carrying banners, others the principal pictures from the church. Five priests head the procession of a large body of nuns and a following of villagers. They are absent for an hour, holding a service on one of the grassy slopes, and the return is heralded by a delirious jangle of bells; the "bar" more frolicsome than ever. There is great jubilation, for after a short delay the thunder-clouds resolve into a heavy rain. Was not the procession effective? But the rain, otherwise so beneficial, prevented our visit to the lunatic asylum under charge of the monastery, a circumstance much to be regretted.

Towards evening we make the visit of farewell to the Lady Superior, the Maïca Staritza, who has taken great pains to collect information about our farther route, especially recommending the rather difficult ascent to the mountain retreat of Siklu.

We eventually visited this place. We had known these kind "religieuses" for two days only, but I think there was a mutual friendliness, and we all, I feel sure, experienced a little pang of regret, as the Staritza kissed and blessed us at parting, that in all human probability we should see that gentle face no more.

We afterwards learnt that this estimable woman had had many difficulties to contend with in establishing a firm and wholesome discipline in place of the more than relaxed practices which formerly prevailed in Roumanian monasteries, but she has held to her better principles, and the little community in her charge may, perhaps, regret the days of her wise government, when a brisk and more worldly ruler shall have succeeded to her staff of authority.

The drive next morning was delightful; the earth refreshed by the heavy rains of the previous night, the abundant wild flowers sparkling with dew. We left Adam at four in the morning, and reached the railway station at Berlad in four hours. Here there was, of course, a "difficulty" with our driver. The Jew, although leaving us as early as eight in the morning, wanted to extort payment for three whole days. A grand altercation ensued, during which our worthy Bar, in impotent wrath, stamps about the station with sounding heels, and the driver seizes the opportunity to purloin a box. Bar appeals to the policeman on duty, who says it is no affair of his. What is to be done? The train is shortly expected. Our energetic friend, Mrs. N., summons the interpreter, springs into a carriage, and dashes to the "Mairie" in the town. The official is polite though highly unsatisfactory, but after rapid and vehement expostulation on both sides, a bargain is concluded for forty-eight francs, hastily paid, the box restored, and our friend rushes up to the station as the passengers are getting into the train. It is a comfortable carriage, and we need it to smooth our ruffled feathers and return to our normal state of placid enjoyment.

The scenery as we roll leisurely over the grassy meadow-land is pleasant, but by no means exciting. The majestic Carpathians are far away on our left-hand, and we must not just yet turn our steps in that direction. Our present aim is Jassy, the former capital of Moldavia. The line branches off at Pashkani, and it is not until ten o'clock at night that we reach the station, and, taking a small carriage, drive to the Hotel de Paris. Here everyone seemed to have gone to bed. After much ringing and delay, a sleepy waiter appeared, and consented to help down the luggage, which he deposited beside us in a small room on the ground-floor, being apparently in a hopeless state of bewilderment. We insist, however, upon the presence of the landlady, to ascertain whether we can really remain in this sleepy place, and she at length appears, evidently just awakened. The attendants, aroused to the exigencies of the situation, show us rooms, bring up tea, and in the end we find ourselves exceedingly comfortable. Notwithstanding the unpromising arrival, we finally decided that the Hotel de Paris is clean; the mistress, a Frenchwoman, very obliging, the service good, the restaurant most excellent, and the charges fairly reasonable.

But we are disappointed in Jassy, one of the most ancient cities in this part of Europe. Turkish tradition, indeed, would ascribe its foundation to a tribe migrated from Turkestan in the time of Abraham; but Roumanian belief, that persistently ignores any earthly being as more remarkable than Trajan, prefers to date the origin of Jassy as due to that celebrated conqueror.

At the present day the principal streets are painfully modern, well laid down in asphalt, with fine shops on either side, and the last Paris fashions displayed on the pavement. There are several hotels, the most imposing building of the sort being the Hotel Trajano. The street carriages are convenient and cheap; you get a small, clean, one-horse cabriolet, going like the wind, for fifty centimes (fivepence) the "course." Two horses cost one franc. To or from the railway the fare is doubled. Amongst the advantages of Jassy the ices must not be forgotten: fifty centimes is the charge for one of the first quality, as large as three ordinary ball-room ices.

Jassy literally swarms with Jews. At the time of our passage there, forty families were leaving to emigrate to America, and the crowds thronging the streets towards the railway station to see them off appeared composed of nearly the entire population of the city.

The old church of Treï Sfetitili, or Treï Ierahi (the three saints), was built by Basile Lupo, Voïvade of Moldavia, by whom it was dedicated to St. John Chrysostom, St. Gregory, and St. Basil. It is one of the most beautiful examples of church ornamentation in the East. It had been set on fire outside at one time by the Turks to melt down the gold lavished on the exquisite mouldings, and thirty years ago was much shaken by an earthquake that caused a great fissure in the wall of the apse. It has since remained a partial ruin and unused, until the Frenchman who is engaged on the renovation of Curtea d'Arghish undertook to restore, also, this beautiful monument. As far as it was possible to judge through scaffolding, the work is being well and tastefully carried out.

The whole exterior of the church is covered with a network of raised carvings, like a rich lace veil thrown from top to bottom, with mouldings, cornices, and courses of the richest colours mingled with gold. Many beautiful fragments of twisted columns lie around. The interior is not easily seen at present, but large frescoes covered by canvas for preservation still remain, and above the entrance door there is a row of exquisite heads of saints. Some low vaulted recesses, also, are framed by beautifully twisted carvings in stone. It is almost worth the journey to Jassy to see this fine monument of Eastern art.

Another ancient church, St. Nicholas, was built by Stephen the Great in the latter half of the fifteenth century. Side chapels were added at a later date, but these are now being taken down, and the original building only will be preserved. Some carving also on the outer wall is being carefully cleared of its disfiguring whitewash. The narthex of this edifice is unusually fine and lofty.

A longer stay would doubtless have shown us some other objects of interest, but I was yearning for the mountains, and felt tempted rather to neglect Jassy, with its fine terraced hills beyond the town sparkling with villas set in their blooming gardens. The wood of Briazo, at the extremity of the plateau, was the refuge of Codréan, a brigand hero—a haïduk —of Roumanian ballad.

## XVII.

### ROUMANIAN MONASTERIES.

#### NO. III.—SÉCU AND SIKLA.

Charming Drive.—The Monastery of Sécu.—The Parenté Arfundărah.—Hospitality.—Foundation of Sécu.—Nestor and Metrofana.—Fortifications.—The former Importance of the Monastery.—The Refectory.—" Mamaliga."—Start for Sikla. —The Bullock Cart.—Our Escort.—Parenté Samuel.—Armed Monks.—Sylvan Glades.—The Forest.—A Wild Mountain Track.—Magnificent Scenery.—An Uncomfortable Slope towards the Precipice.—The Monastery of Sikla.—A Venerable Staritz.—Origin of the Chapel of St. Theodora.—A Peaceful Scene.—Parenté Samuel's Curls.—A Mountain Storm.—Subastria.

About a week after leaving Jassy we were at Balteteshti, a small mineral bathing establishment in Upper Moldavia, and, leaving one of our party to rest in the very comfortable hotel attached to the baths, two of us, with the interpreter, started for a two days' excursion to the monasteries of Sécu and Sikla; taking no luggage, we are able to engage a good carriage and pair for seventeen francs a day.

Our way lies along the road to Monastir Niamtz,

turning off to the left before reaching the monastery. It is beautiful woodland scenery through which we pass—the usual wealth of wild blossoms enamelling the ground, sparkling and waving over every sunlit hillock. After a three hours' drive we stop to rest and to water the horses at one of those picturesque swing-wells so common throughout Roumania, in as lovely a forest glade as can well be imagined; the deep shadows of the noble oaks and beeches relieved against the distant wooded heights that glowed with every tender tint of blue and purple.

On again, through shady winding lanes and across a few shallow streams; then, entering on a more stony track, we endure a few jolts, and presently passing a barrier held open by a peasant, the fortified walls of Sécu come into view, its metal-covered cupolas gleaming like silver.

We drive up to the arched entrance, where a rough-headed monk receives us, rather doubtfully at first, for, as usual, we are the first English who have visited this spot, but, after an instant's inspection, he appears to conclude that we are neither evil nor dangerous; he leads the way up an outer staircase, and, depositing our small bags on the broad verandah, goes off to summon the Parenté Arfundârah, or manager of the guest-house. This official presently arrives, a very burly and altogether jovial personage, with a moist twinkle in his eye, that seemed to appreciate the arrival of foreigners as a source of eventual benefit.

We are shown into the best rooms the guest-house contains, not by any means luxurious, but in travelling it is wisest to think that "variety is charming," and while dinner is being prepared we first pay a visit to the Staritz, or Superior—a very benevolent and very subdued old gentleman—and then proceed to visit the church and the surrounding precincts. As in all Roumanian monasteries, the church occupies the centre of the quadrangle; the guest-house adjoins the cloportnitza, or entrance-gate (usually on the left hand), and the monastic dwellings complete the rest of the enclosure; several of the monks also inhabit detached cottages outside the monastery proper, but within the outer encircling palisades.

We did not ascertain the date of the foundation of the monastery, but it was in the days of the earlier Hospodars that a great Government official, Nestor, coming with his wife Metrofana to bathe in the fine mountain spring, finds here only a solitary hermit. The sick man is cured, and, in gratitude, erects the church and monastery, endowing it with sixteen villages. The reigning Hospodar comes also to this wonderful spring, is greatly benefited, and doubles the gift of the founder; thus Sécu at one time possessed thirty-two villages—a very handsome provision.

Nestor and Metrofana returned here in their old age, to pass their last days and die in the odour of sanctity. Metrofana survived her husband for some time. In the strong corner tower they show a room where the foundress passed the three last years of her life, and where she died. They are both buried in the church, in which is a picture representing them as offering the building. In the choir, on either side, a panel can be removed behind a stall, showing a dark cavity painted in fresco; these are the tombs of Nestor and Metrofana.

The fortifications of Sécu appear to have been at one time very strong, but they have been much damaged and destroyed. During the troubles in connection with the Greek War of Independence (1821), which, in the Principalities, resulted in the overthrow of the Phanariot rule and the reinstalment of the native princes, this monastery was fiercely besieged; but it held out against the Turks until reduced by famine. The tower on the left hand, which is extremely strong, is uninjured; it is loopholed, and capable of a stout resistance. It was at Sécu that Georgaki, an Albanian, one of the chiefs of the movement organised by Ypsilanti, "after extraordinary feats of courage and daring, blew himself up with the remnant of his wild troop."[*] This Georgaki was concerned in the assassination of Vladimiresco.

A very talkative old monk pointed out to us an inscription let into the wall of a dry moat, but we failed to make out its meaning—Bar, as usual, when information was not quite clear, opining that our informant was a "fool-man."

Sécu now numbers sixty monks. We wander round the quadrangle, and visit the great refectory, which testifies to its vanished importance; it is used only on festival days. A large room with two long tables and heavy wooden benches; a gilded and coloured pulpit projects from the wall at one end, raised high above the tables, for the use of the preacher or reader. The kitchen adjoining has an immense vaulted-roofed chimney, with a gigantic cauldron for making the universal national dish—the "mamaliga;" but it all looked poor and neglected, as if the monastery had seen better days, and as if the thirty-two villages were undoubtedly a memory of a distant past.

Our own mamaliga is smoking on the board, and we are summoned up-stairs by Parenté Samuel. The dinner is very good, considering the limited resources of the establishment; the bread — as throughout Roumania — exquisitely delicate, the fowls well cooked, the mamaliga soft. It is cus-

[*] Ubicini.

tomary to serve this—a stiff porridge of maize-flour—on a platter, and to cut it with a string. There is a certain art even in this simple preparation, and it is not everyone who can succeed in making the mamaliga soft. Layers of new cheese are sometimes introduced into this maize pudding.

The burly old gentleman (I think he was Parenté Seraphim) had certainly superintended our repast, if not actually cooked it, for he came up heated and beaming, evidently expecting the compliments which heartily greeted his exertions.

After dinner we sit on the broad verandah to sip our coffee, while endeavouring to understand as much as possible of the history of the place, given through our interpreter. The Parenté showed us also a well-kept visitors'-book. Looking back through several years, I find only Roumanian names, with two exceptions—a French lady and gentleman who had visited Sécu a fortnight previously, and one other Frenchman several years before.

They have already told us that the further excursion to Sikla would be impossible for that afternoon; it would require three or four hours, and to pass the night in that solitary spot would be dangerous. There are only three monks, and the sojourn of strangers might tempt the brigands; but the Superior has promised that on the morrow an ox-cart shall be ready early, and that he will give us two monks, mounted and armed, as an escort.

On the following day we leave Sécu in the early freshness of a morning in July, to reach Sikla, on a still higher summit of the Carpathians. On the wide burnt-up plains bordering the Danube, the heat at this season is intense. Here, the fresh mountain breezes, the luxuriant pastures, the heavy dew, as we brush through the tangled branches of the almost unbroken forest, are wonderfully refreshing and invigorating.

Our little party and escort is thus composed: two ladies seated in a long narrow cart of wooden disjointed planks, which is drawn by four of the beautiful oxen of this country—cream-coloured, with wide-branching horns, and large soft eyes. The cart has a thick lining of hay raised at one end, where it is covered, first with a carpet and then by a soft mattress, forming a delightful seat, although the sitter must struggle against a tendency to subside in a heap in the centre of the vehicle. At the other end of the cart is crouched Parenté Samuel, whom the Superior of Sécu has sent as our special attendant. There is a driver to each pair of oxen, and we are further protected by two powerful-looking monks, mounted and armed—one with a pistol, which he discharges at intervals for the intimidation of possible brigands, the other with a large dagger-knife thrust into his high boot and delicately shaded by a checked handkerchief. These men are dressed in thick brown serge, fastened at the waist by a cord, and wear brown felt brimless caps. Our interpreter, also mounted, hovers round the party.

We roll along very pleasantly at first, over meadows glowing with wild blossoms and tall flowering grasses, through rippling streamlets and up and down a gentle bank or two. The movement of the cart, formed of loose planks that yield and sway with every undulation, softened, also, by the hay and cushions, is delightful. We enter the forest in high spirits. Soon the branches, so gently waving in the more open country, become obtrusive as the path narrows, but Parenté Samuel carefully guides them away. Gradually the surroundings take a wilder and more rugged look, and we begin to ascend a road full of deep ruts and dark marshy bogs: sometimes, a large grey boulder, over which the oxen drag the cart; it strains and shivers in every plank; then a deep hole into which we plunge, while the drivers goad or encourage the oxen for the reascending effort. Parenté Samuel has leapt out some time before; he hangs on to the upper side of the cart whenever the wheels appear too near the edge of the track. Our mounted escort has separated; one rides in front carefully watching the steps of the oxen and the passage of the front wheels, while the other as carefully watches the movement in the rear. They shout directions to the drivers; the drivers scream at the oxen.

The scenery is wildly grand. Gigantic lime-trees, birch, and oak tower above us to an amazing height; then firs and pine-trees only. On every side immense trunks—some with their spreading branches—have fallen, and must decay as they lie, half-buried in grey mosses and hoary beard-like lichens. One monarch of the forest had stretched its splendid length across the track; it has been sawn through, to remove it was impossible.

More fearful dips and agonized jerks upwards, as the oxen strain every nerve and muscle. Now the mountain falls away in a steep precipice on the left, and amidst boulders, rocks, mudholes, quagmires, tangled branches, and fallen trunks, we go slowly on, ever and again with a tendency to overhang the precipice, for the track slopes gently towards the outer edge, and the way is slippery with fallen and sodden leaves. It seems like some forest-clearing in California; the drivers are not unlike squatters in their broad slouch hats and linen wide-sleeved shirts. The directing "fathers" still one in front, one in the rear, watch more carefully now, for we have reached the worst " bit " of the road—a short but very steep ascent, with that uncomfortable slope towards the precipice. More screaming of the drivers, more straining efforts of the goaded beasts; hurried orders, a sickening feeling that a false move, a broken tire-pin, might send us hopelessly down into that measureless abyss—and we are safe! There are more bogs, more boulders, more turnings and windings, and suppressed terrors, but Parenté Samuel has quietly resumed his place amid the hay, and we know that danger is over until our return. Bar, to reassure us, relates how a party of Boyards and ladies, some time before, were on their way to Sikla in a cart drawn by six oxen. At this same point a tire-pin broke; the cart was gently slipping to the verge of the descent, when one of the drivers from the convent, an immensely powerful young man, stopped the movement with his shoulder for a few seconds, while the terrified party threw themselves out on the opposite side. It was comfortable to feel the present safety, but not pleasant to reflect that it was necessary to return by the way we had come, and that the same slight accident might happen without the help of the Samsonian shoulder.

At length the rustic barrier is passed, a pistol is fired off to announce the approach of guests, and on a grassy plateau in the midst of the forest, stands the poor little monastery of Sikla.

A mild-looking "father," who proved to be Staritz, Ecônomo, and Parenté Arfundârah all in one, came forward to greet us, while a pale and rather tattered neophyte helped in releasing the wearied oxen and unloading the cart.

They are three in this dreary solitude, besides a few young boys attending to the cattle; these are all brothers and the nephews of the Staritz. He is a venerable and kindly old man, not in the least fluttered by the arrival of " European" ladies, although the first he has ever seen. He leads us to a very shaky wooden balcony, where we find a rough log table and some planks as benches. " He has," he says, "nothing to offer us but a kindly welcome, good mountain air, and pure water." Later, he brings us a little milk; but Parenté Samuel has taken his precautions, and produces luncheon. They make a " mamaliga; " there is fresh cheese, delicate bread, and a bottle of Father Seraphim's " eau de mélisse," which, sipped incautiously, nearly takes away the roof of my mouth.

We wander on the hillside to sketch. The church of Sikla is a poor little building, entirely of grey wooden planks; the roof also formed of thin strips of wood laid closely row upon row. This is a common style of roofing throughout the country. The small monastery, containing three or four apparently unfurnished rooms above the rude cowsheds; a covered fountain, one or two barns, and a strong log fence occupy the whole of the grassy clearing in the forest. On the right, between the richly clothed mountain peaks, you see the blue vapoury outline of the plain towards Niamtz. On the left rises the bold grey crag, draped with creepers and mountain ash, which overhangs the monastery; on its summit are the little chapel of Saint Theodora and the Hermit's Cave.

The origin of the chapel dates from a very early time. Who this saintly penitent may have been we did not learn. The name of Theodora is generally associated in Byzantine history with records of vice and crime; but this recluse seems to have repented at length, and retired to this wild and beautiful summit of the Carpathians to end her days in sanctity and solitude.

She lived in a natural cavern, and after her death many hermits in succession availed themselves of its peaceful shelter. One day a certain Joanitzo Pashcano, and one of the Cantacuzene family, wandering over the forest in search of game, came upon the rustic hermitage, and, struck with the beauty of the situation, they caused to be built the tiny chapel, which is so small that it can only accommodate ten persons.

Whilst waiting for the party, who have gone up to the summit of the crag, I sit in the calm shade of the church-porch and speculate on the extraordinary strength of the enclosure and its perfect insufficiency as a protection. The fences in these forest districts are made of entire logs of pine woven as it were together with alternate angles; they are scarcely high enough to be a defence against wolves, and would form a nice sort of stairway for the brigands. "Do robbers ever come here?" was asked. "Not now, there is nothing left to take; they came a few years ago, carried off every portable thing, and destroyed the rest."

All is very peaceful now. There is the gentle dripping of the fountain close at hand, a little farther off our oxen are reposing on the soft grass, and Parenté Samuel, sitting on a shaft of the cart, employs the soft leisure of the afternoon in combing his beautiful raven curls. They are a rare adornment and, probably, the secret pride and happiness of his sad, colourless, uneventful life, for this Parenté is one of the saddest-looking of men. A smile would seem impossible to that woe-begone countenance, but he has undoubtedly beautiful curls, hanging round from beneath the brown felt cap. They are black as jet, soft and glossy as satin, and there must be an intense hidden satisfaction in the possession of the shining ringlets, for (to judge by appearances) this care of them is an almost unprecedented experience in the conventual life of Roumanian monks.

On the return of the party, whose voices I have for some time heard echoing above, I find that the good Staritz has picked for my benefit a large bunch of wild strawberries and bilberries; but it is time to leave, and after looking into the church, which can be seen at a glance and contains nothing remarkable, we make a small present to the good old man, for which he is very grateful. He writes our names in the church register, that we may be remembered in their prayers, and a merry peal of bells (an unusual compliment) echoes through the forest as our oxen once more draw us into its wild and tangled shades.

From the monastery of Agâpia there is a way to Sikla much shorter than that from Sécu, but it is a rough and probably difficult horse-track. Our road required about three hours.

In descending, two oxen only were used, the others following, while one driver, with a stout pole, locked the hind wheels of the cart. Sometimes a short dip would be so steep that only the tails and hindquarters of the beasts would be visible. The sudden effort and scramble up the opposite bank just saved us from falling over them.

The worst is past. We are once more on level ground and brushing through the trailing branches. Our team, complete again, are dragging us as briskly as the tortuous road will permit, when a few heavy drops begin to force their way through the leaves. A storm, long threatening, has burst; then a steadier downpour. The thunder rolls majestically, echoing from every mountain peak, nearer and nearer, and the rain, a torrent. Happily we are not far from the little "skite" of Sohastria—a sort of "chapel of ease" depending on Sécu. We turn in that direction, and our team breaks into a splendid gallop as we tear over a broad meadow and arrive in grand style at the enclosing fence. There is no gateway. This is easily remedied; some logs are removed and we dash through (crushing down another division), to remain for some time under the archway waiting for a sign of welcome from the inhabitants. The place is inhabited by seven monks, but they are apparently all absent in the fields or in the forest, and we leave our moist seat to wait on the covered balcony until the storm may pass.

There is freshly mown hay on the greensward around the church, and great trusses of sweet-smelling hay piled on a distant colonnade for shelter. All these the oxen and the horses proceed to demolish with great relish. The injury is not serious, and we would gladly have compensated any one coming forward with the customary welcome, but the absence of the usual cup of coffee showed that the solitary old man, who at length flitted across the shadows in the background, preferred to ignore our presence, so there was no remedy, and we took the opportunity to learn the names of our beautiful Moldavian oxen: Douman, Pluvan, Yello, and Tchokolan.

After an hour's stay, we jolted comfortably back to Sécu, intending to leave again immediately; but Parenté Seraphim's hospitality could not be neglected. A very comfortable dinner had been provided, it must be eaten, the coffee taken reposedly, a farewell visit paid to the Superior, and, above all, the gratifications distributed.

Before leaving, our beaming entertainer contrived to sell me, for two francs, an old wooden rosary which would have been dear at two piastres; but one must sacrifice something for the good of the temporary home where, without charge, the stranger as well as the native receives shelter, a kindly welcome, and entertainment for three days. A beautiful little fishing trap was bought by my friend, which Parenté Seraphim claimed as of his own invention, and to have been in one of the great exhibitions at Paris. We purchased also some very rough wooden spoons and a bottle of what he called eau de mélisse, equally concocted by himself.

It was not until the sun was throwing long shadows across the mountains that we finally turned from the fortress monastery of Sécu. The drive was delightful, the horses fresh, the road excellent. Passing the outskirts of Niamtz, we followed the high road leading south, and reached Balteteshti late in the evening.

## XVIII.

### ROUMANIAN MONASTERIES.

#### NO. IV.—DURÂU, TCHAKLÂU, THE BISTRITZA.

From Piatra.—Picturesque Environs.—The Monastery of Bistritza.—Tomb of Alexander the Good.—A Beautiful Church.—Bisericanu.—Pingaraciora.—Village of Hangû.—Moldavian Peasantry.—Costume.—Difficult Mountain Track.—The Monastery of Durâu.—A Tradition of Tourists.—From the Little Balcony.—Parenté Hilarion and the Neophyte.—Transylvanian Peasants.—Eidelweis.—A Little Miser.—Floats along the Troughs.—Repchiuni.—Leisurely Construction of the Raft.—Obstructions.—Lowering Clouds.—The Master Raftsman.—Rain and Rapids.—Skilful Guidance.—The Eddies.—A Sad Landing.—A Compassionate Traveller.—At Piatra.—Maritza.—Zeckler Harvesters.—Homewards.

THE four little horses had been tinkling their bells and shaking their rope harness since three o'clock in the morning before the door of the Bistritza Hotel at Piatra; they had been ordered for five, and at that hour precisely we are ready to start. The garçon of the restaurant had brought up small cups of the very weakest coffee, with fingers of bread, and Maritza helps to stow away our light travelling gear into the shambling, disjointed sort of hooded chaise that is to convey us partly up the ascent of the highest peak in this district of the Carpathians—Tchaklâu—some 8,000 feet above the sea-level.

We rattle down the almost deserted street, crossing the untidy market-place, and, passing round the base of the old fire-tower, are quickly in the fresh, cool suburbs. The breeze from the rapid river comes over gardens laden with the perfume of roses and mignonette; the birds are trilling joyously; the bees issue from their hives under the broad verandahs as, here and there, a peasant's cottage gleams out like snow against its background of orchard and leafy slopes, the invariable columns supporting the deep-eaved roof, the walls of the dwelling and the broad clay seat beside the door looking as fresh as the last coat of whitewash could make them, with the embellishment of a blue band marking the square of the tiny windows. On the farther side of the river—the Bistritza—the mountains rise and fall with broad meadows and sunny homesteads on the lower slopes; then thick forest growth of oak and beech, and, finally, the pine-clad summit. Beyond all this the pale grey peaks and crags of Tchaklâu tower above the mountain range and melt into the vapoury distance. The road is good, the expedition is delightful.

Less than an hour's drive brings us to a shady road sloping upwards on the right hand, and we see the bright cupolas of the large monastery of Bistritza in a setting of forest-clad mountains. We alight in the grassy precincts of the church, unwilling to disturb the monastic inhabitants at this early hour; but our arrival is immediately known, and it is not long before the Superior comes down to welcome the unlooked-for guests, while an attendant monk hands the tray of " dulces " and coffee.

The monastery of Bistritza is one of the most important of those still existing in Roumania. It was founded by Alexander the Good (Alexandru celŭ Bunŭ), " Domnu," or Voïvade, of Moldavia in 1430. His tomb, as well as that of his first wife, Domna Ana, may be seen on the left-hand side of a large and richly decorated ante-chapel. The tomb of a son of Stephen the Great stands on the right of the entrance.

The church of Bistritza is very handsome, painted and gilded throughout, even to the summit of the cupolas; the screen is a blaze of gold and colours, but this is relieved by the rich brown of the carved stalls and by the soft tone of the beautifully sculptured doorways and finely carved arch of the windows.

The Superior of the convent is a good-looking and very courteous man in the prime of life; his sylvan retreat is by no means a seclusion, as the place is much visited by Roumanians. Its neighbourhood to Piatra—a busy, populous town—and the fresh beauty of the scenery, render it a favourite point for excursions and holiday-making.

Not so the large monastery that came into view round the next spur of the mountains as we left Bistritza, and turned once more into the high road. It looked beautiful: the shining cupolas and whitened towers of the irregular building, like a cluster of snowdrops in billowy masses of rich foliage; but Bisericanu is no longer a monastery, but a convict prison, as is also another edifice on a neighbouring wooded height—a strong-looking, turreted, grey fortress, once the monastery of Pingaraciora. We passed a prisoner on the road, manacled, between two soldiers. Very many of the convents in Roumania have—since the secularisation of monastic property in 1864—been converted into hospitals, prisons, or asylums.

We continue our way; on the right the forest-clad mountains, on the left, at some distance below, the river Bistritza, swirling and seething over some slight rapids, along which the rafts are shooting with a sure and steady but rapid movement. We are to return to Piatra on one of these rafts, and are not sorry to watch the skilful way in which they are handled.

The road has been fairly good, crossing the water two or three times on good solid bridges, until we reach the straggling village of Hangû, when a violent storm—never long absent in these mountain passes—drives us for shelter to a rough wayside inn. It is also a " bakal's " shop, where everything is sold (including English starch and Colman's mustard), except the first necessary of life—bread. The people would appear to feed solely on mamaliga, with an abundance of rich milk. Butter is unknown; the only preparation of it is salted cheese, and sometimes sweet curds. I doubt if they ever eat meat, but they seem to do very well on their frugal diet; the men are strong and vigorous, the women upright and healthy-looking, taking more than their full share in all heavy manual labour.

A rustic wedding was going on somewhere in the environs, and several peasants in gala dress watched us as we endeavoured to sketch the scene from the pillared platform in front of the "locanda"—some low-roofed cottages, a wandering irregular fence, a swing-well with its bold graceful curve, and the grey peak of Tchaklâu towering into the clouds as a background. Mrs. N—— bought of one of the young women a complete costume, for which she drove a very successful bargain. It consisted of a long linen garment embroidered about the throat and sleeves; a large stiff apron, also embroidered, and much adorned with spangles; a girdle of many colours, several strings of beads, and a long scarf-veil that is wound about the head very gracefully and becomingly. There is much less of costume to be met with in Moldavia than in Wallachia, where the wise and patriotic example of the Queen encourages the retention of the national dress, which is one of the most beautiful in Europe, although there is a hard struggle against the encroaching influence of French fashions.

The rain clearing off, we start once more on our road to the secluded monastery of Durâu, where we intend to pass the night and the following day, Sunday. Here begins the more difficult part of our progress. The well-made road ceased at Hangû, to give place to a rough, stony mountain track intersected by innumerable streamlets; these are not deep, but, as the driver seems uncertain of his road and misty in his judgment as to the proper fords, carrying the shaky little carriage over impossible boulders and across rotten planks, two of us jumped out to lighten the strain for the weary little horses. They had been almost without food the whole day, and became at length so weak that they stopped and would have slid back at every rise in the ground, necessitating on each occasion a rapid and undignified descent into the mud.

We now pass a large saw-mill in full activity, from which the freshly hewn planks are floated down to the river in wooden troughs, raised about a foot from the ground. Sometimes a workman will take passage on one of these planks, balancing with wonderful dexterity, and shooting out of sight like lightning.

We learn at the mill that the convent is still at half-an-hour's distance, but it is cheering to be assured that we have not strayed in this beautiful but interminable wilderness, and before long a rustic barrier proclaims the entry of the monastic domains. Here respectability requires a dignified advance. The broad meadow is smooth and flat; the driver hints at savage dogs, and we creep for the last time into the old hooded cabriolet, drive solemnly under the cloportnitza, and stop in the grassy precincts of the church. We have been accompanied across the meadow by a magnificent dog, not unlike a St. Bernard. Far from showing enmity, he first inspects the party with anxious and careful inquiry, decides that we are innocent and friendly, and ends by escorting us to the door of a balconied dwelling where a venerable and slightly astonished " padré " comes forward to welcome us. The greeting is kindly, calm, dignified, but the possible accommodation almost *nil*. The Staritz explains the situation. The monastery of Duràu does not, as in the case of other monasteries, draw any allowance from the State for the entertainment of strangers. It stands on the property of the Stourdza family, and having been long utterly neglected and forgotten by the proprietor—lately dead in Paris, the owner of untold millions—the poor little community is reduced to its own resources for a bare subsistence. Strangers rarely visit the place; foreigners and tourists are legendary. They have a tradition that about five-and-twenty years ago a shooting party of gentlemen from Galatz came here and climbed the summit of Tchaklâu. It happened that I was able to identify two of these sportsmen, and, meeting them the other day in London, they were interested to learn that after this quarter of a century they are still remembered in this distant convent of the Carpathians, where no subsequent arrivals of our countrymen have occurred to confuse the recollection. May we dwell as pleasantly in the memories of that little group of kindly, simple-hearted old men! The community numbers twenty monks, living in the precincts and in detached cottages embowered in orchards.

They gave us of their best, but it was needful here to put in stern practice the wisest theory of a genuine traveller—cheerful resignation to unavoidable inconvenience. There was no bread to be procured, no meat, no fowl; only mamaliga, milk, cheese, and a few eggs. Our host, an archimandrite, prepares the dinner, waits upon us at table—with the help of a neophyte—and then sits with us for company.

From the wooden verandah before our windows we look upon scenery of mountain and primeval forest, the majestic ruggedness of Tchaklâu, now shrouded in tossing vapours, now lighted with dazzling sunshine as it falls on the granite peaks, or on the velvet sward carpeting the narrow gullies; below, the encircling belt of sombre pine-forest, shutting in the monastery as in an amphitheatre; then the brighter tone of chestnut, beech, and oak breaks into clearings of soft meadow-land, across which rude fences wander, and so on to the peaceful oases of the convent enclosure. It breaks away on the right, behind the deep-eaved cottages, where the rush of unseen water rises from the leafy ravine. On the left of our verandah stands the inevitable whitewashed church. It is, as an object, the only blot in the picture, but we try to forget it in the charm of sylvan beauty around the humble little fountain in front; the bell-tower farther back; behind that, again, the cloportnitza. On either side the monastic cottages with their broad verandahs, some with the basement and the grey wooden pilasters half smothered in pink and crimson roses, with tall white heads of lily and trailing wreaths of clematis; all sweet odours that mingle with the scent of new-made hay from the grassy slopes in front. Now and then a dark-robed figure wanders over the grass; he goes, perhaps, to the church, or to fill a "cofitza" at the ever-dripping fountain; they are mostly very old and infirm. Parenté Hilarion, in the next cottage to ours, has a distressing cough. As we sit on his verandah and endeavour to retain in our sketch-books the memory of this calm sweet rest, he can be heard between his paroxysms instructing a young neophyte in the elements of monastic literature. The boy, Georghi, having finished his lesson, comes out to stare at us, and remains calmly enough while we turn the pencils on him.

Soon after this our scene is animated by brighter figures—a dozen or so of Transylvanians, men and women. They have crossed the border, very near to this part, in search of harvesting work; they will sleep one night in the monastery, go to mass in the morning, and pursue their road over the lower spurs of Tchaklâu. There is little difference in dress to distinguish these people from the Roumanians, but the race is fairer; two of the women had light hair and blue eyes; one was exceedingly pretty. A man and his wife were persuaded by the promise of coin to stand still for a few minutes, but they were impatient to follow their friends, who with bags slung over their shoulders were wending their way across the grass, so the sketch was hastily finished, the coin grasped, and the whole cheerful party disappeared through the broad archway of the cloportnitza.

The next day, Sunday, a time of perfect rest; at

intervals the deep silence broken by the bell from the wooden bell-tower, or the more familiar call to prayer—a monk passing slowly round the church striking the long bar of wood with a mallet. Then some worshippers gather from the cottages around, adjusting their black veils before entering the sacred edifice. There is a poor old man nearly bent double with age and rheumatism; another who is lame; then the possessor of that fearful cough. He shrouds himself as well as may be from the drenching rain, for a heavy mountain shower is falling; he is followed by his little pupil, Georghi.

Some one had sent us in the morning a splendid lily stuck in a piece of honeycomb. I think it was this Parenté Hilarion. He is a cousin of the good Staritz of Sikla, who had sent, by us, many messages of friendly greeting.

We had given up the attempt to climb to the rocky summit of Tchaklâu, the highest peak in this part of the Carpathians, but advised our interpreter to go up with a guide, both mounted, to search for the great iron cross said to have been erected on it. Towards evening he came back, reporting the way very difficult. He had seen the iron cross, but the return road was so steep and slippery that he made the whole of it on foot. I have been told that the view from the highest point, looking down upon a forest of needle-like crags, is most remarkable.

Our envoy brought back with him large tufts of moss and flowers, amongst them several specimens of the eidelweis.

Whilst waiting for the ox-cart which is to take us away early on Monday morning, we go up to inspect the new building, intended as a guest-house, over the arched gateway of the enclosure. The guests probably are almost entirely composed of the peasants passing across the frontier in search of work. The dwelling consists of four rooms, very solidly constructed of pine planking. Wood has little value here, and the labour is supplied on the spot.

By eight o'clock we have once again mounted into an ox-cart, this time drawn by only two beasts. We have received fresh presents of lilies, and have taken a regretful leave of our host, the Staritz, of one or two of the poor old fathers, and of the beautiful dog, who throughout our visit has expressed his cordial, though dignified, approval of the unusual strangers. Our worthy interpreter was so much impressed by the piety and charity of the Staritz that he could hardly tear himself away, and we saw them, as the cart turned into the leafy forest, exchanging the kiss of peace and of farewell. Can nothing be done to give this neglected community in the heart of the Carpathians some small particle of the glittering millions that the lord of these vast forests could not carry with him to his grave?

The cart jolts on, but not unpleasantly; it is safer than the weakly cabriolet of our arrival, for the heavy rains have swollen the streamlets, and the cart can stand all sorts of ruts and pitfalls without upsetting.

We follow the beautiful forest road, with its turns and windings among thick trees, with the luxuriant carpeting of tall grasses and ferns. The driver's little son, at first in pursuit of a refractory cow, gives up the chase and devotes himself to opening the barriers, for which eventually he receives a small silver piece, presumably *the first* silver that he has ever seen, for after a look of astonishment, he sinks upon the ground, in a futile attempt to secrete the treasure from his mamma, who is now seen striding over a hedge from a neighbouring cottage. The conflict is sharp but short; the mother whips up the infantine miser under one of her sturdy arms, and carries him, wildly struggling, to his home.

We have passed the saw-mills, and the road is bounded on one side by the raised trough down which the planks are rushing towards the river Bistritza, where the floats are made up, and the wood thus conveyed to the Sereth, and thence to the Danube. A great proportion of it is shipped at Galatz. Every now and then there is a block in the trough; the planks accumulate, and, when hard pressed, tumble over, but a passing workman soon sets them again upon their travels.

Before reaching Repchiuni we stop the cart, and go up through a neglected orchard to inspect a half-ruined building, which proves to be the "skite" of Hanghû. It has a round tower, and in a country so rich in beautiful scenery the situation is not remarkable. A peasant who had charge of the place talked incessantly to our interpreter. He had apparently some interminable grievance to narrate, but, I am sorry to say, his listener, not quite making out the wearisome complaint, expressed his usual sentiment: he was a "fool" man. We were further informed that this place was the supposed refuge of some heroine in one of Dumas' novels.

At 11.30 we arrived at Repchiuni, where we dismissed our escort, and sat down outside a rude hut to wait for the raft. We had previously met the forester who had so kindly called upon us at Piatra and planned out our route. He came with us to the starting-place, gave orders that everything should be properly arranged, directed that his best raftsman should go with us, and took a polite leave, saying that the construction of the raft would require an hour, and that in about three hours from the time of starting we should reach our destination.

We wait tranquilly and patiently, but after a long time we begin vaguely to perceive that the men are not of the same mind as the master. An hour has passed, yet there is scarcely any progress in our float. First they come to a standstill for wood, and two men are sent to some distant point up stream; they do not return, and our energetic friend, starting across a broad meadow to discover the reason, finds them quietly seated on the brink of the river smoking. They start up and pretend haste, but still our float is very hard to build. When all is finished and apparently ready, it is announced that some formalities have to be gone through—the consignment of the wood to be verified, and a signature obtained, but the registrar is not to be found. Another expedition in search of the missing official: more patience! The clouds are lowering ominously, and we begin to feel anxious. We beguile the time in examining the raft. It is very long, and worked at both ends by paddles loosely attached between wooden pegs. In the centre a broad platform had been arranged with raised back and sides, and a very deep seat, where natives would have crouched; had we done so, much of our subsequent tribulation might have been avoided. This platform should have been roofed with boughs, but there is no sun to incommode us, and we forego that embellishment, though regretting the loss of the picturesque effect.

At last! At past three o'clock we start, and float down for about a mile, when something gives way in the paddle serving as rudder. We are pulled to shore, steadied by a heavy stone on the rope, and lose another half-hour while the men are leisurely repairing the mishap. It is fortunate that all three travellers are well acquainted with life in the East, where inexhaustible patience is the first necessary of existence. After events threw some light on these repeated hindrances to our progress down the Bistritza, and we have since concluded that our men did not intend to reach Piatra that evening, but had agreed between themselves to stop at a wayside hamlet, where some great festivity was going on.

Our principal raftsman was, without doubt, exceedingly skilful. Although quite a small young man, he had wonderful muscular power in his tiny bronze-coloured hands, and bare feet, and ankles like a slender girl's. He looked like a gipsy. The man who worked the rudder was an unkempt, rough being, who, our little man declared with contempt, was not a " maéstro " (skilled raftsman).

Now begins the first serious trouble in our otherwise prosperous journey. It was, to the day, one month since we had started, and we felt thankful that our little expedition—we might almost call it a pioneering party—had been hitherto exceptionally bright and successful; but now the rain, a disaster in our exposed situation, begins steadily. It pours down in such torrents that we think it *must* soon cease; but no, it continues—it continues for hours, and two of us are drenched through and through.

We sit in pools of water; water eddies up over our feet; our small baggage is soaking. This heavy downpour streaming from the mountains on all sides has " churned up " the river with wonderful rapidity, making it much more "rough" than we had expected. It is well to try to remember that we are taking a pleasure trip (!) on the lovely Bistritza, and that the scenery *should* have been glorious, bathed in evening sunlight. It is very fine, even seen through the rain. The mountains, grandly wooded to the water's edge, leave sometimes quite a narrow gorge. There are windings innumerable, and many rapids which increase in strength as we advance, and the Bistritza is swollen by the wild rushing waters of the Bicassu. The rapids have the appearance of a miniature boiling sea with curling wavelets, hissing and seething round the points of rock; they seem to advance to meet the float. Suddenly the front man is churning the waves with a circular sweep of the long paddle. One leg high in air, every nerve and tendon quivering, the whole weight of the little, lithe, muscular body is thrown on to the pole, that bends and threatens to snap with the strain; then a swirl round, and instantly, the paddle immovable! and calm, swift gliding onward.

Hours pass on, and still we turn bend after bend of the river. Now we are running straight for a great buttress of black rock rising menacingly before our frail raft; the swift current rushes, tossed and seething, round its base; the point of the float almost touches the dark, jagged headland, is caught by the descending rush of foaming waters, and sent quivering, but safe, almost into mid-stream. Then more eddies, with the planks of the raft gleaming through the froth and foam.

In our course we had passed many smaller rafts stranded and more or less dilapidated; and our float in less skilful hands might well have met with some disaster, but at length our gipsy declares that we cannot reach Piatra that night; we must be landed at the nearest convenient spot. Protest was useless. The day was fast sinking—gloom was settling dark and drear over the swollen river and the forest-clad mountains. In sad silence the raft is steered on to a muddy bank, up which a forlorn and bedraggled party climb and stumble to reach a small hamlet on the high-road.

Here they tell us that we may perhaps get a conveyance into the town if fortunate enough to capture a passing vehicle, and we enter meanwhile a cottage of very questionable appearance to wait for this slender chance. It is crowded with soldiers in undress, some peasants, and a group of pretty Moldavian girls. The place reeks with "raki" and smoke. We conclude that this festive gathering has been the real aim of our raftsmen throughout the day.

A small chaise comes rattling along, and stops for a minute. Can we find place there? It is a private conveyance; the owner sits behind his coachman; the small space remaining is crowded with parcels, but he will make room for one. We are three ladies; we must go together or not at all, yet to remain in that uncanny drinking-house is not to be thought of. The owner of the little chaise, with a kindness that will be long remembered, compassionates our distress, and we crowd up five where three should be. Happily the frail carriage does not break down, and the little wiry horse trots along with his increased load as if nothing unusual had happened.

It is ten o'clock before we reach Piatra, in a fearfully limp and helpless condition. I had unexpectedly collapsed, am put rapidly to bed with hot bricks to the feet, and the compassionate landlady proceeds to energetic remedies—strong friction with vinegar to restore circulation. She works with untiring vigour over all my various bruises until I groan with agony, for one cannot get up and down bullock-carts quite unscathed. They are all very kind, however, and do their utmost for us, according to their lights.

Not least among the small trials of the succeeding

days of weakness was the infliction of a brass band in the garden of the restaurant belonging to the hotel. There were times when it "executed," with short intervals, during the whole day and evening, the "repertoire," decidedly limited—chiefly native airs, which are in themselves beautiful, but this rendering was excruciating.

On the eighth day after our wet voyage down the Bistritza we prepared to leave Piatra to seek medical advice and rest among the comforts and civilisation of Vienna, giving up with much regret the latter part of our scheme of travel. It had been planned to turn southwards to visit the mineral baths of Slanik and the great salt-mines of Okna, and so by carriage to Krondstadt and Hermandstadt to visit the Southern Carpathians, and reach the Austrian capital by the Danube.

We left Piatra with many mutual expressions of good-will. The expenses of our stay in the Hotel Bistritza were very moderate, and we felt really sorry to say good-bye to these worthy people, particularly to the household drudge, Maritza, who had tears in her eyes as she looked after us from the doorstep. She generally pattered about with bare feet, and her usual attire might have been more in order; but a very gentle, loving heart beat beneath that faded cotton jacket. We gave her our photographs in a group (done on the premises). "Taré biné! taré biné! moltè frumosi!" she exclaimed over and over again as it was slipped into her pocket, and I verily believe that the poor soul valued this remembrance as much as the very substantial parting fee she had so well earned by her untiring and cheerful service.

It was an extremely dirty, but otherwise fairly good, carriage that took us to Romàn, the nearest station on the railway to Vienna. The country is undulating and well cultivated, but the beautiful mountain peaks are fading in the distance, and the wealth of wild flowers has diminished.

We chiefly note the passage of large parties of Zecklers, winding along the road in their slow bullock-carts, in search of harvesting work. The women are very fair, with masses of flaxen hair, which the unmarried girls arrange in the most grotesque fashion, tying it very high up, where it is divided, twisted tightly round some stiff band, and then forms two monstrous rings, standing as wide out from the head as possible.

We reach Romàn after a drive of five hours, paying as we pass the barrier the toll that is exacted at the entrance of all Roumanian towns; at the same time the coachman is required to remove the bells from the horses' heads.

## XIX.

### IN CRETE.

#### NO. I.—CANEA AND ITS ENVIRONS.

In the Harbour of Canea.—Rethymo.—Brother Geronimo.—Arrival at Canea.—The Convent Parlour.—An Improvised Home.—A Street Scene.—Our Opposite Neighbour.—The Grocer's Shop. — Cretan Costume. — Funerals. — Twelve o'clock. — The former Lords of the Island. — Ancient Costumes.—Raouf Pasha.—Unusual Visitors.—The Rhiza and he White Mountains.—Aloes.

ONE bright May morning, a few years since, I entered the harbour of Candia, on board a steamer of the Austrian Lloyds; the anchor was cast between the massive battlemented walls of the Venetian fortifications that formerly protected the entrance of the port.

What a picturesque scene! What a singular mingling of East and West does this port of Candia offer to the spectator! The immense vaulted ruins of the arsenal recall the vanished glories of Venetian galleys that once found shelter there; while the Lion of St. Mark—boldly sculptured on the wall of the great bastion—seems still to defy the dreamy East, with its golden sunlight, its palm-trees, seen here and there above the battlements; the turbans, the veils, the languor, the neglect, the decay of all surrounding objects. The little boats scattered over the blue waters of the port make no choice between these contrasting claims, and elude the question by painting, on either side of the rudder, the lion of the past and the crescent of to-day.

At the foot of the great tower some old bronze cannon—relics of the Venetian occupation—lie on the shore, half buried in fallen stones and sand; a few Turkish soldiers are seated on them, swinging their feet and munching their lumps of black bread; other idlers, grouped on a block of masonry that has lain there for centuries, gaze vacantly at the steamer; and all is reflected in water of the deepest azure, that sends a joyous sparkling ripple across the streak of sunlight.

The boat that carries the weekly mails between Syra and the Cretan coast, does not remain in harbour a sufficient time to allow of visiting the city, the Greek name of which is Megàlo Kastron (the Great Fortress); the Venetians called it Candia, a name that is used also for the island, which the Turks call Kirit, and the Europeans, either Candia or Crete, indifferently.

Some hours later the boat stopped in the roadstead before Rethymo, at the foot of the fortress that crowns a high rocky eminence on the west; two or three palm-trees, and some minarets, varied by glittering church crosses, show the position of the town. Around the bay a few swelling hills pleasantly wooded, country houses, olives and vineyards, a small fort upon the shore, and—far off amongst the clouds—the vague outline of Mount Ida, compose all the impression that can be formed of Rethymo, before yielding once more to the agitated character of these Cretan waters.

At length the rolling slackens; the breeze, always, at this season, strong during the afternoon, sinks as the sun nears the horizon; the traveller—who may be a bad sailor—comes back to mundane interests, and climbing on to the deck, quickly loses all remembrance of past discomfort under the renovating influence of the cool starry heavens, and the mysterious vapoury outlines of the coast.

A group of persons, talking briskly in Italian, drew me to that part of the deck, and I discover that we have taken on board at Candia a Latin archbishop, going to Canea, with three Franciscan brethren in full costume of woollen robes, girdles, and sandals. The worthy archbishop is explaining, gently and rather slowly, that Canea does not possess a hotel for travellers, but he proposes to offer us the use of an empty house, in the enclosure of the convent, and beside the dwelling occupied by the

Sisters of St. Joseph. This offer is briskly urged by Brother Geronimo—a Sicilian, quick, active, merry, and most obliging—who, as soon as the harbour is reached, superintends the disembarkation of a large amount of luggage, which he passes through the custom house without examination, as goods going to the convent. It may be observed that it was then the rule that all goods arriving in a Turkish port, destined for the use of a religious house or of a Christian mission, were entirely exempt from duty.

In a few minutes we are quietly threading, towards midnight, the silent streets of Canea—a little procession of two ladies, with a servant, escorted by an archbishop and by three barefooted friars! The great door of the convent is soon reached, and we are conducted to the reception-room, where the reverend Father Superior receives us with the greatest politeness. Black coffee is served; and conversation, at first animated, begins to languish, then continues with long pauses, during which we ask ourselves, wearily, what can have become of the promised house, the longed-for rest?

Alas! we hear a whisper that our dwelling is, as yet, absolutely empty! The telegram sent from Rethymo had preceded our arrival only by a few minutes! What was to be done? resign ourselves to the inevitable? Doubtless; for the Sicilian brother is rushing about, hastening the preparations. He carries off part of the simple furniture of the convent; he borrows of the Sisters, of the neighbours; he arranges and disposes everything, with so much activity and good-will, that one could not show impatience. The next day, other furniture, hired in the neighbourhood, completed our installation.

The first glance from the window is a disappointment: there is no *view!* A small side glimpse of azure mountains promises fine scenery; but the real subject of the picture is a narrow street, the principal artery of commerce in Canea. Well, let us be satisfied, even with these limited attractions. The passers-by in a strange country are always interesting, and the sketch of one morning will serve to describe all the mornings during our six weeks' stay, so quiet and prosperous seems the life here, in spite of political agitations and of the restless, discontented nature of the Cretan population.

At six o'clock the street begins to awake. A heavy shop shutter is thrown up with a clang and fixed; then other shutters, some fastened sideways. A few foot passengers, donkeys, and mules clatter along the rough pavement. One hears a heavy, irregular rumble; it is the dust-cart, for the chief streets of Canea are carefully kept.

There is talking under our window; let us look out. On the opposite side of the street stands a well-built house. The ground floor is divided into three shops—a chemist's, a grocer's, and a small café. The first floor stands back in the shadow of a broad balcony, but towards seven o'clock a glass door opens, and the lady of the house, a Greek, comes out and leans upon the balustrade. She wears a French dressing-gown, and her splendid hair falls in thick braids upon her shoulders, whilst she slowly sips her black coffee, indifferent to the early studies of little hands that are playing, somewhere in the background, an air from "Norma," followed by "La Mère Angot," quite out of time and with numerous false notes.

Beneath the balcony the grocer's shop gradually becomes animated. On the open front, olives, soap, and leather fill the places of honour, sustained by rolls of cord, barrels of rice, slices of dried mutton, and clusters of candles. The grocer himself, carelessly seated on a sack of flour, reads his newspaper, whilst a little Arab blacks his great boots—a real little Arab, wearing a yellow-white turban. A mountaineer from Sphakia examines the squares of leather. He is a tall, handsome youth, straight, vigorous, and energetic; he carries a goat's-hair sack, hanging round the neck, and has boots up to the knees—the yellow boots of the country, excessively supple, and supposed to protect the wearer from the bite of serpents. The Cretan costume, with the exception of these high boots, differs little from that of the other inhabitants of the Greek islands: a sleeveless waistcoat, laced in the back and very much open on the breast, wide pantaloons in blue cotton, and the red fez, soft and long, with a great blue tassel hanging on the shoulder.

Two or three idlers crouched on small stools at the door of the café are smoking, while they discuss the news freshly arrived from Syra and Athens, or listen open-mouthed to a Greek peasant in "fustanelle" and long shoes, their points strongly curved upwards and adorned with large black tassels.

Suddenly everyone moves at the cry of a group of negro hamals, who advance slowly and with difficulty, carrying, suspended between long poles, a great bale of leather, which nearly fills the street, and sways in an alarming manner. The negro porters encourage their effort by a sort of measured howl.

The population of Canea is by this time in movement. The Arab women flit by enveloped in white winding-sheets; the negresses display their gay colouring amid their floating draperies; the Turk wears the turban or the fez, according to his preference for ancient or modern customs; coaches roll noisily over the stones; there are equipages and even street carriages at Canea.

A chant which reaches us from the neighbouring

mosque announces the passage of a Mussulman funeral. This procession differs in many respects from those at Constantinople; they seem to have preserved here some customs of the Christian rite—the coffin is preceded by two boys carrying incense, and is followed by a great crowd of Greeks and of Mussulman Cretans. The bier is covered with red silk veils and gauze, above the usual shawls, and a garland of artificial flowers, mixed with gold, surrounds the pointed end which marks the head and is carried forwards. It 'is a woman's funeral, and while it passes a monotonous chant is kept up by the funeral train. The porters of the bier change almost at every minute; for them it is both a sacred duty and a meritorious action.

Funeral processions are frequent in this street, that leads from the great mosque to the gate of the city and the Mussulman cemetery adjoining. A little later and the funeral chant is again heard. This time it is a man's bier, recognisable by the turban on the high point of the coffin, which is covered in black cloth embroidered in large Arabic characters. A man carrying two bunches of flowers fixed in earthen pots opens the procession; he is followed by the incense-bearers.

In the neighbourhood of our house the sonorous voice of a large clock announces the Turkish hour. On the stroke of twelve (sunset) all the shops are closed as if by magic; shutters are again clapped down, deep silence falls on the busy street, and the profound peace is only broken at rare intervals by the roll of a belated coach, the whistle of the night watchman, or the feeble tremor of the telegraph wires.

Canea—called by the Turks Khânia—is the centre of government for the island. You find there the konak, or residence of the governor, the consulates, the steamboat offices, and the chief commercial houses. The consuls, as also some families of wealthy merchants, have their private dwellings at Khalépa, a village covering a rising ground at half-an-hour's distance to the south-east of the city.

The principal streets—especially those inhabited by the Mussulmans, the most ancient portion of Canea—are well paved and clean; named and numbered. In these old quarters many of the massive stone houses still bear the coats-of-arms of their former Venetian occupants, sculptured above the great entrance-gates, most of the old Cretan families having had a Greek or Italian origin. The language in general use is Greek.

The island of Crete, so celebrated in the fables of mythology and in the Greek and Roman annals, was sold to the Venetians in 1204 by Baldwin, Marquis of Montferrat. It was colonised half a century later. The Venetians raised the fine fortifications that still surround the town, and Canea became at that time a place of considerable importance.

In 1669 Crete fell under the Turkish domination, and at a later time was given by Sultan Mahmoud to the celebrated Mehemet Ali Pasha, Viceroy of Egypt. It subsequently became once more a part of the Ottoman Empire.

The principal wealth of the island consists of olives, oranges, wine, soap, and the cheeses of Sphakia: all these articles are largely exported throughout the Levant. Canea is the centre of Cretan commerce, but the chief industry of the city appears to be the manufacture of leather boots and shoes, which are renowned for their durability and softness. The women, both Mussulman and Christian, spin and weave a strong cloth, as well as very handsome many-coloured striped coverlets of woollen or cotton.

In the districts removed from European innovations, some of the old costumes may still be found: women's garments, richly embroidered in colours, the designs bearing evident traces of Venetian taste and style; but these curious relics of high-art needle-work are not much in favour with the Cretan dames, who prefer any modern tinsel to the heavy splendours of their grandmothers. Mr. Sandwith, lately H.B.M. Consul in Crete, made, during his long residence in the island, a very large and beautiful collection of these ancient embroideries, bought at a very high price, for the Cretan peasant woman knows how to make a large profit on her "antiquities," if she sets small store by them as wearing apparel.

Canea owes much of its present comfort and prosperity to Raouf Pasha, who has been three times Vali, or Governor, of the island, where his gentle, conciliatory rule gained him universal good-will. Amongst other important undertakings—such as the establishment and encouragement of schools and industrial enterprises—he has bestowed on the town a fine public garden outside the fortifications; some good roads—that especially leading to the great natural harbour of Suda Bay; a service of street carriages, very well organised, and (if I mistake not) the electric telegraph, street lighting, and other minor improvements. These signs of progress have conferred on Canea an appearance of civilisation that the traveller would scarcely expect.

A good hotel is still wanting in this capital of old Crete; without it tourists can make no stay in this charming and healthy spot. From time to time a yacht will cast its anchor in the port of Canea; the visitors skim over the environs, and probably examine the arsenal at Suda, but they do not extend their excursions to the mountains, and shortly re-embarking, the yacht spreads its white wings for other shores. Strangers, especially ladies, coming

to Crete with the intention of making a few weeks'
stay, are so unusual, that our installation produced
an extraordinary sensation, which served the gossips
for conversation and conjecture until a fresh event
startled the town. Surprises came thickly. A gentleman had landed the previous night from the
steamer: an English tourist, who was also endeavouring to find a lodging for a few weeks!
What *could* these unexpected arrivals mean? The
new-comer began in the most inoffensive manner to
make painted studies of the types and costumes of
the country; he was perfectly quiet and unobtrusive;
but—but—in short, what *can* have brought him to
Crete? Very evidently there was a mystery.

I have as yet spoken only of the town, but I
longed to see, to explore, those sun-bathed slopes,
that the small opening in the street displayed under
a thousand fairy-like tints; to have a nearer enjoyment of those aromatic plants that perfumed even
the narrow roadway of the city; and one balmy
evening, soon after our arrival, I took an open
carriage at the station beyond the ramparts, and
rolled easily along the good road towards Suda Bay.

I had left the town, passing at first through a
rough street, and by the sombre vaulted passage
under the Venetian fortifications, which is at all
times encumbered by horses and mules, by Cretans,
Levantines, Arabs, negroes, and negresses: on the

outer side is a small market-place for fruits and vegetables. The road follows for a few minutes the line of the moat, then by a sudden turn to the right brings you to the public garden. But one can have no thought for this garden, however pretty it may be: the open country spreads before us its illimitable beauties, dazzling, majestic, or tender, as the eye may fall on the beautifully wooded plain, with its villages and " tchiftliks" half buried in the rich masses of foliage; or rise to the high uplands of the Riza, clothed with a verdure tenderly veiled by distance. Above these heights again the eye follows with delight the gigantic outline of the White Mountains of Sphakia, every golden crag and peak rising from the azure and violet haze of its deep gorges, and reposes at length upon the highest summits, scarcely traced upon the blue heavens by lines of eternal snow.

The high road, as also many smaller lanes, are bordered by hedges of aloes, which here attain to an extraordinary height and strength: these hedges, frequently mixed with cactus, form a perfectly impenetrable barrier. Many of the aloes were on the point of flowering, throwing up their flower-stalks, tall and straight as the masts of a small ship, and already budding with yellow-grey blossoms. These stalks reach to 15 or 20 feet of height; the massive flowers measure more than half a yard in diameter.

The great abundance of the aloe in Crete, makes one regret that the inhabitants should not, as yet, have turned the fibre to profitable use. It is employed by the women of Cephalonia to make a delicate but rather perishable sort of lace.

The Cretans regard as a fable the idea so generally received, that the aloe blossoms but once in a century; they declare that the plant produces its flowers with an interval of a few years; but they add a fable of their own invention, according to which they predict misfortunes and public disasters whenever the aloe hedges are more than usually flourishing. During the summer of our visit the aloes around Canea were loaded with blossom.

## XX.

### IN CRETE.

#### NO. II.—CANEA AND ITS ENVIRONS.

Church Mosques.—The Ancient Arsenal of the Galleys.—Venetian Fortifications.—The Negro Village.—Arab Huts.—Street Carriages.—The Leper Settlement.—Red Earth and Olive-trees.—Murniés.—Yorghi, the Coffee-seller.—Honey and Travelling Bees.—"Lâvdanum."—The Spring of Perivoglia.—View from the Terrace.—The Garden of Munir Agha.—Fine Orange-trees.—Khalépa.

THREE of the principal mosques of Canea are especially worthy of notice as having been formerly Christian churches. That in the high street, once the cathedral of the city, stands near the Latin convent. The interior of the nave is long and narrow. It is separated from its side aisles by pillars with sculptured capitals ; the exterior shows remains of a square tower, ornamented by small columns.

The second church-mosque, which still bears traces of fine Gothic work, has been almost destroyed by earthquake ; but the third monument that we visited possesses a side chapel in such good preservation, with its high pointed arches and groined roof, that one almost expects to hear the solemn strains of a Christian chant, and, quitting the twilight of the deserted chapel for the brilliant sunshine of the portico, it is difficult at first to realise the situation. On one side of this half-ruined monument are found the remains of an ancient monastery, and of a cemetery surrounded by Gothic cloisters.

It is in the harbour of Canea that the finest remains of those high vaults, built by the Venetians for the use of their galleys, may still be seen. Nine of these, in good preservation, form two sides of the interior basin, and serve as an admirable foreground to the picturesque masses of the ancient city—its houses of old stone, bronzed by the burning sun of this southern climate; its wooden dwellings, blue or rose-coloured; its terraced roofs or spreading eaves; all this warmth and brilliancy repeated in the still waters, and backed by the majestic range of the snowy mountains of Sphakia.

The Venetian fortifications still defend Canea on the south and east by moat and rampart and noble bastions. On the massive tower that protects the eastern entrance a stone entablature displays St. Mark's "Lion" in his most bellicose aspect: he hurls defiance at the negro village grouped at the foot of the southern fort.

This village, composed of small, square, flat-roofed houses, is inhabited by the negro colony originally transported hither by Mehemet Ali, of Egypt. A small mosque occupies the centre of the little settlement. It is whitewashed all over (as are the houses), with the exception of the minaret, that shoots upwards coloured a flaming red. Two houses of the village, belonging to brothers who had enriched themselves by their work, put forth some pretension to superiority. All this negro population is industrious.

The negroes have planted their village on the seashore. The Arabs, faithful to their native taste, constructed theirs on a great bare space of sand, rather farther inland and on the other side of the high road between Canea and Khalépa. Their huts, wattled and deeply thatched, are sometimes surrounded by palisades. Here and there an Arab, majestically draped in a dirty blanket, contemplates the stranger for a distance without deigning to manifest curiosity or surprise. A native of Benghazi passes with a floating movement of his beautiful creamy bournous; some children, neatly dressed in earrings and necklace of glass beads, make mud-pies and clamour for "backshish," apparently for the trouble of having looked up. It is a little morsel of Africa, transported to Crete to give one more touch of exotic originality to the plains at the foot of the lofty peak of Akrotiri.

Let us turn now towards the west, following the moat of the great Venetian ramparts. We are soon at the office for street carriages, established by Raouf Pasha. These coaches can be taken by distance or by the hour; the fares are exceedingly moderate and strictly regulated. It is high civilisation; and if you do not propose to pass beyond the Bay of Suda or the immediate environs of Canea, the roads and the conveyance are perfect. But if you attempt to follow the ancient tracks, the fearful plunges with which all travellers in the East are familiar, begin at once. However, the real traveller will resign himself willingly to this suffering, that is leading him towards points of beauty unknown to the fastidious tourist. We will leave the smooth highway, and traverse, without unnecessary delay, the third hamlet in the environs of the city. To the inhabitants of these sad dwellings, more even than to those of the negro and Arab settlements, it is forbidden to live in the town. These miserable people may not so much as enter it; it is the *leper* village!

Small white cottages bordering a lane hedged by aloes and cactus; some lofty trees; a beautiful open country, with white and snowy mountains in the distance; here and there a horse, a donkey, or a goat cropping the soft grass under the hedge; fowls pecking about; some pretty children playing in the sunshine, and even young girls neatly dressed, who suspend their household labours to gaze at the passing stranger: such is the scene, that causes an impression of pleased surprise, too soon, alas! dissipated. A second glance will reveal the sad aspect of this abode of misfortune. Afflicted beings enveloped, in spite of the great heat, in thick cloaks of coarse wool, the hoods pulled low over the face, drag their feeble limbs, or crouch on matting or in the dust, begging vaguely. Some ask alms for occupation, for the Government allows to each leper one large loaf a day, and some amongst them have owned olive-fields, vineyards, and property, the produce of which is brought to them by friends.

The lepers assembled at the gates of Canea have been brought from all the surrounding districts. As soon as the first symptoms of this fearful malady become evident, the person so terribly afflicted is doomed to leave, at once and for ever, home and family, and to make his abode amidst those living spectres. Young women are here, still preserving an appearance of youth and personal attractions; children are born here, rosy and fresh, and seemingly in rude health. All, alas! are doomed to slow and hideous decay. The skin becomes discoloured and takes a livid hue; the fingers, the hands, the features gradually disappear, eaten by the leprosy, and the last sad state of a being who has no longer human form is hidden from all eyes by the enshrouding cloak and the concealing hood.

In the centre of the poor hamlet there is a well

used by the lepers, and it is here that friends lay down their offerings; they cannot be otherwise given.

The people of this country attribute the existence of leprosy principally to the unwholesome food of the mass of the population, and particularly of the Greeks. They live almost entirely on salted meat and fish, and use immoderate quantities of olive oil. They take this oil with everything; a morsel of bread even is never eaten without it. Oil is one of the chief products of Crete, which can be procured with fatal ease.

The town of Candia, and also (as I believe) Rethymo, have outside their gates leper villages similar to that at Canea.

One breathes more freely after leaving these sad homes of suffering. Ah! how fresh and beautiful is the open country! The road crosses a little bridge turning in the direction of the Rhiza—the green and smiling spurs of the high Sphakiote mountains. The air is fragrant with the scent of thousands of aromatic plants that carpet the rough ground; then you reach vast fields of olives—tall, full, and leafy as forest trees—that throw the shadow of their spreading branches across the bright red earth. So red, indeed, is it, that the tuft of grass or the shoot of young corn appears by contrast tinged with a fine sky-blue. I have nowhere remarked earth so deeply red as that of Crete: may it be for this reason that the olive here attains a height and strength far superior to the olive growth in southern France or Italy? Many of the stately trees date from the Venetian times; they may be recognised by their enormous trunks, bent and twisted into a thousand strange and picturesque coils.

The road soon afterwards sinks between orange plantations, protected by hedges where the aloe and cactus are mingled with high bushes of myrtle in full flower; and as we gradually draw near the hills, the deep ravines (at present dry) blush with the rich colouring of the oleander; on the edge of the gully the waving plumes of tall ferns and of the dwarf palm complete the graceful picture.

We reach the village of Murniés, and the carriage stops under the vine trellis that serves as entrance to a rustic " café." The " câvedji " comes out in haste; he wears the Cretan dress: sleeveless waistcoat, large red waistband, the soft fez, and the high yellow boots. He offers the glass of water that precedes the coffee; it is perfumed with orange flower, and the coffee itself partakes of this national essence, which harmonises but badly with its natural aroma.

This man is an active, enterprising spirit, uniting many callings, as an inspector of rural police, the guide of occasional strangers, the master of the village coffee-house, and the owner of various houses and gardens, orange and olive groves. When troubles broke out in Crete, in 1866, Yorghi *went away* (as they say here, to indicate politely the condition of an insurgent), and it was from this village —perhaps even from his hand—that the first shot was fired which began the war. When peace was made he came home, married, and seemed to settle down. They gave him a small post of authority, in order to keep him in hand. His friends affirm that in spite of the wife, and the orange groves, and his official dignity, the fiery Yorghi is quite ready to go away again at the first opportunity; but, whilst awaiting a more brilliant destiny, he discharges his peaceful duties as "câvedji" and guide, to the complete satisfaction of the public. It is evident, however, that recollections of past struggles often recur to him; they are especially vivid before the ruins of a chapel, where thirty of the enemy had taken refuge. He boasts of having made three prisoners, whom he took to the mountains; "but he did not kill them," explains a friendly apologist; and Yorghi, suddenly remembering that he, an inspector of police, is treading on dangerous ground, adroitly changes the conversation. "I can show you the most beautiful fountain in these parts," said he. "Oh! such beautiful water! It is quite near, in the shade of those lime-trees." What can be more innocent than a peaceful fountain? It is infinitely more delightful to contemplate than the scene of a bloody struggle, and—the dangerous reminiscences are forgotten.*

Much honey is made in the environs of Murniés and of Perivoglia, a charming village on the mountain side, embosomed in orange groves, plane-trees, and olives. The hives are baskets, reversed, and thatched with heather. The quality of the honey is most excellent, for the peasants, not satisfied with the great abundance of aromatic plants that cover the ground, send their bees in their hives, for change of air and nourishment, to the perfumed slopes of the Akrotiri.

In this part of the country the myrtle hedges are very luxuriant, and (in the season) covered with the delicate perfumed blossoms; but the shrub which principally scents the air, and which is found here in profusion, is the "lâvdanum," mentioned by old authors as a Cretan production. The leaves of this shrub exude a thick gum, which is collected by whipping the branches with leather thongs. This gum is supposed to possess medicinal virtues.

Above the village of Perivoglia you may see the spring of water that supplies Canea and the environs: it rushes from the heart of the mountain into a

---

* A few years later, I was again in Crete, and once more visited the beautiful slopes of Perivoglia. Yorghi was there, looking very much dilapidated, and with a great sword-cut disfiguring his left cheek: he had evidently *been away* to some purpose in the interval.

natural basin at the end of a short subterranean passage, and thence into the plain by a series of well-constructed conduits. On the terrace beside the spring a little café has been established in the angle of a grey rock, where a large vaulted niche, partly natural, shows, as the key-stone of the arch, a sculptured head which seems of ancient date. It is said that this spot is the site of the summer palace of the Venetian governors.

This terrace of Perivoglia is a favourite rendezvous for holiday-makers from Canea. It is delightful to rest in the shadow of its spreading plane-trees, soothed by the cool ripple of the spring, and to gaze down on the heaving billows of foliage that cover the slopes and spread out at the foot of the mountain until they melt in the broad stretch of yellow sand that marks the shore and completes the exquisite colouring of the picture by its contrast with the deep ultramarine of the wide expanse of the Mediterranean. Against this azure background the red ramparts and snowy minarets of Canea stand out in clear relief: on the right, the chain of the Akrotiri stretches its bold promontory, and ends in a majestic crag of extraordinary beauty of outline.

One of the finest gardens near Murniés belongs to a certain Munir Agha, whose son, Ali Bey, most politely showed us over it. This garden is not so vast as the property of Hamdy Bey, that everyone agrees to extol, but it is infinitely better cultivated. The paths, bordered with rose-trees heavy with blossom, surround large square plots, where oranges in every variety, lemon, citron, apricot, peach, plum, and nectarine, flourish in perfection.

Orange-trees here reach the height of 45 or 50 feet. The crop varies very much according to the season: a tree may give two or three hundred oranges, as it may produce at another time three thousand. Ali Bey showed us a tree that had once yielded as many as five thousand oranges. The fruit, which is of the finest quality and flavour, is sold on the spot for one Turkish pound (18s. 2d.) the thousand; it is exported in large quantities to Constantinople and to all the ports of the Levant.

The extreme purity of the air in Crete is remarked by all travellers, and the invigorating, vivifying nature of the climate of the hills and the breezy uplands can scarcely be surpassed; but a residence in the low-lying grounds, in the midst of beautiful but rank vegetation, is extremely unhealthy: the winter torrents rushing from the mountains form (during several months of the year) stagnant swamps, the inevitable source of intermittent fevers.

In the environs of Canea the finest and most salubrious air is found at Khalépa, a hill-side rather stony, rather wanting in trees, compared to the luxuriant vegetation of the plain and of the lower slopes of the Rhiza; but this bareness is forgotten before the magnificent panorama of the bay of Canea and of the point of Suda. From a healthy eminence, scented by a multitude of aromatic plants, that rises behind the English Consulate, the view is magnificent; and those who have once gazed on it, and who may have enjoyed the frank and cordial hospitality of that stone house in the midst of the heather, will carry with them from Canea, and above all, from Khalépa, a happy and imperishable remembrance.

THE END.

PRINTED BY J. S. VIRTUE AND CO., LIMITED, CITY ROAD, LONDON.

11, HENRIETTA STREET, COVENT GARDEN, W.C.

APRIL, 1886.

A

# 𝕮𝖆𝖙𝖆𝖑𝖔𝖌𝖚𝖊 𝖔𝖋 𝕭𝖔𝖔𝖐𝖘

PUBLISHED BY

## CHAPMAN & HALL, LIMITED,

INCLUDING

*Drawing Examples, Diagrams, Models, Instruments, etc.,*

ISSUED UNDER THE AUTHORITY OF

### THE SCIENCE AND ART DEPARTMENT, SOUTH KENSINGTON,

FOR THE USE OF SCHOOLS AND ART AND SCIENCE CLASSES.

# THOMAS CARLYLE'S WORKS.

Messrs. CHAPMAN & HALL beg to announce that an entirely New Edition of the Writings of Mr. Carlyle, to be completed in Seventeen Volumes, demy 8vo, is now publishing, called

## THE ASHBURTON EDITION.

This Edition is handsomely printed and contains the Portraits and Illustrations, and is issued in Monthly Volumes, at Eight Shillings a Volume, viz. :

| Vol. | | | |
|---|---|---|---|
| 1. | THE FRENCH REVOLUTION. Vol. 1. | | [*Ready*. |
| 2. | THE FRENCH REVOLUTION AND PAST AND PRESENT. | | [*Ready*. |
| 3. | SARTOR RESARTUS; HEROES AND HERO WORSHIP. | | [*Ready*. |
| 4. | LIFE OF JOHN STERLING—LIFE OF SCHILLER. | | [*Ready*. |
| 5. | LATTER-DAY PAMPHLETS—EARLY KINGS OF NORWAY—ESSAY ON THE PORTRAIT OF JOHN KNOX. | | [*Ready*. |
| 6. | LETTERS AND SPEECHES OF OLIVER CROMWELL. Vol. 1. | | [*Ready*. |
| 7. | Ditto ditto ,, 2. | | [*Ready*. |
| 8. | Ditto ditto ,, 3. | | [*Ready*. |
| 9. | HISTORY OF FREDERICK THE GREAT. Vol. 1. | | [*Ready*. |
| 10. | Ditto ditto ,, 2. | | [*Ready*. |
| 11. | Ditto ditto ,, 3. | | |
| 12. | Ditto ditto ,, 4. | | |
| 13. | Ditto ditto ,, 5. | | |
| 14. | Ditto ditto ,, 6. | | |
| 15. | CRITICAL AND MISCELLANEOUS ESSAYS. Vol. 1. | | |
| 16. | Ditto ditto ,, 2. | | |
| 17. | Ditto ditto ,, 3. | | |

Ten Volumes are now ready.

# BOOKS

PUBLISHED BY

# CHAPMAN & HALL, LIMITED.

*ABLETT (T. R.)—*
WRITTEN DESIGN. Oblong, sewed, 6d.

*ABOUT (EDMOND)—*
HANDBOOK OF SOCIAL ECONOMY; OR, THE WORKER'S A B C. From the French. With a Biographical and Critical Introduction by W. FRASER RAE. Second Edition, revised. Crown 8vo, 4s.

THE ARMIES OF THE NATIVE STATES OF INDIA. Reprinted from the *Times* by permission. Crown 8vo, 4s.

*BADEN-POWELL (GEORGE)—*
STATE AID AND STATE INTERFERENCE. Illustrated by Results in Commerce and Industry. Crown 8vo, 9s.

*BARTLEY (G. C. T.)—*
A HANDY BOOK FOR GUARDIANS OF THE POOR. Crown 8vo, cloth, 3s.

BAYARD: HISTORY OF THE GOOD CHEVALIER, SANS PEUR ET SANS REPROCHE. Compiled by the LOYAL SERVITEUR; translated into English from the French of Loredan Larchey. With over 200 Illustrations. Royal 8vo, 21s.

*BELL (DR. JAMES), Principal of the Somerset House Laboratory—*
THE CHEMISTRY OF FOODS. With Microscopic Illustrations.
PART I. TEA, COFFEE, SUGAR, ETC. Large crown 8vo, 2s. 6d.
PART II. MILK BUTTER, CEREALS, PREPARED STARCHES, ETC. Large crown 8vo, 3s.

BENNET (WILLIAM)—

 KING OF THE PEAK: a Romance. With Portrait.
 Crown 8vo, 6s.

BENSON (W.)—

 MANUAL OF THE SCIENCE OF COLOUR. Coloured
 Frontispiece and Illustrations. 12mo, cloth, 2s. 6d.

 PRINCIPLES OF THE SCIENCE OF COLOUR. Small
 4to, cloth, 15s.

BINGHAM (CAPT. THE HON. D.)—

 A SELECTION FROM THE LETTERS AND
 DESPATCHES OF THE FIRST NAPOLEON. With Explanatory Notes.
 3 vols. demy 8vo, £2 2s.

 THE BASTILLE: Its History and Chronicles. [In the Press.

BIRDWOOD (SIR GEORGE C. M.), C.S.I.—

 THE INDUSTRIAL ARTS OF INDIA. With Map and
 174 Illustrations. New Edition. Demy 8vo, 14s.

BLACKIE (JOHN STUART), F.R.S.E.—

 THE SCOTTISH HIGHLANDERS AND THE LAND
 LAWS. Demy 8vo, 9s.

 ALTAVONA: FACT AND FICTION FROM MY LIFE
 IN THE HIGHLANDS. Third Edition. Crown 8vo, 6s.

BLATHERWICK (DR.)—

 PERSONAL RECOLLECTIONS OF PETER STONNOR,
 Esq. With Illustrations by JAMES GUTHRIE and A. S. BOYD. Large crown 8vo, 6s.

BLOOMFIELD'S (BENJAMIN LORD), MEMOIR OF—
 MISSION TO THE COURT OF BERNADOTTE. Edited by GEORGIANA,
 BARONESS BLOOMFIELD, Author of "Reminiscences of Court and Diplomatic Life."
 With Portraits. 2 Vols. demy 8vo, 28s.

BOYLE (FREDERICK)—

 ON THE BORDERLAND—BETWIXT THE REALMS
 OF FACT AND FANCY. Crown 8vo, 10s. 6d.

BOULGER (DEMETRIUS C.)—

 GENERAL GORDON'S LETTERS FROM THE
 CRIMEA, THE DANUBE, AND ARMENIA. 2nd Edition. Crown 8vo, 5s.

**BRADLEY (THOMAS),** *of the Royal Military Academy, Woolwich—*

    ELEMENTS OF GEOMETRICAL DRAWING. In Two
        Parts, with Sixty Plates. Oblong folio, half bound, each Part 16s.

**BRAY (MRS.)—**

    AUTOBIOGRAPHY OF (born 1789, died 1883).
        Author of the "Life of Thomas Stothard, R.A.," "The White Hoods," &c.
        Edited by JOHN A. KEMPE. With Portraits. Crown 8vo, 10s. 6d.

## MRS. BRAY'S NOVELS AND ROMANCES.

*New and Revised Editions, with Frontispieces.* 3s. 6d. each.

THE WHITE HOODS; a Romance of Flanders.
DE FOIX; a Romance of Bearn.
THE TALBA; or, The Moor of Portugal.
THE PROTESTANT; a Tale of the Times of Queen Mary.

### NOVELS FOUNDED ON TRADITIONS OF DEVON AND CORNWALL.

FITZ OF FITZFORD; a Tale of Destiny.
HENRY DE POMEROY; or, the Eve of St. John.
TRELAWNY OF TRELAWNE; or, a Romance of the West.
WARLEIGH; or, The Fatal Oak.
COURTENAY OF WALREDDON; a Romance of the West.
HARTLAND FOREST AND ROSE-TEAGUE.

### MISCELLANEOUS TALES.

A FATHER'S CURSE AND A DAUGHTER'S SACRIFICE.
TRIALS OF THE HEART.

**BROADLEY (A. M.)—**

    HOW WE DEFENDED ARABI AND HIS FRIENDS.
        A Story of Egypt and the Egyptians. Illustrated by FREDERICK VILLIERS.
        Demy 8vo, 12s.

**BROMLEY-DAVENPORT** *(the late W.), M.P.—*

    SPORT: Fox Hunting, Salmon Fishing, Covert Shooting,
        Deer Stalking. With numerous Illustrations by General CREALOCK, C.B.
        Small 4to, 21s.
    A New and Cheaper Edition. Crown 8vo, 6s.

**BUCKLAND (FRANK)—**

    LOG-BOOK OF A FISHERMAN AND ZOOLOGIST.
        With numerous Illustrations. Fourth Thousand. Crown 8vo, 5s.

**BURCHETT (R.)—**

**DEFINITIONS OF GEOMETRY.** New Edition. 24mo, cloth, 5d.

**LINEAR PERSPECTIVE,** for the Use of Schools of Art. New Edition. With Illustrations. Post 8vo, cloth, 7s.

**PRACTICAL GEOMETRY:** The Course of Construction of Plane Geometrical Figures. With 137 Diagrams. Eighteenth Edition. Post 8vo, cloth, 5s.

**BURLEIGH (BENNET G.)—**

**DESERT WARFARE:** Being the Chronicle of the Eastern Soudan Campaign. With Maps. Demy 8vo, 12s.

**CAMPION (J. S.).—**

**ON THE FRONTIER.** Reminiscences of Wild Sports, Personal Adventures, and Strange Scenes. With Illustrations. Second Edition. Demy 8vo, 16s.

**ON FOOT IN SPAIN.** With Illustrations. Second Edition. Demy 8vo, 16s.

**CARLYLE BIRTHDAY BOOK.** Second Edition. Small fcap. 8vo, 3s.

**CHAMPEAUX (ALFRED)—**

**TAPESTRY.** With Woodcuts. Cloth, 2s. 6d.

**CHURCH (A. H.), M.A., Oxon.—**

**ENGLISH PORCELAIN.** A Handbook to the China made in England during the Eighteenth Century, as illustrated by Specimens chiefly in the National Collection. With numerous Illustrations. Large crown 8vo, 3s.

**ENGLISH EARTHENWARE.** A Handbook to the Wares made in England during the 17th and 18th Centuries, as illustrated by Specimens in the National Collections. With 49 Illustrations. Crown 8vo, 3s.

**PLAIN WORDS ABOUT WATER.** Illustrated. Crown 8vo, sewed, 6d.

**FOOD:** A Short Account of the Sources, Constituents, and Uses of Food. Crown 8vo, cloth, 3s.

**PRECIOUS STONES:** considered in their Scientific and Artistic Relations. With Illustrations. Crown 8vo, 2s. 6d.

CLINTON (R. H.)—
> A COMPENDIUM OF ENGLISH HISTORY, from the Earliest Times to A.D. 1872. With Copious Quotations on the Leading Events and the Constitutional History, together with Appendices. Post 8vo, 7s. 6d.

COBDEN, RICHARD, LIFE OF. By JOHN MORLEY. With Portrait. 2 vols. Demy 8vo, 32s.
> New Edition. Portrait. Crown 8vo, 7s. 6d.
> Popular Edition, with Portrait, sewed, 1s.; cloth, 2s.

---

## CHAPMAN & HALL'S ONE SHILLING SERIES OF BOOKS.—*Crown 8vo, sewed.*

MEMOIRS OF A STOMACH. Written by Himself, that all who eat may read. Edited by a Minister of the Interior. 1s.
FAST AND LOOSE. A Novel. By ARTHUR GRIFFITHS, Author of "The Chronicles of Newgate." 1s.
A SINGER'S STORY, as related by the Author of "Flitters, Tatters, and the Counsellor." 1s.
NUMBER NINETY-NINE. A Novel. By ARTHUR GRIFFITHS. 1s.
THE CASE OF REUBEN MALACHI. By H. SUTHERLAND EDWARDS. 1s.
SARTOR RESARTUS. By THOMAS CARLYLE. Crown 8vo, sewed, 1s.

---

## CHAPMAN & HALL'S SERIES OF POPULAR NOVELS.
*New and Cheaper Editions of Popular Novels. Crown 8vo.*

KARMA. By A. P. SINNETT. 3s. 6d.
MOLOCH. A Story of Sacrifice. By MRS. CAMPBELL PRAED, Author of "Nadine." 6s.
FAUCIT OF BALLIOL. By HERMAN MERIVALE. 6s.
AN AUSTRALIAN HEROINE. By MRS. CAMPBELL PRAED. 6s.
STORY OF AN AFRICAN FARM. By RALPH IRON. 5s.
TO LEEWARD. By F. MARION CRAWFORD. New Edition. 5s.
AN AMERICAN POLITICIAN. By F. MARION CRAWFORD. 5s.
TIE AND TRICK. By HAWLEY SMART. 6s.

---

COOKERY—
> THE PYTCHLEY BOOK OF REFINED COOKERY AND BILLS OF FARE. By MAJOR L——. Second Edition. Large crown 8vo, 8s.
> OFFICIAL HANDBOOK FOR THE NATIONAL TRAINING SCHOOL FOR COOKERY. Containing Lessons on Cookery; forming the Course of Instruction in the School. Compiled by "R. O. C." Fourteenth Thousand. Large crown 8vo, 8s.
> BREAKFAST AND SAVOURY DISHES. By "R. O. C." Seventh Thousand. Crown 8vo, 1s.

*COOKERY—Continued—*

>HOW TO COOK FISH. A Series of Lessons in Cookery, from the Official Handbook to the National Training School for Cookery, South Kensington. Compiled by "R. O. C." Crown 8vo, sewed, 3d.
>
>SICK-ROOM COOKERY. From the Official Handbook to the National School for Cookery, South Kensington. Compiled by "R. O. C." Crown 8vo, sewed, 6d.
>
>THE KINGSWOOD COOKERY BOOK. By H. F. WICKEN. Crown 8vo, 2s.

*COURTNEY (W. L.)—*

>CONSTRUCTIVE ETHICS: A Review of Modern Philosophy and its Three Stages of Interpretation, Criticism, and Reconstruction. Demy 8vo. [*In April.*

*CRAIK (GEORGE LILLIE)—*

>ENGLISH OF SHAKESPEARE. Illustrated in a Philological Commentary on his "Julius Cæsar." Seventh Edition. Post 8vo, cloth, 5s.
>
>OUTLINES OF THE HISTORY OF THE ENGLISH LANGUAGE. Tenth Edition. Post 8vo, cloth, 2s. 6d.

*CRAWFORD (F. MARION)—*

>TO LEEWARD. Crown 8vo, 5s.
>
>AN AMERICAN POLITICIAN. Crown 8vo, 5s.

*CRIPPS (WILFRED)—*

>COLLEGE AND CORPORATION PLATE. A Handbook for the Reproduction of Silver Plate. With numerous Illustrations. Large crown 8vo, cloth, 2s. 6d.

*DAVITT (MICHAEL)—*

>LEAVES FROM A PRISON DIARY; or, Lectures to a Solitary Audience. 2 vols. Crown 8vo, 21s.
>In one vol. Crown 8vo, cloth, 6s.
>Cheap Edition. Crown 8vo, sewed, Ninth Thousand, 1s. 6d.

*DAUBOURG (E.)—*

>INTERIOR ARCHITECTURE. Doors, Vestibules, Staircases, Anterooms, Drawing, Dining, and Bed Rooms, Libraries, Bank and Newspaper Offices, Shop Fronts and Interiors. Half-imperial, cloth, £2 12s. 6d.

*DAVIDSON (ELLIS A.)—*

>PRETTY ARTS FOR THE EMPLOYMENT OF LEISURE HOURS. A Book for Ladies. With Illustrations. Demy 8vo, 6s.

*DAY (WILLIAM)—*

>THE RACEHORSE IN TRAINING, with Hints on Racing and Racing Reform, to which is added a Chapter on Shoeing. Fifth Edition. 8vo, 9s.

**D'HAUSSONVILLE (VICOMTE)—**
    SALON OF MADAME NECKER. Translated by H. M. TROLLOPE. 2 vols. Crown 8vo, 18s.

**DE KONINCK (L. L.) and DIETZ (E.)—**
    PRACTICAL MANUAL OF CHEMICAL ASSAYING, as applied to the Manufacture of Iron. Edited, with notes, by ROBERT MALLET. Post 8vo, cloth, 6s.

**DICKENS (CHARLES)—See pages 32—38.**
    THE LETTERS OF CHARLES DICKENS. Edited by his Sister-in-Law and his Eldest Daughter. Two vols, uniform with "The Charles Dickens Edition" of his Works. Crown 8vo, 8s.
    THE CHARLES DICKENS BIRTHDAY BOOK. Compiled and Edited by his Eldest Daughter. With Five Illustrations by his Youngest Daughter. In a handsome fcap. 4to volume, 12s.

**DRAGE (GEOFFREY)—**
    CRIMINAL CODE OF THE GERMAN EMPIRE. Translated with Prolegomena, and a Commentary, by G. DRAGE. Crown 8vo, 8s.

**DRAYSON (LIEUT.-COL. A. W.)—**
    THE CAUSE OF THE SUPPOSED PROPER MOTION OF THE FIXED STARS. Demy 8vo, cloth, 10s.
    PRACTICAL MILITARY SURVEYING AND SKETCHING. Fifth Edition. Post 8vo, cloth, 4s. 6d.

**DREAMS BY A FRENCH FIRESIDE.** Translated from the German by MARY O'CALLAGHAN. Illustrated by Fred Roe. Crown 8vo, 7s. 6d.

**DUPANLOUP, MONSEIGNEUR (BISHOP OF ORLEANS),** LIFE OF. By ABBÉ F. LAGRANGE. Translated from the French by LADY HERBERT. With Two Portraits. 2 vols. 8vo, 32s.

**DYCE'S COLLECTION.** A Catalogue of Printed Books and Manuscripts bequeathed by the REV. ALEXANDER DYCE to the South Kensington Museum. 2 vols. Royal 8vo, half-morocco, 14s.
    A Collection of Paintings, Miniatures, Drawings, Engravings, Rings, and Miscellaneous Objects, bequeathed by the REV. ALEXANDER DYCE to the South Kensington Museum. Royal 8vo, half-morocco, 6s. 6d.

**DYCE (WILLIAM), R.A.—**
    DRAWING-BOOK OF THE GOVERNMENT SCHOOL OF DESIGN; OR, ELEMENTARY OUTLINES OF ORNAMENT. Fifty selected Plates. Folio, sewed, 5s.; 18s.
        Text to Ditto. Sewed, 6d.

*EDWARDS, H. SUTHERLAND—*
> FAMOUS FIRST-NIGHT REPRESENTATIONS.
> [*In the Press.*

*EGYPTIAN ART—*
> A HISTORY OF ART IN ANCIENT EGYPT. By G. Perrot and C. Chipiez. Translated by Walter Armstrong. With over 600 Illustrations. 2 vols. Imperial 8vo, £2 2s.

*ELLIS (A. B., Major 1st West India Regiment)—*
> WEST AFRICAN ISLANDS. Demy 8vo. 14s.
>
> THE HISTORY OF THE WEST INDIA REGIMENT. With Maps and Coloured Frontispiece and Title-page. Demy 8vo. 18s.
>
> THE LAND OF FETISH. Demy 8vo. 12s.

*ENGEL (CARL)—*
> A DESCRIPTIVE AND ILLUSTRATED CATALOGUE OF THE MUSICAL INSTRUMENTS in the SOUTH KENSINGTON MUSEUM, preceded by an Essay on the History of Musical Instruments. Second Edition. Royal 8vo, half-morocco, 12s.
>
> MUSICAL INSTRUMENTS. With numerous Woodcuts. Large crown 8vo, cloth, 2s. 6d.

*ESCOTT (T. H. S.)—*
> ENGLAND. ITS PEOPLE, POLITY, AND PURSUITS. New and Revised Edition. Fifth Thousand. 8vo, 8s.
>
> PILLARS OF THE EMPIRE: Short Biographical Sketches. 8vo, 10s. 6d.

*EWALD (ALEXANDER CHARLES), F.S.A.—*
> REPRESENTATIVE STATESMEN: Political Studies. 2 vols. Large crown 8vo, £1 4s.
>
> SIR ROBERT WALPOLE. A Political Biography, 1676-1745. Demy 8vo, 18s.

*FANE (VIOLET)—*
> QUEEN OF THE FAIRIES (A Village Story), and other Poems. Crown 8vo, 6s.
>
> ANTHONY BABINGTON: a Drama. Crown 8vo, 6s.

*FEARNLEY (W.)—*
> LESSONS IN HORSE JUDGING, AND THE SUMMERING OF HUNTERS. With Illustrations. Crown 8vo, 4s.

*FLEMING (GEORGE), F.R.C.S.—*

> ANIMAL PLAGUES: THEIR HISTORY, NATURE, AND PREVENTION. 8vo, cloth, 15s.
>
> PRACTICAL HORSE-SHOEING. With 37 Illustrations. Fifth Edition, enlarged. 8vo, sewed, 2s.
>
> RABIES AND HYDROPHOBIA: THEIR HISTORY, NATURE, CAUSES, SYMPTOMS, AND PREVENTION. With 8 Illustrations. 8vo, cloth, 15s.

*FORSTER (JOHN), M.P. for Berwick—*

> THE CHRONICLE OF JAMES I., KING OF ARAGON, SURNAMED THE CONQUEROR. Written by Himself. Translated from the Catalan by the late JOHN FORSTER, M.P. for Berwick. With an Historical Introduction by DON PASCUAL DE GAYANGOS. 2 vols. Royal 8vo, 28s.

*FORSTER (JOHN)—*

> THE LIFE OF CHARLES DICKENS. With Portraits and other Illustrations. 3 vols. 8vo, cloth, £2 2s.
>
> THE LIFE OF CHARLES DICKENS. Uniform with the Illustrated Library Edition of Dickens's Works. 2 vols. Demy 8vo, £1 8s.
>
> THE LIFE OF CHARLES DICKENS. Uniform with the Library Edition. Post 8vo, 10s. 6d.
>
> THE LIFE OF CHARLES DICKENS. Uniform with the "C. D." Edition. With Numerous Illustrations. 2 vols. 7s.
>
> THE LIFE OF CHARLES DICKENS. Uniform with the Household Edition. With Illustrations by F. BARNARD. Crown 4to, cloth, 5s.
>
> WALTER SAVAGE LANDOR: a Biography, 1775-1864. With Portrait. A New and Revised Edition. Demy 8vo, 12s.

*FORTNIGHTLY REVIEW—*

> FORTNIGHTLY REVIEW.—First Series, May, 1865, to Dec. 1866. 6 vols. Cloth, 13s. each.
>
> New Series, 1867 to 1872. In Half-yearly Volumes. Cloth, 13s. each.
>
> From January, 1873, to the present time, in Half-yearly Volumes. Cloth, 16s. each.
>
> CONTENTS OF FORTNIGHTLY REVIEW. From the commencement to end of 1878. Sewed, 2s.

*FORTNUM (C. D. E.)*—

> A DESCRIPTIVE AND ILLUSTRATED CATALOGUE OF THE BRONZES OF EUROPEAN ORIGIN in the SOUTH KENSINGTON MUSEUM, with an Introductory Notice. Royal 8vo, half-morocco, £1 10s.
>
> A DESCRIPTIVE AND ILLUSTRATED CATALOGUE OF MAIOLICA, HISPANO-MORESCO, PERSIAN, DAMASCUS, AND RHODIAN WARES in the SOUTH KENSINGTON MUSEUM. Royal 8vo, half-morocco, £2.
>
> MAIOLICA. With numerous Woodcuts. Large crown 8vo, cloth, 2s. 6d.
>
> BRONZES. With numerous Woodcuts. Large crown 8vo, cloth, 2s. 6d.

*FRANCATELLI (C. E.)*—

> ROYAL CONFECTIONER: English and Foreign. A Practical Treatise. Fourth Edition. With Illustrations. Crown 8vo, 5s.

*FRANKS (A. W.)*—

> JAPANESE POTTERY. Being a Native Report. Numerous Illustrations and Marks. Large crown 8vo, cloth, 2s. 6d.

*GALLENGA (ANTONIO)*—

> EPISODES OF MY SECOND LIFE. 2 vols. Demy 8vo, 28s.
>
> IBERIAN REMINISCENCES. Fifteen Years' Travelling Impressions of Spain and Portugal. With a Map. 2 vols. Demy 8vo, 32s.

*GASNAULT (PAUL) and GARNIER (ED.)*—

> FRENCH POTTERY. With Illustrations. Crown 8vo, 3s.

*GORDON (GENERAL)*—

> LETTERS FROM THE CRIMEA, THE DANUBE, AND ARMENIA. Edited by DEMETRIUS C. BOULGER. Second Edition. Crown 8vo, 5s.

*GORST (J. E.), Q.C., M.P.*—

> An ELECTION MANUAL. Containing the Parliamentary Elections (Corrupt and Illegal Practices) Act, 1883, with Notes. Third Edition. Crown 8vo, 1s. 6d.

GRESWELL (WILLIAM), M.A., F.R.C.I.—

> OUR SOUTH AFRICAN EMPIRE. With Map. 2 vols. Crown 8vo, 21s.

GRIFFIN (SIR LEPEL HENRY), K.C.S.I.—

> THE GREAT REPUBLIC. Second Edition. Crown 8vo, 4s. 6d.

GRIFFITHS (MAJOR ARTHUR), H.M. Inspector of Prisons—

> CHRONICLES OF NEWGATE. Illustrated. New Edition. Demy 8vo, 16s.
>
> MEMORIALS OF MILLBANK: or, Chapters in Prison History. With Illustrations by R. Goff and Author. New Edition. Demy 8vo, 12s.

HALL (SIDNEY)—

> A TRAVELLING ATLAS OF THE ENGLISH COUN-TIES. Fifty Maps, coloured. New Edition, including the Railways, corrected up to the present date. Demy 8vo, in roan tuck, 10s. 6d.

HARDY (LADY DUFFUS)—

> DOWN SOUTH. Demy 8vo. 14s.
>
> THROUGH CITIES AND PRAIRIE LANDS. Sketches of an American Tour. Demy 8vo, 14s.

HATTON (JOSEPH) and HARVEY (REV. M.)—

> NEWFOUNDLAND. The Oldest British Colony. Its History, Past and Present, and its Prospects in the Future. Illustrated from Photographs and Sketches specially made for this work. Demy 8vo, 18s.
>
> TO-DAY IN AMERICA. Studies for the Old World and the New. 2 vols. Crown 8vo, 18s.

HAWKINS (FREDERICK)—

> ANNALS OF THE FRENCH STAGE: FROM ITS ORIGIN TO THE DEATH OF RACINE. 4 Portraits. 2 vols. Demy 8vo, 28s.

HILDEBRAND (HANS)—

> INDUSTRIAL ARTS OF SCANDINAVIA IN THE PAGAN TIME. Illustrated. Crown 8vo, 6d.

HILL (MISS G.)—
>   THE PLEASURES AND PROFITS OF OUR LITTLE
>   POULTRY FARM. Small 8vo, 3s.

HOLBEIN—
>   TWELVE HEADS AFTER HOLBEIN. Selected from
>   Drawings in Her Majesty's Collection at Windsor. Reproduced in Autotype, in portfolio. £1 16s.

HOLLINGSHEAD (JOHN)—
>   FOOTLIGHTS. Crown 8vo. 7s. 6d.

HOVELACQUE (ABEL)—
>   THE SCIENCE OF LANGUAGE: LINGUISTICS,
>   PHILOLOGY, AND ETYMOLOGY. With Maps. Large crown 8vo, cloth, 5s.

HUMPHRIS (H. D.)—
>   PRINCIPLES OF PERSPECTIVE. Illustrated in a
>   Series of Examples. Oblong folio, half-bound, and Text 8vo, cloth, £1 1s.

INTERNATIONAL POLICY: Essay on the Foreign Relations
of England. By FREDERIC HARRISON, PROF. BEESLEY, RICHARD CONGREVE, and others. New Edition. Crown 8vo, 2s. 6d.

IRON (RALPH)—
>   THE STORY OF AN AFRICAN FARM. New Edition.
>   Crown 8vo, 5s.

JARRY (GENERAL)—
>   OUTPOST DUTY. Translated, with TREATISES ON
>   MILITARY RECONNAISSANCE AND ON ROAD-MAKING. By Major-Gen. W. C. E. NAPIER. Third Edition. Crown 8vo, 5s.

JEANS (W. T.)—
>   CREATORS OF THE AGE OF STEEL. Memoirs of
>   Sir W. Siemens, Sir H. Bessemer, Sir J. Whitworth, Sir J. Brown, and other Inventors. Second Edition. Crown 8vo, 7s. 6d.

JOHNSON (DR. SAMUEL)—
>   LIFE AND CONVERSATIONS OF DR. SAMUEL
>   JOHNSON. By A. MAIN. Crown 8vo, 10s. 6d.

JONES (CAPTAIN DOUGLAS), R.A.—
   NOTES ON MILITARY LAW. Crown 8vo, 4s.

JONES COLLECTION (HANDBOOK OF THE) IN THE SOUTH
   KENSINGTON MUSEUM. Illustrated. Large crown 8vo, 2s. 6d.

KEMPIS (THOMAS À)—
   OF THE IMITATION OF CHRIST. Four Books.
   Beautifully Illustrated Edition. Demy 8vo, 16s.

KENNARD (MRS. EDWARD)—
   TWILIGHT TALES. Illustrated by EDITH ELLISON.
   Crown 8vo, 7s. 6d.

KENT (CHARLES)—
   HUMOUR AND PATHOS OF CHARLES DICKENS,
   WITH ILLUSTRATIONS OF HIS MASTERY OF THE TERRIBLE
   AND PICTURESQUE. Portrait. Crown 8vo, 6s.

KLACZKO (M. JULIAN)—
   TWO CHANCELLORS: PRINCE GORTCHAKOF AND
   PRINCE BISMARCK. Translated by MRS. TAIT. New and cheaper Edition, 6s.

LACORDAIRE'S JESUS CHRIST; GOD; AND GOD AND
   MAN. Conferences delivered at Notre Dame in Paris. New Edition in 1 vol.
   Crown 8vo, 6s.

LAING (S.)—
   MODERN SCIENCE AND MODERN THOUGHT.
   Third Edition. With a Supplementary Chapter on Gladstone's "Dawn of Creation"
   and Drummond's "Natural Law of the Spiritual World." Demy 8vo, 7s. 6d.

LAVELEYE (ÉMILE DE)—
   THE ELEMENTS OF POLITICAL ECONOMY.
   Translated by W. POLLARD, B.A., St. John's College, Oxford. Crown 8vo, 6s.

LANDOR'S WORKS. 8 vols. Demy 8vo, 14s. each volume.
   All the Volumes can be supplied excepting Vol. II., *which is out of print*.

LECTURES ON AGRICULTURAL SCIENCE, AND OTHER
   PROCEEDINGS OF THE INSTITUTE OF AGRICULTURE, SOUTH
   KENSINGTON, 1883-4. Crown 8vo, sewed, 2s.

*LEFÈVRE (ANDRÉ)—*

 PHILOSOPHY, Historical and Critical. Translated, with an Introduction, by A. W. Keane, B.A. Large crown 8vo, 7s. 6d.

*LESLIE (R. C.)—*

 A SEA PAINTER'S LOG. With Illustrations by the Author. Crown 8vo.   [*In the Press.*

*LETOURNEAU (DR. CHARLES)—*

 SOCIOLOGY. Based upon Ethnology. Translated by Henry M. Trollope. Large crown 8vo, 10s.

 BIOLOGY. Translated by William MacCall. With Illustrations. Large crown 8vo, 6s.

*LILLY (W. S.)—*

 SOME CHAPTERS ON EUROPEAN HISTORY. With an Introductory Dialogue on the Philosophy of History. 2 vols. Demy 8vo, 21s.

 ANCIENT RELIGION AND MODERN THOUGHT. A New and Revised Edition. Demy 8vo, 12s.

*LONG (JAMES)—*

 DAIRY FARMING. To which is added a Description of the Chief Continental Systems. With numerous Illustrations. Crown 8vo, 9s.

*LOW (C. R.)—*

 SOLDIERS OF THE VICTORIAN AGE. 2 vols. Demy 8vo, £1 10s.

*LYTTON (ROBERT, EARL)—*

 POETICAL WORKS—

  FABLES IN SONG. 2 vols. Fcap 8vo, 12s.
  THE WANDERER. Fcap. 8vo, 6s.
  POEMS, HISTORICAL AND CHARACTERISTIC. Fcap. 6s.

*MALLET (ROBERT)—*

 PRACTICAL MANUAL OF CHEMICAL ASSAYING, as applied to the Manufacture of Iron. By L. L. De Koninck and E. Dietz. Edited, with notes, by Robert Mallet. Post 8vo, cloth, 6s.

*MASKELL (ALFRED)*—

> RUSSIAN ART AND ART OBJECTS IN RUSSIA. A Handbook to the Reproduction of Goldsmiths' Work, &c., from that Country. Crown 8vo, 4s. 6d.

*MASKELL (WILLIAM)*—

> A DESCRIPTION OF THE IVORIES, ANCIENT AND MEDIÆVAL, in the SOUTH KENSINGTON MUSEUM, with a Preface. With numerous Photographs and Woodcuts. Royal 8vo, half-morocco, £1 1s.
>
> IVORIES: ANCIENT AND MEDIÆVAL. With numerous Woodcuts. Large crown 8vo, cloth, 2s. 6d.
>
> HANDBOOK TO THE DYCE AND FORSTER COLLECTIONS. With Illustrations. Large crown 8vo, cloth, 2s. 6d.

*MEREDITH (GEORGE)*—

> MODERN LOVE AND POEMS OF THE ENGLISH ROADSIDE, WITH POEMS AND BALLADS. Fcap. cloth, 6s.

---

## GEORGE MEREDITH'S WORKS.

*A New and Uniform Edition. In Six-Shilling Volumes. Crown 8vo:*

DIANA OF THE CROSSWAYS. [Ready.
EVAN HARRINGTON. [Ready.
THE ORDEAL OF RICHARD FEVEREL. A History of a Father and Son. [Ready.
THE ADVENTURES OF HARRY RICHMOND. [Ready.
SANDRA BELLONI. Originally EMILIA IN ENGLAND [Ready.
VITTORIA. [Ready.
RHODA FLEMING.
BEAUCHAMP'S CAREER.
THE EGOIST.

---

*MERIVALE (HERMAN CHARLES)*—

> BINKO'S BLUES. A Tale for Children of all Growths. Illustrated by EDGAR GIBERNE. Small crown 8vo, 5s.
>
> THE WHITE PILGRIM, and other Poems. Crown 8vo, 9s.
>
> FAUCIT OF BALLIOL. Crown 8vo, 6s.

## MILITARY BIOGRAPHIES—

**FREDERICK THE GREAT.** By Col. C. B. Brackenbury; with Maps and Portrait. Large crown 8vo, 4s.

**LOUDON.** A Sketch of the Military Life of Gideon Ernest, Freicherr von Loudon, sometime Generalissimo of the Austrian Forces. By Col. G. B. Malleson, C.S.I. With Portrait and Maps. Large crown 8vo, 4s.

**TURENNE.** By H. M. Hozier. With Portrait and Two Maps. Large crown 8vo, 4s.

**PARLIAMENTARY GENERALS OF THE GREAT CIVIL WAR.** By Major Walford, R.A. With Maps. Crown 8vo, 4s.

## MOLESWORTH (W. NASSAU)—

**HISTORY OF ENGLAND FROM THE YEAR 1830 TO THE RESIGNATION OF THE GLADSTONE MINISTRY, 1874.** Twelfth Thousand. 3 vols. Crown 8vo, 18s.

**ABRIDGED EDITION.** Large crown, 7s. 6d.

## MOLTKE (FIELD-MARSHAL COUNT VON)—

**POLAND: AN HISTORICAL SKETCH.** An Authorised Translation, with Biographical Notice by E. S. Buchheim. Crown 8vo, 4s. 6d.

## MORLEY (HENRY)—

**TABLES OF ENGLISH LITERATURE.** Containing 20 Charts. Second Edition, with Index. Royal 4to, cloth, 12s.

In Three Parts. Parts I. and II., containing Three Charts, each 1s. 6d. Part III. in Sections, 1, 2, and 5, 1s. 6d. each; 3 and 4 together, 3s.

\*\*\* The Charts sold separately.

## MORLEY (JOHN)—

**LIFE AND CORRESPONDENCE OF RICHARD COBDEN.** Fourth Thousand. 2 vols. Demy 8vo £1 12s.

Popular Edition. With Portrait. 4to, sewed, 1s. Bound in cloth, 2s.

## MUNTZ (EUGÈNE), From the French of—

**RAPHAEL: HIS LIFE, WORKS, AND TIMES.** Edited by W. Armstrong. With 155 Wood Engravings and 41 Full-page Plates. Imperial 8vo, 36s.

## MURPHY (J. M.)—

**RAMBLES IN NORTH-WEST AMERICA.** With Frontispiece and Map. 8vo, 16s.

## URRAY (ANDREW), F.L.S.—

**ECONOMIC ENTOMOLOGY.** Aptera. With numerous Illustrations. Large crown 8vo, 7s. 6d.

NAPIER (MAJ.-GEN. W. C. E.)—
>TRANSLATION OF GEN. JARRY'S OUTPOST DUTY. With TREATISES ON MILITARY RECONNAISSANCE AND ON ROAD-MAKING. Third Edition. Crown 8vo, 5s.

NAPOLEON. A Selection from the Letters and Despatches of the First Napoleon. With Explanatory Notes by Captain the Hon. D. BINGHAM. 3 vols. Demy 8vo, £2 2s.

NECKER (MADAME)—
>THE SALON OF MADAME NECKER. By VICOMTE D'HAUSSONVILLE. Translated by H. M. TROLLOPE. 2 vols. Crown 8vo, 18s.

NESBITT (ALEXANDER)—
>GLASS. Illustrated. Crown 8vo, cloth, 2s. 6d.

NEVINSON (HENRY)—
>A SKETCH OF HERDER AND HIS TIMES. With a Portrait. Demy 8vo, 14s.

NEWTON (E. TULLEY), F.G.S.—
>THE TYPICAL PARTS IN THE SKELETONS OF A CAT, DUCK, AND CODFISH, being a Catalogue with Comparative Description arranged in a Tabular form. Demy 8vo, cloth, 3s.

NORMAN (C. B.), late of the 90th Light Infantry and Bengal Staff Corps—
>TONKIN; OR, FRANCE IN THE FAR EAST. With Maps. Demy 8vo, 14s.

O'GRADY (STANDISH)—
>TORYISM AND THE TORY DEMOCRACY. Crown 8vo, 5s.

OLIVER (PROFESSOR), F.R.S., &c.—
>ILLUSTRATIONS OF THE PRINCIPAL NATURAL ORDERS OF THE VEGETABLE KINGDOM, PREPARED FOR THE SCIENCE AND ART DEPARTMENT, SOUTH KENSINGTON. With 109 Plates. Oblong 8vo, plain, 16s.; coloured, £1 6s.

OXENHAM (REV. H. N.)—
>MEMOIR OF LIEUTENANT RUDOLPH DE LISLE, R.N., OF THE NAVAL BRIGADE. [In the Press.
>
>SHORT STUDIES, ETHICAL AND RELIGIOUS. Demy 8vo. 12s.
>
>SHORT STUDIES IN ECCLESIASTICAL HISTORY AND BIOGRAPHY. Demy 8vo, 12s.

*PERROT (GEORGES) and CHIPIEZ (CHARLES)—*

> A HISTORY OF ANCIENT ART IN PHŒNICIA AND ITS DEPENDENCIES. Translated from the French by WALTER ARMSTRONG, B.A. Oxon. Containing 644 Illustrations in the text, and 10 Steel and Coloured Plates. 2 vols. Imperial 8vo, 42s.
>
> A HISTORY OF ART IN CHALDÆA AND ASSYRIA. Translated by WALTER ARMSTRONG, B.A. Oxon. With 452 Illustrations. 2 vols. Imperial 8vo, 42s.
>
> A HISTORY OF ART IN ANCIENT EGYPT. Translated from the French by W. ARMSTRONG, B A. Oxon. With over 600 Illustrations. 2 vols. Imperial 8vo, 42s.

*PIASSETSKY (P.)—*

> RUSSIAN TRAVELLERS IN MONGOLIA AND CHINA. Translated by GORDON-CUMMING. With 75 Illustrations. 2 vols. Crown 8vo, 24s.

*PITT TAYLOR (FRANK)—*

> THE CANTERBURY TALES. Selections from the Tales of GEOFFREY CHAUCER rendered into Modern English, with close adherence to the language of the Poet. With Frontispiece. Crown 8vo, 6s.

*POLLEN (J. H.)—*

> ANCIENT AND MODERN FURNITURE AND WOODWORK IN THE SOUTH KENSINGTON MUSEUM. With an Introduction, and Illustrated with numerous Coloured Photographs and Woodcuts. Royal 8vo, half-morocco, £1 1s.
>
> GOLD AND SILVER SMITH'S WORK. With numerous Woodcuts. Large crown 8vo, cloth, 2s. 6d.
>
> ANCIENT AND MODERN FURNITURE AND WOODWORK. With numerous Woodcuts. Large crown 8vo, cloth, 2s. 6d.

*POYNTER (E. J.), R.A.—*

> TEN LECTURES ON ART. Third Edition. [*In the Press.*

*PRAED (MRS. CAMPBELL)—*

AUSTRALIAN LIFE: Black and White. With Illustration. Crown 8vo, 8s.

AN AUSTRALIAN HEROINE. Crown 8vo, 6s.

MOLOCH. A Story of Sacrifice. Crown 8vo, 6s.

*PRINSEP (VAL), A.R.A.—*

IMPERIAL INDIA. Containing numerous Illustrations and Maps. Second Edition. Demy 8vo, £1 1s.

PYTCHLEY COOKERY BOOK—
THE PYTCHLEY BOOK OF REFINED COOKERY AND BILLS OF FARE. By Major L——. Second Edition. Large crown 8vo, 8s.

RADICAL PROGRAMME, THE. From the *Fortnightly Review*, with additions. With a Preface by the Right Hon. J. Chamberlain, M.P. Thirteenth Thousand. Crown 8vo, 2s. 6d.

*RAMSDEN (LADY GWENDOLEN)—*

A BIRTHDAY BOOK. Illustrated. Containing 46 Illustrations from Original Drawings, and numerous other Illustrations. Royal 8vo, 21s.

*REDGRAVE (GILBERT)—*

OUTLINES OF HISTORIC ORNAMENT. Translated from the German. Edited by Gilbert Redgrave. With numerous Illustrations. Crown 8vo, 4s.

*REDGRAVE (GILBERT R.)—*

MANUAL OF DESIGN, compiled from the Writings and Addresses of Richard Redgrave, R.A. With Woodcuts. Large crown 8vo, cloth, 2s. 6d.

*REDGRAVE (RICHARD)—*

ELEMENTARY MANUAL OF COLOUR, with a Catechism on Colour. 24mo, cloth, 9d.

*REDGRAVE (SAMUEL)—*

A DESCRIPTIVE CATALOGUE OF THE HISTORICAL COLLECTION OF WATER-COLOUR PAINTINGS IN THE SOUTH KENSINGTON MUSEUM. With numerous Chromo-lithographs and other Illustrations. Royal 8vo, £1 1s.

RENAN (ERNEST)—

> RECOLLECTIONS OF MY YOUTH. Translated from the original French, and revised by MADAME RENAN. Crown 8vo, 8s.

RIANO (JUAN F.)—

> THE INDUSTRIAL ARTS IN SPAIN. Illustrated. Large crown 8vo, cloth, 4s.

ROBINSON (JAMES F.)—

> BRITISH BEE FARMING. Its Profits and Pleasures. Large crown 8vo, 5s.

ROBINSON (J. C.)—

> ITALIAN SCULPTURE OF THE MIDDLE AGES AND PERIOD OF THE REVIVAL OF ART. With 20 Engravings. Royal 8vo, cloth, 7s. 6d.

ROBSON (GEORGE)—

> ELEMENTARY BUILDING CONSTRUCTION. Illustrated by a Design for an Entrance Lodge and Gate. 15 Plates. Oblong folio, sewed, 8s.

ROBSON (REV. J. H.), M.A., LL.M.—

> AN ELEMENTARY TREATISE ON ALGEBRA. Post 8vo, 6s.

ROCK (THE VERY REV. CANON), D.D.—

> ON TEXTILE FABRICS. A Descriptive and Illustrated Catalogue of the Collection of Church Vestments, Dresses, Silk Stuffs, Needlework, and Tapestries in the South Kensington Museum. Royal 8vo, half-morocco, £1 11s. 6d.
>
> TEXTILE FABRICS. With numerous Woodcuts. Crown 8vo, cloth, 2s. 6d.

*ROLAND (ARTHUR)—*

> **FARMING FOR PLEASURE AND PROFIT.** Edited by William Ablett. 8 vols. Crown 8vo, 5s. each.
>
>> DAIRY-FARMING, MANAGEMENT OF COWS, &c.
>> POULTRY-KEEPING.
>> TREE-PLANTING, FOR ORNAMENTATION OR PROFIT.
>> STOCK-KEEPING AND CATTLE-REARING.
>> DRAINAGE OF LAND, IRRIGATION, MANURES, &c.
>> ROOT-GROWING, HOPS, &c.
>> MANAGEMENT OF GRASS LANDS, LAYING DOWN GRASS, ARTIFICIAL GRASSES, &c.
>> MARKET GARDENING, HUSBANDRY FOR FARMERS AND GENERAL CULTIVATORS.

*RUSDEN (G. W.), for many years Clerk of the Parliament in Victoria—*

> **A HISTORY OF AUSTRALIA.** With a Coloured Map. 3 vols. Demy 8vo, 50s.
>
> **A HISTORY OF NEW ZEALAND.** With Maps. 3 vols. Demy 8vo, 50s.

*SCOTT (A. DE C., MAJOR-GENERAL, late Royal Engineers)—*

> **LONDON WATER: a Review of the Present Condition and** Suggested Improvements of the Metropolitan Water Supply. Crown 8vo, sewed, 2s.

*SCOTT-STEVENSON (MRS.)—*

> **ON SUMMER SEAS.** Including the Mediterranean, the Ægean, the Ionian, and the Euxine, and a voyage down the Danube. With a Map. Demy 8vo, 16s.
>
> **OUR HOME IN CYPRUS.** With a Map and Illustrations. Third Edition. Demy 8vo, 14s.
>
> **OUR RIDE THROUGH ASIA MINOR.** With Map. Demy 8vo, 18s.

*SHEPHERD (MAJOR), R.E.—*

> **PRAIRIE EXPERIENCES IN HANDLING CATTLE AND SHEEP.** With Illustrations and Map. Demy 8vo, 10s. 6d.

*SHIRREFF (MISS)—*

> **HOME EDUCATION IN RELATION TO THE KINDERGARTEN.** Two Lectures. Crown 8vo, 1s. 6d.

*SIMMONDS (T. L.)—*
>ANIMAL PRODUCTS: their Preparation, Commercial Uses, and Value. With numerous Illustrations. Large crown 8vo, 7s. 6d.

*SINNETT (A. P.)—*
>ESOTERIC BUDDHISM. Annotated and enlarged by the Author. Fifth Edition. Crown 8vo, 6s.
>
>KARMA. A Novel. New Edition. Crown 8vo, 3s. 6d.

*SINNETT (MRS.)—*
>THE PURPOSE OF THEOSOPHY. Crown 8vo, 3s.

*SMART (HAWLEY)—*
>TIE AND TRICK. Crown 8vo, 6s.

*SMITH (MAJOR R. MURDOCK), R.E.—*
>PERSIAN ART. Second Edition, with additional Illustrations. Large crown 8vo, 2s.

*STORY (W. W.)—*
>ROBA DI ROMA. Seventh Edition, with Additions and Portrait. Crown 8vo, cloth, 10s. 6d.
>
>CASTLE ST. ANGELO. With Illustrations. Crown 8vo, 10s. 6d.

*SUTCLIFFE (JOHN)—*
>THE SCULPTOR AND ART STUDENT'S GUIDE to the Proportions of the Human Form, with Measurements in feet and inches of Full-Grown Figures of Both Sexes and of Various Ages. By Dr. G. SCHADOW, Member of the Academies, Stockholm, Dresden, Rome, &c. &c. Translated by J. J. WRIGHT. Plates reproduced by J. SUTCLIFFE. Oblong folio, 31s. 6d.

*TAINE (H. A.)—*
>NOTES ON ENGLAND. Translated, with Introduction, by W. FRASER RAE. Eighth Edition. With Portrait. Crown 8vo, 5s.

*TANNER (PROFESSOR), F.C.S.—*
>HOLT CASTLE; or, Threefold Interest in Land. Crown 8vo, 4s. 6d.
>
>JACK'S EDUCATION; OR, HOW HE LEARNT FARMING. Second Edition. Crown 8vo, 3s. 6d.

*TEMPLE (SIR RICHARD), BART., M.P., G.C.S.I.—*
>COSMOPOLITAN ESSAYS. With Maps. Demy 8vo.
>[*In the Press.*

*TOPINARD (DR. PAUL)—*

    ANTHROPOLOGY. With a Preface by Professor PAUL BROCA. With numerous Illustrations. Large crown 8vo, 7s. 6d.

*TOVEY (LIEUT.-COL., R.E.)—*

    MARTIAL LAW AND CUSTOM OF WAR; or, Military Law and Jurisdiction in Troublous Times. Crown 8vo, 6s.

*TRAILL (H. D.)—*

    THE NEW LUCIAN. Being a Series of Dialogues of the Dead. Demy 8vo, 12s.

*TROLLOPE (ANTHONY)—*

    AYALA'S ANGEL. Crown 8vo. 6s.

    LIFE OF CICERO. 2 vols. 8vo. £1 4s.

    THE CHRONICLES OF BARSETSHIRE. A Uniform Edition, in 8 vols., large crown 8vo, handsomely printed, each vol. containing Frontispiece. 6s. each.

    THE WARDEN and BARCHESTER TOWERS. 2 vols.
    DR. THORNE.
    FRAMLEY PARSONAGE.
    THE SMALL HOUSE AT ALLINGTON. 2 vols.
    LAST CHRONICLE OF BARSET. 2 vols.

*UNIVERSAL—*

    UNIVERSAL CATALOGUE OF BOOKS ON ART. Compiled for the use of the National Art Library, and the Schools of Art in the United Kingdom. In 2 vols. Crown 4to, half-morocco, £2 2s.

    Supplemental Volume to Ditto. Crown 8vo, 8s. nett.

*VERON (EUGENE)—*

    ÆSTHETICS. Translated by W. H. ARMSTRONG. Large crown 8vo, 7s. 6d.

*WALE (REV. HENRY JOHN), M.A.—*

    MY GRANDFATHER'S POCKET BOOK, from 1701 to 1796. Author of "Sword and Surplice." Demy 8vo, 12s.

*WALKER (MRS.)—*

    EASTERN LIFE AND SCENERY, with Excursions to Asia Minor, Mitylene, Crete, and Roumania. 2 vols., crown 8vo.
                                                        [*In the Press.*

*WESTWOOD (J. O.), M.A., F.L.S., &c.—*

    CATALOGUE OF THE FICTILE IVORIES IN THE SOUTH KENSINGTON MUSEUM. With an Account of the Continental Collections of Classical and Mediæval Ivories. Royal 8vo, half-morocco, £1 4s.

WHIST HANDBOOKS. By AQUARIUS—

    THE HANDS AT WHIST. 32mo, cloth gilt, 1s.

    EASY WHIST. 32mo, cloth gilt, 1s.

    ADVANCED WHIST. 32mo, cloth gilt, 1s.

*WHITE (WALTER)*—

    A MONTH IN YORKSHIRE. With a Map. Fifth Edition. Post 8vo, 4s.

    A LONDONER'S WALK TO THE LAND'S END, AND A TRIP TO THE SCILLY ISLES. With 4 Maps. Third Edition. Post 8vo, 4s.

*WICKEN (H. F.)*—

    THE KINGSWOOD COOKERY BOOK. Crown 8vo, 2s.

WILL-O'-THE-WISPS, THE. Translated from the German of Marie Petersen by CHARLOTTE J. HART. With Illustrations. Crown 8vo, 7s. 6d.

*WORNUM (R. N.)*—

    ANALYSIS OF ORNAMENT: THE CHARACTERISTICS OF STYLES. An Introduction to the History of Ornamental Art. With many Illustrations. Ninth Edition. Royal 8vo, cloth, 8s.

*WORSAAE (J. J. A.)*—

    INDUSTRIAL ARTS OF DENMARK, FROM THE EARLIEST TIMES TO THE DANISH CONQUEST OF ENGLAND. With Maps and Illustrations. Crown 8vo, 3s. 6d.

*YEO (DR. J. BURNEY)*—

    CLIMATE AND HEALTH RESORTS. New Edition. Crown 8vo, 10s. 6d.

*YOUNGE (C. D.)*—

    PARALLEL LIVES OF ANCIENT AND MODERN HEROES. New Edition. 12mo, cloth, 4s. 6d.

## SOUTH KENSINGTON MUSEUM

## DESCRIPTIVE AND ILLUSTRATED CATALOGUES.

*Royal 8vo, half-bound.*

BRONZES OF EUROPEAN ORIGIN. By C. D. E. Fortnum. £1 10s.

DYCE'S COLLECTION OF PRINTED BOOKS AND MANUSCRIPTS. 2 vols. 14s.

DYCE'S COLLECTION OF PAINTINGS, ENGRAVINGS, &c. 6s. 6d.

FURNITURE AND WOODWORK, ANCIENT AND MODERN. By J. H. Pollen. £1 1s.

GLASS VESSELS. By A. Nesbitt. 18s.

GOLD AND SILVER SMITH'S WORK. By J. G. Pollen. £1 6s.

IVORIES, ANCIENT AND MEDIÆVAL. By W. Maskell. 21s.

IVORIES, FICTILE. By J. O. Westwood. £1 4s.

MAIOLICA, HISPANO-MORESCO, PERSIAN, DAMASCUS AND RHODIAN WARES. By C. D. E. Fortnum. £2.

MUSICAL INSTRUMENTS. By C. Engel. 12s.

SCULPTURE, ITALIAN SCULPTURE OF THE MIDDLE AGES. By J. C. Robinson. Cloth, 7s. 6d.

SWISS COINS. By R. S. Poole. £2 10s.

TEXTILE FABRICS. By Rev. D. Rock. £1 11s. 6d.

WATER-COLOUR PAINTING. By S. Redgrave. £1 1s.

UNIVERSAL CATALOGUE OF BOOKS ON ART. 2 vols. Small 4to, £1 1s. each.

UNIVERSAL CATALOGUE OF BOOKS ON ART. Supplementary vol. 8s. nett.

## SOUTH KENSINGTON MUSEUM SCIENCE AND ART HANDBOOKS.

Handsomely printed in large crown 8vo.

*Published for the Committee of the Council on Education.*

THE ART OF THE SARACENS IN EGYPT. By STANLEY LANE POOLE. With Illustrations. [*In the Press.*

ENGLISH PORCELAIN. By A. H. CHURCH, M.A. With numerous Illustrations. 3s.

RUSSIAN ART AND ART OBJECTS IN RUSSIA. By ALFRED MASKELL. With Illustrations. 4s. 6d.

FRENCH POTTERY. By PAUL GASNAULT and EDOUARD GARNIER. With Illustrations and marks. 3s.

ENGLISH EARTHENWARE: A Handbook to the Wares made in England during the 17th and 18th Centuries. By PROF. CHURCH. With Illustrations. 3s.

INDUSTRIAL ARTS OF DENMARK. From the Earliest Times to the Danish Conquest of England. By J. J. A. WORSAAE, Hon. F.S.A., &c. &c. With Illustrations. 3s. 6d.

INDUSTRIAL ARTS OF SCANDINAVIA IN THE PAGAN TIME. By HANS HILDEBRAND, Royal Antiquary of Sweden. With Illustrations. 2s. 6d.

PRECIOUS STONES. By PROFESSOR CHURCH. With Illustrations. 2s. 6d.

INDUSTRIAL ARTS OF INDIA. By Sir GEORGE C. M. BIRDWOOD, C.S.I. With Map and Illustrations. Demy 8vo, 14s.

HANDBOOK TO THE DYCE AND FORSTER COLLECTIONS. By W. MASKELL. With Illustrations. 2s. 6d.

INDUSTRIAL ARTS IN SPAIN. By JUAN F. RIANO. With Illustrations. 4s.

GLASS. By ALEXANDER NESBITT. With Illustrations. 2s. 6d.

GOLD AND SILVER SMITH'S WORK. By JOHN HUNGERFORD POLLEN. With Illustrations. 2s. 6d.

TAPESTRY. By ALFRED CHAMPEAUX. With Illustrations. 2s. 6d.

BRONZES. By C. DRURY E. FORTNUM, F.S.A. With Illustrations. 2s. 6d.

PLAIN WORDS ABOUT WATER. By A. H. CHURCH, M.A. Oxon. With Illustrations. Sewed, 6d.

SOUTH KENSINGTON MUSEUM SCIENCE & ART HANDBOOKS—*Continued*.

ANIMAL PRODUCTS: their Preparation, Commercial Uses, and Value. By T. L. SIMMONDS. With Illustrations. 7s. 6d.

FOOD: A Short Account of the Sources, Constituents, and Uses of Food. By A. H. CHURCH, M.A. Oxon. 3s.

ECONOMIC ENTOMOLOGY. By ANDREW MURRAY, F.L.S. APTERA. With Illustrations. 7s. 6d.

JAPANESE POTTERY. Being a Native Report. Edited by A. W. FRANKS. With Illustrations and Marks. 2s. 6d.

HANDBOOK TO THE SPECIAL LOAN COLLECTION of Scientific Apparatus. 3s.

INDUSTRIAL ARTS: Historical Sketches. With Illustrations. 3s.

TEXTILE FABRICS. By the Very Rev. DANIEL ROCK, D.D. With Illustrations. 2s. 6d.

JONES COLLECTION IN THE SOUTH KENSINGTON MUSEUM. With Portrait and Illustrations. 2s. 6d.

COLLEGE AND CORPORATION PLATE. By WILFRED CRIPPS. With Illustrations. Cloth, 2s. 6d.

IVORIES: ANCIENT AND MEDIÆVAL. By WILLIAM MASKELL. With Illustrations. 2s. 6d.

ANCIENT AND MODERN FURNITURE AND WOODWORK. By JOHN HUNGERFORD POLLEN. With Illustrations. 2s. 6d.

MAIOLICA. By C. DRURY E. FORTNUM, F.S.A. With Illustrations. 2s. 6d.

THE CHEMISTRY OF FOODS. With Microscopic Illustrations. By JAMES BELL, Principal of the Somerset House Laboratory. Part I.—Tea, Coffee, Cocoa, Sugar, &c. 2s. 6d. Part II.—Milk, Butter, Cereals, Prepared Starches, &c. 3s.

MUSICAL INSTRUMENTS. By CARL ENGEL. With Illustrations. 2s. 6d.

MANUAL OF DESIGN, compiled from the Writings and Addresses of RICHARD REDGRAVE, R.A. By GILBERT R. REDGRAVE. With Illustrations. 2s. 6d.

PERSIAN ART. By MAJOR R. MURDOCK SMITH, R.E. Second Edition, with additional Illustrations. 2s.

# CARLYLE'S (THOMAS) WORKS.

## THE ASHBURTON EDITION.

An entirely New Edition of the Writings of Mr. CARLYLE, to be completed in Seventeen Volumes, demy 8vo, is now publishing. For Particulars see page 2.

## CHEAP AND UNIFORM EDITION.

*23 vols., Crown 8vo, cloth, £7 5s.*

THE FRENCH REVOLUTION: A History. 2 vols., 12s.

OLIVER CROMWELL'S LETTERS AND SPEECHES, with Elucidations, &c. 3 vols., 18s.

LIVES OF SCHILLER AND JOHN STERLING. 1 vol., 6s.

CRITICAL AND MISCELLANEOUS ESSAYS. 4 vols., £1 4s.

SARTOR RESARTUS AND LECTURES ON HEROES. 1 vol., 6s.

LATTER-DAY PAMPHLETS. 1 vol., 6s.

CHARTISM AND PAST AND PRESENT. 1 vol., 6s.

TRANSLATIONS FROM THE GERMAN OF MUSÆUS, TIECK, AND RICHTER. 1 vol., 6s.

WILHELM MEISTER, by Göethe. A Translation. 2 vols., 12s.

HISTORY OF FRIEDRICH THE SECOND, called Frederick the Great. 7 vols., £2 9s.

## LIBRARY EDITION COMPLETE.

Handsomely printed in 34 vols., demy 8vo, cloth, £15 3s.

SARTOR RESARTUS. With a Portrait, 7s. 6d.

THE FRENCH REVOLUTION. A History. 3 vols., each 9s.

LIFE OF FREDERICK SCHILLER AND EXAMINATION OF HIS WORKS. With Supplement of 1872. Portrait and Plates, 9s.

CRITICAL AND MISCELLANEOUS ESSAYS. With Portrait. 6 vols., each 9s.

ON HEROES, HERO WORSHIP, AND THE HEROIC IN HISTORY. 7s. 6d.

PAST AND PRESENT. 9s.

**CARLYLE'S (THOMAS) WORKS.**—LIBRARY EDITION—*Continued.*

OLIVER CROMWELL'S LETTERS AND SPEECHES. With Portraits. 5 vols., each 9s.

LATTER-DAY PAMPHLETS. 9s.

LIFE OF JOHN STERLING. With Portrait, 9s.

HISTORY OF FREDERICK THE SECOND. 10 vols., each 9s.

TRANSLATIONS FROM THE GERMAN. 3 vols., each 9s.

EARLY KINGS OF NORWAY; ESSAY ON THE PORTRAITS OF JOHN KNOX; AND GENERAL INDEX. With Portrait Illustrations. 8vo, cloth, 9s.

---

### PEOPLE'S EDITION.

*37 vols., small 8vo, 2s. each vol.; or in sets, 37 vols. in 19, cloth gilt, £3 14s.*

SARTOR RESARTUS.

FRENCH REVOLUTION. 3 vols.

LIFE OF JOHN STERLING.

OLIVER CROMWELL'S LETTERS AND SPEECHES. 5 vols.

ON HEROES AND HERO WORSHIP.

PAST AND PRESENT.

CRITICAL AND MISCELLANEOUS ESSAYS. 7 vols.

LATTER-DAY PAMPHLETS.

LIFE OF SCHILLER.

FREDERICK THE GREAT. 10 vols.

WILHELM MEISTER. 3 vols.

TRANSLATIONS FROM MUSÆUS, TIECK, AND RICHTER. 2 vols.

THE EARLY KINGS OF NORWAY; Essay on the Portraits of Knox; and General Index.

---

SARTOR RESARTUS. Cheap Edition, crown 8vo, sewed, 1s.

---

### SIXPENNY EDITION.
*4to, sewed.*

SARTOR RESARTUS. Eightieth Thousand.

HEROES AND HERO WORSHIP.

ESSAYS: BURNS, JOHNSON, SCOTT, THE DIAMOND NECKLACE.

*The above in 1 vol., cloth, 2s. 6d.*

# DICKENS'S (CHARLES) WORKS.

## ORIGINAL EDITIONS.

*In demy 8vo.*

THE MYSTERY OF EDWIN DROOD. With Illustrations by S. L. Fildes, and a Portrait engraved by Baker. Cloth, 7s. 6d.

OUR MUTUAL FRIEND. With Forty Illustrations by Marcus Stone. Cloth, £1 1s.

THE PICKWICK PAPERS. With Forty-three Illustrations by Seymour and Phiz. Cloth, £1 1s.

NICHOLAS NICKLEBY. With Forty Illustrations by Phiz. Cloth, £1 1s.

SKETCHES BY "BOZ." With Forty Illustrations by George Cruikshank. Cloth, £1 1s.

MARTIN CHUZZLEWIT. With Forty Illustrations by Phiz. Cloth, £1 1s.

DOMBEY AND SON. With Forty Illustrations by Phiz. Cloth, £1 1s.

DAVID COPPERFIELD. With Forty Illustrations by Phiz. Cloth, £1 1s.

BLEAK HOUSE. With Forty Illustrations by Phiz. Cloth, £1 1s.

LITTLE DORRIT. With Forty Illustrations by Phiz. Cloth, £1 1s.

THE OLD CURIOSITY SHOP. With Seventy-five Illustrations by George Cattermole and H. K. Browne. A New Edition. Uniform with the other volumes, £1 1s.

BARNABY RUDGE: a Tale of the Riots of 'Eighty. With Seventy-eight Illustrations by George Cattermole and H. K. Browne. Uniform with the other volumes, £1 1s.

CHRISTMAS BOOKS: Containing—The Christmas Carol; The Cricket on the Hearth; The Chimes; The Battle of Life; The Haunted House. With all the original Illustrations. Cloth, 12s.

OLIVER TWIST and TALE OF TWO CITIES. In one volume. Cloth, £1 1s.

OLIVER TWIST. Separately. With Twenty-four Illustrations by George Cruikshank Cloth, 11s.

A TALE OF TWO CITIES. Separately. With Sixteen Illustrations by Phiz. Cloth, 9s.

\*\*\* *The remainder of Dickens's Works were not originally printed in demy 8vo.*

## DICKENS'S (CHARLES) WORKS.

### LIBRARY EDITION.

*In post 8vo. With the Original Illustrations, 30 vols., cloth, £12.*

|  |  |  |  | *s* | *d* |
|---|---|---|---|---|---|
| PICKWICK PAPERS ... | 43 Illustrns., | 2 vols. | 16 | 0 |
| NICHOLAS NICKLEBY | 39 | ,, | 2 vols. | 16 | 0 |
| MARTIN CHUZZLEWIT | 40 | ,, | 2 vols. | 16 | 0 |
| OLD CURIOSITY SHOP & REPRINTED PIECES | 36 | ,, | 2 vols. | 16 | 0 |
| BARNABY RUDGE and HARD TIMES | 36 | ,, | 2 vols. | 16 | 0 |
| BLEAK HOUSE ... | 40 | ,, | 2 vols. | 16 | 0 |
| LITTLE DORRIT | 40 | ,, | 2 vols. | 16 | 0 |
| DOMBEY AND SON | 38 | ,, | 2 vols. | 16 | 0 |
| DAVID COPPERFIELD | 38 | ,, | 2 vols. | 16 | 0 |
| OUR MUTUAL FRIEND | 40 | ,, | 2 vols. | 16 | 0 |
| SKETCHES BY "BOZ" | 39 | ,, | 1 vol. | 8 | 0 |
| OLIVER TWIST | 24 | ,, | 1 vol. | 8 | 0 |
| CHRISTMAS BOOKS | 17 | ,, | 1 vol. | 8 | 0 |
| A TALE OF TWO CITIES | 16 | ,, | 1 vol. | 8 | 0 |
| GREAT EXPECTATIONS | 8 | ,, | 1 vol. | 8 | 0 |
| PICTURES FROM ITALY & AMERICAN NOTES | 8 | ,, | 1 vol. | 8 | 0 |
| UNCOMMERCIAL TRAVELLER ... | 8 | ,, | 1 vol. | 8 | 0 |
| CHILD'S HISTORY OF ENGLAND | 8 | ,, | 1 vol. | 8 | 0 |
| EDWIN DROOD and MISCELLANIES ... | 12 | ,, | 1 vol. | 8 | 0 |
| CHRISTMAS STORIES from "Household Words," &c. | 14 | ,, | 1 vol. | 8 | 0 |

THE LIFE OF CHARLES DICKENS. By JOHN FORSTER. With Illustrations. Uniform with this Edition. 10s. 6d.

**A NEW EDITION OF ABOVE, WITH THE ORIGINAL ILLUSTRATIONS, IN CROWN 8vo, 30 VOLS. IN SETS ONLY.**

# DICKENS'S (CHARLES) WORKS.

## THE "CHARLES DICKENS" EDITION.

*In Crown 8vo. In 21 vols., cloth, with Illustrations, £3 16s.*

|  |  | s. | d. |
|---|---|---|---|
| PICKWICK PAPERS | 8 Illustrations | 4 | 0 |
| MARTIN CHUZZLEWIT | 8 ,, | 4 | 0 |
| DOMBEY AND SON | 8 ,, | 4 | 0 |
| NICHOLAS NICKLEBY | 8 ,, | 4 | 0 |
| DAVID COPPERFIELD | 8 ,, | 4 | 0 |
| BLEAK HOUSE | 8 ,, | 4 | 0 |
| LITTLE DORRIT | 8 ,, | 4 | 0 |
| OUR MUTUAL FRIEND | 8 ,, | 4 | 0 |
| BARNABY RUDGE | 8 ,, | 3 | 6 |
| OLD CURIOSITY SHOP | 8 ,, | 3 | 6 |
| A CHILD'S HISTORY OF ENGLAND | 4 ,, | 3 | 6 |
| EDWIN DROOD and OTHER STORIES | 8 ,, | 3 | 6 |
| CHRISTMAS STORIES, from "Household Words" | 8 ,, | 3 | 6 |
| SKETCHES BY "BOZ" | 8 ,, | 3 | 0 |
| AMERICAN NOTES and REPRINTED PIECES | 8 ,, | 3 | 6 |
| CHRISTMAS BOOKS | 8 ,, | 3 | 6 |
| OLIVER TWIST | 8 ,, | 3 | 6 |
| GREAT EXPECTATIONS | 8 ,, | 3 | 6 |
| TALE OF TWO CITIES | 8 ,, | 3 | 0 |
| HARD TIMES and PICTURES FROM ITALY | 8 ,, | 3 | 0 |
| UNCOMMERCIAL TRAVELLER | 4 ,, | 3 | 0 |
| THE LIFE OF CHARLES DICKENS. Numerous Illustrations. | 2 vols. | 7 | 0 |
| THE LETTERS OF CHARLES DICKENS | 2 vols. | 8 | 0 |

## DICKENS'S (CHARLES) WORKS.

## THE ILLUSTRATED LIBRARY EDITION.

*Complete in 30 Volumes. Demy 8vo, 10s. each; or set, £15.*

This Edition is printed on a finer paper and in a larger type than has been employed in any previous edition. The type has been cast especially for it, and the page is of a size to admit of the introduction of all the original illustrations.

No such attractive issue has been made of the writings of Mr. Dickens, which, various as have been the forms of publication adapted to the demands of an ever widely-increasing popularity, have never yet been worthily presented in a really handsome library form.

The collection comprises all the minor writings it was Mr. Dickens's wish to preserve.

SKETCHES BY "BOZ." With 40 Illustrations by George Cruikshank.

PICKWICK PAPERS. 2 vols. With 42 Illustrations by Phiz.

OLIVER TWIST. With 24 Illustrations by Cruikshank.

NICHOLAS NICKLEBY. 2 vols. With 40 Illustrations by Phiz.

OLD CURIOSITY SHOP and REPRINTED PIECES. 2 vols. With Illustrations by Cattermole, &c.

BARNABY RUDGE and HARD TIMES. 2 vols. With Illustrations by Cattermole, &c.

MARTIN CHUZZLEWIT. 2 vols. With 40 Illustrations by Phiz.

AMERICAN NOTES and PICTURES FROM ITALY. 1 vol. With 8 Illustrations.

DOMBEY AND SON. 2 vols. With 40 Illustrations by Phiz.

DAVID COPPERFIELD. 2 vols. With 40 Illustrations by Phiz.

BLEAK HOUSE. 2 vols. With 40 Illustrations by Phiz.

LITTLE DORRIT. 2 vols. With 40 Illustrations by Phiz.

A TALE OF TWO CITIES. With 16 Illustrations by Phiz.

THE UNCOMMERCIAL TRAVELLER. With 8 Illustrations by Marcus Stone.

GREAT EXPECTATIONS. With 8 Illustrations by Marcus Stone.

OUR MUTUAL FRIEND. 2 vols. With 40 Illustrations by Marcus Stone.

CHRISTMAS BOOKS. With 17 Illustrations by Sir Edwin Landseer, R.A., Maclise, R.A., &c. &c.

HISTORY OF ENGLAND. With 8 Illustrations by Marcus Stone.

CHRISTMAS STORIES. (From "Household Words" and "All the Year Round.") With 14 Illustrations.

EDWIN DROOD AND OTHER STORIES. With 12 Illustrations by S. L. Fildes.

DICKENS'S (CHARLES) WORKS.

# THE POPULAR LIBRARY EDITION
## OF THE WORKS OF
# CHARLES DICKENS,

*In* 30 *Vols., large crown* 8*vo, price* £6; *separate Vols.* 4*s. each.*

An Edition printed on good paper, each volume containing 16 full-page Illustrations, selected from the Household Edition, on Plate Paper.

SKETCHES BY "BOZ."
PICKWICK. 2 vols.
OLIVER TWIST.
NICHOLAS NICKLEBY. 2 vols.
MARTIN CHUZZLEWIT. 2 vols.
DOMBEY AND SON. 2 vols.
DAVID COPPERFIELD. 2 vols.
CHRISTMAS BOOKS.
OUR MUTUAL FRIEND. 2 vols.
CHRISTMAS STORIES.
BLEAK HOUSE. 2 vols.
LITTLE DORRIT. 2 vols.
OLD CURIOSITY SHOP AND REPRINTED PIECES. 2 vols.
BARNABY RUDGE. 2 vols.
UNCOMMERCIAL TRAVELLER.
GREAT EXPECTATIONS.
TALE OF TWO CITIES.
CHILD'S HISTORY OF ENGLAND.
EDWIN DROOD AND MISCELLANIES.
PICTURES FROM ITALY AND AMERICAN NOTES.

## DICKENS'S (CHARLES) WORKS.

## HOUSEHOLD EDITION.

*In 22 Volumes.  Crown 4to, cloth, £4 8s. 6d.*

MARTIN CHUZZLEWIT, with 59 Illustrations, cloth, 5s.

DAVID COPPERFIELD, with 60 Illustrations and a Portrait, cloth, 5s.

BLEAK HOUSE, with 61 Illustrations, cloth, 5s.

LITTLE DORRIT, with 58 Illustrations, cloth, 5s.

PICKWICK PAPERS, with 56 Illustrations, cloth, 5s.

OUR MUTUAL FRIEND, with 58 Illustrations, cloth, 5s.

NICHOLAS NICKLEBY, with 59 Illustrations, cloth, 5s.

DOMBEY AND SON, with 61 Illustrations, cloth, 5s.

EDWIN DROOD; REPRINTED PIECES; and other Stories, with 30 Illustrations, cloth, 5s.

THE LIFE OF DICKENS. By JOHN FORSTER. With 40 Illustrations. Cloth, 5s.

BARNABY RUDGE, with 46 Illustrations, cloth, 4s.

OLD CURIOSITY SHOP, with 32 Illustrations, cloth, 4s.

CHRISTMAS STORIES, with 23 Illustrations, cloth, 4s.

OLIVER TWIST, with 28 Illustrations, cloth, 3s.

GREAT EXPECTATIONS, with 26 Illustrations, cloth, 3s.

SKETCHES BY "BOZ," with 36 Illustrations, cloth, 3s.

UNCOMMERCIAL TRAVELLER, with 26 Illustrations, cloth, 3s.

CHRISTMAS BOOKS, with 28 Illustrations, cloth, 3s.

THE HISTORY OF ENGLAND, with 15 Illustrations, cloth, 3s.

AMERICAN NOTES and PICTURES FROM ITALY, with 18 Illustrations, cloth, 3s.

A TALE OF TWO CITIES, with 25 Illustrations, cloth, 3s.

HARD TIMES, with 20 Illustrations, cloth, 2s. 6d.

*A New Edition of*

# CHARLES DICKENS'S WORKS.

Messrs. CHAPMAN & HALL beg to announce an Edition of CHARLES DICKENS'S WORKS, entitled:—

## THE CABINET EDITION.

To be completed in 30 vols. small fcap. 8vo, Marble Paper Sides, Cloth Backs, with uncut edges, price Eighteenpence each.

A Complete Work will be Published every Month and each Volume will contain Eight Illustrations reproduced from the Originals.

CHRISTMAS BOOKS, One Vol.,
MARTIN CHUZZLEWIT, Two Vols.,
DAVID COPPERFIELD, Two Vols.,
*Are now Ready.*

---

## DICKENS'S (CHARLES) WORKS.
### MR. DICKENS'S READINGS.
*Fcap. 8vo, sewed.*

CHRISTMAS CAROL IN PROSE. 1s.
CRICKET ON THE HEARTH. 1s.
CHIMES: A GOBLIN STORY. 1s.
STORY OF LITTLE DOMBEY. 1s.
POOR TRAVELLER, BOOTS AT THE HOLLY-TREE INN, and MRS. GAMP. 1s.

---

A CHRISTMAS CAROL, with the Original Coloured Plates, being a reprint of the Original Edition. Small 8vo, red cloth, gilt edges, 5s.

---

ONE SHILLING EACH.   Reprinted from the Original Plates.

A CHRISTMAS CAROL. Fcap. cloth, 1s.
THE CHIMES: A Goblin Story. Fcap. cloth, 1s.

---

*The Cheapest and Handiest Edition of*

## THE WORKS OF CHARLES DICKENS.

The Pocket-Volume Edition of Charles Dickens's Works.
*In 30 Vols. small fcap. 8vo, £2 5s.*

---

*New and Cheap Issue of*

## THE WORKS OF CHARLES DICKENS.
In pocket volumes.

PICKWICK PAPERS, with 8 Illustrations, cloth, 2s.
NICHOLAS NICKLEBY, with 8 Illustrations, cloth, 2s.
OLIVER TWIST, with 8 Illustrations, cloth, 1s.
SKETCHES BY "BOZ," with 8 Illustrations, cloth, 1s.
OLD CURIOSITY SHOP, with 8 Illustrations, cloth, 2s.
BARNABY RUDGE, with 16 Illustrations, cloth, 2s.
AMERICAN NOTES AND PICTURES FROM ITALY, with 8 Illustrations, cloth, 1s.6d.
CHRISTMAS BOOKS, with 8 Illustrations, cloth, 1s. 6d.
MARTIN CHUZZLEWIT, with 8 Illustrations, cloth, 2s.

*List of Books, Drawing Examples, Diagrams, Models, Instruments, etc.,*

INCLUDING

THOSE ISSUED UNDER THE AUTHORITY OF THE SCIENCE AND ART DEPARTMENT, SOUTH KENSINGTON, FOR THE USE OF SCHOOLS AND ART AND SCIENCE CLASSES.

---

CATALOGUE OF MODERN WORKS ON SCIENCE AND TECHNOLOGY. 8vo, sewed, 1s.

BENSON (W.)—

PRINCIPLES OF THE SCIENCE OF COLOUR. Small 4to, 15s.

MANUAL OF THE SCIENCE OF COLOUR. Coloured Frontispiece and Illustrations. 12mo, 2s. 6d.

BRADLEY (THOMAS), *of the Royal Military Academy, Woolwich—*.

ELEMENTS OF GEOMETRICAL DRAWING. In Two Parts, with 60 Plates. Oblong folio, half-bound, each part 16s.
Selections (from the above) of 20 Plates, for the use of the Royal Military Academy, Woolwich. Oblong folio, half-bound, 16s.

BURCHETT—

LINEAR PERSPECTIVE. With Illustrations. Post 8vo, 7s.

PRACTICAL GEOMETRY. Post 8vo, 5s.

DEFINITIONS OF GEOMETRY. Third Edition. 24mo, sewed, 5d.

CARROLL (JOHN)—

FREEHAND DRAWING LESSONS FOR THE BLACK BOARD. 6s.

*CUBLEY (W. H.)—*

> A SYSTEM OF ELEMENTARY DRAWING. With Illustrations and Examples. Imperial 4to, sewed, 3s. 6d.

*DAVISON (ELLIS A.)—*

> DRAWING FOR ELEMENTARY SCHOOLS. Post 8vo, 3s.
>
> MODEL DRAWING. 12mo, 3s.

*DELAMOTTE (P. H.)—*

> PROGRESSIVE DRAWING-BOOK FOR BEGINNERS. 12mo, 3s. 6d.

*DYCE—*

> DRAWING-BOOK OF THE GOVERNMENT SCHOOL OF DESIGN: ELEMENTARY OUTLINES OF ORNAMENT. 50 Plates. Small folio, sewed, 5s.; mounted, 18s.
>
> INTRODUCTION TO DITTO. Fcap. 8vo, 6d.

*FOSTER (VERE)—*

> DRAWING-BOOKS:
> Forty-six Numbers, at 2d. each.
>
> DRAWING-CARDS:
> Freehand Drawing: First Grade, Sets I., II., III., 1s. each.
> Second Grade, Set I., 2s.

*HENSLOW (PROFESSOR)—*

> ILLUSTRATIONS TO BE EMPLOYED IN THE PRACTICAL LESSONS ON BOTANY. Post 8vo, sewed, 6d.

*JACOBSTHAL (E.)—*

> GRAMMATIK DER ORNAMENTE, in 7 Parts of 20 Plates each. Unmounted, £3 13s. 6d.; mounted on cardboard, £11 4s. The Parts can be had separately.

*JEWITT—*

>HANDBOOK OF PRACTICAL PERSPECTIVE. 18mo, 1s. 6d.

*LINDLEY (JOHN)—*

>SYMMETRY OF VEGETATION: Principles to be Observed in the Delineation of Plants. 12mo, sewed, 1s.

*MARSHALL—*

>HUMAN BODY. Text and Plates reduced from the large Diagrams. 2 vols., £1 1s.

*NEWTON (E. TULLEY), F.G.S.—*

>THE TYPICAL PARTS IN THE SKELETONS OF A CAT, DUCK, AND CODFISH, being a Catalogue with Comparative Descriptions arranged in a Tabular Form. Demy 8vo, 3s.

*OLIVER (PROFESSOR)—*

>ILLUSTRATIONS OF THE VEGETABLE KINGDOM. 109 Plates. Oblong 8vo. Plain, 16s.; coloured, £1 6s.

*POYNTER (E. J.), R.A., issued under the superintendence of—*

>THE SOUTH KENSINGTON DRAWING SERIES.
>
>>FREEHAND—ELEMENTARY ORNAMENT: books 6d., cards, 9d. each.
>>
>>FREEHAND—FIRST GRADE: books 6d., cards 1s. each.
>>
>>FREEHAND—SECOND GRADE: books 1s., cards 1s. 6d. each.
>>
>>FREEHAND—PLANTS FROM NATURE: books 6d., cards, 1s. each.
>>
>>FREEHAND—HUMAN FIGURE, ELEMENTARY: books 6d.
>>
>>FREEHAND—HUMAN FIGURE, ADVANCED: books 2s. each.
>>
>>FREEHAND—FIGURES FROM THE CARTOONS OF RAPHAEL: four books, 2s. each.
>>
>>FREEHAND—ELEMENTARY PERSPECTIVE DRAWING. By S. J. CARTLIDGE, F.R.Hist.S. Books 1s. each; or one volume, cloth, 5s.

REDGRAVE—
> MANUAL AND CATECHISM ON COLOUR. Fifth Edition. 24mo, sewed, 9d.

ROBSON (GEORGE)—
> ELEMENTARY BUILDING CONSTRUCTION. Oblong folio, sewed, 8s.

WALLIS (GEORGE)—
> DRAWING-BOOK. Oblong, sewed, 3s. 6d.; mounted, 8s.

WORNUM (R. N.)—
> THE CHARACTERISTICS OF STYLES: An Introduction to the Study of the History of Ornamental Art. Royal 8vo, 8s.

ELEMENTARY DRAWING COPY-BOOKS, for the Use of Children from four years old and upwards, in Schools and Families. Compiled by a Student certificated by the Science and Art Department as an Art Teacher. Seven Books in 4to, sewed:

Book I. Letters, 8d.
" II. Ditto, 8d.
" III. Geometrical and Ornamental Forms, 8d.
Book IV. Objects, 8d.
" V. Leaves, 8d.
" VI. Birds, Animals, &c., 8d.
" VII. Leaves, Flowers, and Sprays, 8d.

\*\*\* Or in Sets of Seven Books, 4s. 6d.

PRINCIPLES OF DECORATIVE ART. Folio, sewed, 1s.

DIAGRAM OF THE COLOURS OF THE SPECTRUM, with Explanatory Letterpress, on roller, 5s.

COPIES FOR OUTLINE DRAWING:
> LARGE FREEHAND EXAMPLES FOR CLASS TEACHING. Specially prepared under the authority of the Science and Art Department. Six Sheets. Size 60 by 40. 9s.
>
> DYCE'S ELEMENTARY OUTLINES OF ORNAMENT, 50 Selected Plates, mounted back and front, 18s.; unmounted, sewed, 5s.
>
> WEITBRICHT'S OUTLINES OF ORNAMENT, reproduced by Herman, 12 Plates, mounted back and front, 8s. 6d.; unmounted, 2s.
>
> MORGHEN'S OUTLINES OF THE HUMAN FIGURE, reproduced by Herman, 20 Plates, mounted back and front, 15s.; unmounted, 3s. 4d.
>
> TARSIA, from Gruner, Four Plates, mounted, 3s. 6d., unmounted, 7d.
>
> ALBERTOLLI'S FOLIAGE, Four Plates, mounted, 3s. 6d.; unmounted, 5d.
>
> OUTLINE OF TRAJAN FRIEZE, mounted, 1s.
>
> WALLIS'S DRAWING-BOOK, mounted, 8s., unmounted, 3s. 6d.
>
> OUTLINE DRAWINGS OF FLOWERS. Eight Plates, mounted, 3s. 6d.; unmounted, 8d.

## COPIES FOR SHADED DRAWING:

COURSE OF DESIGN. By CH. BARGUE (French), 20 Sheets, £2 9s.

ARCHITECTURAL STUDIES. By J. B. TRIPON. 10 Plates, £1.

MECHANICAL STUDIES. By J. B. TRIPON. 15s. per dozen.

FOLIATED SCROLL FROM THE VATICAN, unmounted, 5d.; mounted, 1s. 3d.

TWELVE HEADS after Holbein, selected from his Drawings in Her Majesty's Collection at Windsor. Reproduced in Autotype. Half imperial, £1 16s.

## COLOURED EXAMPLES:

A SMALL DIAGRAM OF COLOUR, mounted, 1s. 6d.; unmounted, 9d.

COTMAN'S PENCIL LANDSCAPES (set of 9), mounted, 15s.

,, SEPIA DRAWINGS (set of 5), mounted, £1.

ALLONGE'S LANDSCAPES IN CHARCOAL (Six), at 4s. each, or the set £1 4s.

RADDE COLOUR SCALE, in case, £1.

## SOLID MODELS, &c.:

*Box of Models, £1 4s.

A Stand with a universal joint, to show the solid models, &c., £1 18s.

*One Wire Quadrangle, with a circle and cross within it, and one straight wire. One solid cube. One Skeleton Wire Cube. One Sphere. One Cone. One Cylinder. One Hexagonal Prism. £2 2s.

Skeleton Cube in wood, 3s. 6d.

18-inch Skeleton Cube in wood, 12s.

*Three objects of *form* in Pottery:

Indian Jar,
Celadon Jar,  } 18s. 6d.
Bottle,

*Five selected Vases in Majolica Ware, £2 11s.

*Three selected Vases in Earthenware, 18s.

Imperial Deal Frames, glazed, without sunk rings, 10s. each.

*Davidson's Smaller Solid Models, in Box, £2, containing—

| | | |
|---|---|---|
| 2 Square Slabs. | Octagon Prism. | Triangular Prism. |
| 9 Oblong Blocks (steps). | Cylinder. | Pyramid, Equilateral. |
| 2 Cubes. | Cone. | Pyramid, Isosceles. |
| Square Blocks. | Jointed Cross. | Square Block |

## SOLID MODELS, &c.—*Continued.*

*Davidson's Advanced Drawing Models, £9.—The following is a brief description of the Models:—An Obelisk—composed of 2 Octagonal Slabs, 26 and 20 inches across, and each 3 inches high; 1 Cube, 12 inches edge; 1 Monolith (forming the body of the obelisk) 3 feet high; 1 Pyramid, 6 inches base; the complete object is thus nearly 5 feet high. A Market Cross—composed of 3 Slabs, 24, 18, and 12 inches across, and each 3 inches high; 1 Upright, 3 feet high; 2 Cross Arms, united by mortise and tenon joints; complete height, 3 feet 9 inches. A Step-Ladder, 23 inches high. A Kitchen Table, 14½ inches high. A Chair to correspond. A Four-legged Stool, with projecting top and cross rails, height 14 inches. A Tub, with handles and projecting hoops, and the divisions between the staves plainly marked. A strong Trestle, 18 inches high. A Hollow Cylinder, 9 inches in diameter, and 12 inches long, divided lengthwise. A Hollow Sphere, 9 inches in diameter, divided into semi-spheres, one of which is again divided into quarters; the semi-sphere, when placed on the cylinder, gives the form and principles of shading a dome, whilst one of the quarters placed on half the cylinder forms a niche.

*Davidson's Apparatus for Teaching Practical Geometry (22 models), £5.

*Binn's Models for Illustrating the Elementary Principles of Orthographic Projection as applied to Mechanical Drawing, in box, £1 10s.

Miller's Class Drawing Models.—These Models are particularly adapted for teaching large classes; the stand is very strong, and the universal joint will hold the Models in any position. *Wood Models*: Square Prism, 12 inches side, 18 inches high; Hexagonal Prism, 14 inches side, 18 inches high; Cube, 14 inches side; Cylinder, 13 inches diameter, 16 inches high; Hexagon Pyramid, 14 inches diameter, 22½ inches side; Square Pyramid, 14 inches side, 22½ inches side; Cone, 13 inches diameter, 22½ inches side; Skeleton Cube, 19 inches solid wood 1¾ inch square; Intersecting Circles, 19 inches solid wood 2¼ by 1½ inches. *Wire Models*: Triangular Prism, 17 inches side, 22 inches high; Square Prism, 14 inches side, 20 inches high; Hexagonal Prism, 16 inches diameter, 21 inches high; Cylinder, 14 inches diameter, 21 inches high; Hexagon Pyramid, 18 inches diameter, 24 inches high; Square Pyramid, 17 inches side, 24 inches high; Cone, 17 inches side, 24 inches high; Skeleton Cube, 19 inches side; Intersecting Circles, 19 inches side; Plain Circle, 19 inches side; Plain Square, 19 inches side. Table, 27 inches by 21½ inches. Stand. The set complete, £14 13s.

Large Compasses, with chalk-holder, 5s.

*Slip, two set squares and **T** square, 5s.

*Parkes's Case of Instruments, containing 6-inch compasses with pen and pencil leg, 5s.

*Prize Instrument Case, with 6-inch compasses pen and pencil leg, 2 small compasses, pen and scale, 18s.

6-inch Compasses, with shifting pen and point, 4s. 6d.

\* Models, &c., entered as sets, can only be supplied in sets.

# LARGE DIAGRAMS.

## ASTRONOMICAL:

TWELVE SHEETS. By JOHN DREW, Ph. Dr., F.R.S.A. Sheets, £2 8s.; on rollers and varnished, £4 4s.

## BOTANICAL:

NINE SHEETS. Illustrating a Practical Method of Teaching Botany. By Professor HENSLOW, F.L.S. £2; on rollers and varnished, £3 3s.

| CLASS. | DIVISION. | SECTION. | DIAGRAM. |
|---|---|---|---|
| Dicotyledon | Angiospermous | Thalamifloral | 1 |
| | | Calycifloral | 2 & 3 |
| | | Corollifloral | 4 |
| | | Incomplete | 5 |
| | Gymnospermous | | 6 |
| Monocotyledons | Petaloid | Superior | 7 |
| | | Inferior | 8 |
| | Glumaceous | | 9 |

\* Models, &c., entered as sets, can only be supplied in sets.

## BUILDING CONSTRUCTION:

TEN SHEETS. By WILLIAM J. GLENNY. £1 1s.

LAXTON'S EXAMPLES OF BUILDING CONSTRUCTION, containing 32 Imperial Plates, £1.

BUSBRIDGE'S DRAWING OF BUILDING CONSTRUCTION. 36 Sheets, 9s. Mounted on cardboard, 18s.

## GEOLOGICAL:

DIAGRAM OF BRITISH STRATA. By H. W. BRISTOW, F.R.S., F.G.S. A Sheet, 4s.; on roller and varnished, 7s. 6d.

## MECHANICAL:

DIAGRAMS OF THE MECHANICAL POWERS, AND THEIR APPLICATIONS IN MACHINERY AND THE ARTS GENERALLY. By Dr. JOHN ANDERSON. 8 Diagrams, highly coloured, on stout paper, 3 feet 6 inches by 2 feet 6 inches. Sheets £1; mounted on rollers, £2.

DIAGRAMS OF THE STEAM-ENGINE. By Prof. GOODEVE and Prof. SHELLEY. Stout paper, 40 inches by 27 inches, highly coloured. 41 Diagrams (52½ Sheets), £6 6s.; varnished and mounted on rollers, £11 11s.

MACHINE DETAILS. By Prof. UNWIN. 16 Coloured Diagrams. Sheets, £2 2s.; mounted on rollers and varnished, £3 14s.

SELECTED EXAMPLES OF MACHINES, OF IRON AND WOOD (French). By STANISLAS PETTIT. 60 Sheets, £3 5s.; 13s. per dozen.

BUSBRIDGE'S DRAWINGS OF MACHINE CONSTRUCTION. 50 Sheets, 12s. 6d. Mounted £1 5s.

## PHYSIOLOGICAL:

ELEVEN SHEETS. Illustrating Human Physiology, Life Size and Coloured from Nature. Prepared under the direction of JOHN MARSHALL, F.R.S., F.R.C.S., &c. Each Sheet, 12s. 6d. On canvas and rollers, varnished, £1 1s.

1. THE SKELETON AND LIGAMENTS.
2. THE MUSCLES, JOINTS, AND ANIMAL MECHANICS.
3. THE VISCERA IN POSITION.—THE STRUCTURE OF THE LUNGS.
4. THE ORGANS OF CIRCULATION.
5. THE LYMPHATICS OR ABSORBENTS.
6. THE ORGANS OF DIGESTION.
7. THE BRAIN AND NERVES.—THE ORGANS OF THE VOICE.
8 & 9. THE ORGANS OF THE SENSES.
10 & 11. THE MICROSCOPIC STRUCTURE OF THE TEXTURES AND ORGANS.

---

HUMAN BODY, LIFE SIZE. By JOHN MARSHALL, F.R.S., F.R.C.S. Each Sheet, 12s. 6d.; on canvas and rollers, varnished, £1 1s. Explanatory Key, 1s.

1, 2, 3. THE SKELETON, Front, Back, and Side View.
5, 6, 7. THE MUSCLES, Front, Back, and Side View.

## ZOOLOGICAL:

TEN SHEETS. Illustrating the Classification of Animals. By ROBERT PATTERSON. £2; on canvas and rollers, varnished, £3 10s.

---

## PHYSIOLOGY AND ANATOMY OF THE HONEY BEE.
Two Diagrams. 7s. 6d.

# NEW NOVELS.

(To be had at all Libraries.)

---

BY THE HON. MRS. HENRY CHETWYND.

MRS. DORRIMAN. By the Hon. Mrs. Henry Chetwynd. 3 vols.

BY GEORGE GISSING.

ISABEL CLARENDON. By George Gissing. 2 vols.
*[In April.*

BY MRS. BERENS.

A WOMAN WITH A PAST. By Mrs. Berens. 3 vols.
*[In April.*

BY S. LAING.

A SPORTING QUIXOTE: or, The Life and Adventures of the Hon. Augustus Fitzmuddle, afterwards Earl of Muddleton. By S. Laing. 2 vols.

BY ARTHUR GRIFFITHS.

THE THIN RED LINE. By Arthur Griffiths. 2 vols.
*[In April.*

BY COLONEL FIFE-COOKSON.

BAYLERBAY; or, STRANGERS IN TURKEY. By Colonel Fife-Cookson. 2 vols.
*[In April.*

BY MRS. EDWARD KENNARD.

KILLED IN THE OPEN. By Mrs. Edward Kennard. Author of "The Right Sort," "Straight as a Die," etc., etc. 3 vols.

# THE FORTNIGHTLY REVIEW.

### Edited by T. H. S. ESCOTT.

THE FORTNIGHTLY REVIEW is published on the 1st of every month, and a Volume is completed every Six Months.

*The following are among the Contributors:—*

SIR RUTHERFORD ALCOCK.
MATHEW ARNOLD.
PROFESSOR BAIN.
SIR SAMUEL BAKER.
PROFESSOR BEESLY.
PAUL BERT.
BARON GEORGETON BUNSEN.
DR. BRIDGES.
HON. GEORGE C. BRODRICK.
JAMES BRYCE, M.P.
THOMAS BURT, M.P.
SIR GEORGE CAMPBELL, M.P.
THE EARL OF CARNARVON.
EMILIO CASTELAR.
RT. HON. J. CHAMBERLAIN, M.P.
PROFESSOR SIDNEY COLVIN.
MONTAGUE COOKSON, Q.C.
L. H. COURTNEY, M.P.
G. H. DARWIN.
SIR GEORGE W. DASENT.
PROFESSOR A. V. DICEY.
RIGHT HON. H. FAWCETT, M.P.
EDWARD A. FREEMAN.
SIR BARTLE FRERE, BART.
J. A. FROUDE.
MRS. GARRET-ANDERSON.
J. W. L. GLAISHER, F.R.S.
M. E. GRANT DUFF, M.P.
THOMAS HARE.
F. HARRISON.
LORD HOUGHTON.
PROFESSOR HUXLEY.
PROFESSOR R. C. JEBB.
PROFESSOR JEVONS.
ANDREW LANG.
EMILE DE LAVELEYE.

T. E. CLIFFE LESLIE.
SIR JOHN LUBBOCK, M.P.
THE EARL LYTTON.
SIR H. S. MAINE.
DR. MAUDSLEY.
PROFESSOR MAX MÜLLER.
G. OSBORNE MORGAN, Q.C., M.P.
PROFESSOR HENRY MORLEY.
WILLIAM MORRIS.
PROFESSOR H. N. MOSELEY.
F. W. H. MYERS.
F. W. NEWMAN.
PROFESSOR JOHN NICHOL.
W. G. PALGRAVE.
WALTER H. PATER.
RT. HON. LYON PLAYFAIR, M.P.
DANTE GABRIEL ROSSETTI.
LORD SHERBROOKE.
HERBERT SPENCER.
HON. E. L. STANLEY.
SIR J. FITZJAMES STEPHEN, Q.C.
LESLIE STEPHEN.
J. HUTCHISON STIRLING.
A. C. SWINBURNE.
DR. VON SYBEL.
J. A. SYMONDS.
THE REV. EDWARD F. TALBOT
 (WARDEN OF KEBLE COLLEGE).
SIR RICHARD TEMPLE, BART.
W. T. THORNTON
HON. LIONEL A. TOLLEMACHE.
H. D. TRAILL.
ANTHONY TROLLOPE.
PROFESSOR TYNDALL.
A. J. WILSON.
THE EDITOR.

&c. &c. &c.

THE FORTNIGHTLY REVIEW *is published at* 2s. 6d.

CHAPMAN & HALL, LIMITED, 11, HENRIETTA STREET, COVENT GARDEN, W.C.

[CHARLES DICKENS AND EVANS,]     [CRYSTAL PALACE PRESS.

www.ingramcontent.com/pod-product-compliance
Lightning Source LLC
Chambersburg PA
CBHW032353230426
43672CB00007B/686